Deliberative Democra

MW01241036

This book is a pioneering analysis of the deliberative systems approach in Taiwan, extending our understanding of Taiwanese democratic politics and consolidating links between theoretical development and the practical application of deliberative practices.

As a front-runner of new democracies in Asia and a relatively open society, Taiwan provides a model for deliberative governance, with a view towards institutional innovation and increasing democratisation. This book considers how components within the intricate web of micro- and macro-deliberative systems perform different functions, complement each other and contribute both to policy change and democratic and deliberative innovations. Specific cases are provided – such as participatory budgeting in Taipei City and the government–academia alliance model – to demonstrate the long-term systemic effects of mini-publics and citizen actions. In addition, the book proposes the possibility of deliberative democracy for other countries in the world, alongside various policy issues, including mini-publics, e-participation, co-governance, citizen science, negotiation mechanisms and the deliberative practices of indigenous peoples.

Deliberative Democracy in Taiwan will appeal to students and scholars of East Asian studies, Taiwanese politics, political science and social movement studies.

Mei-Fang Fan is Professor at the Institute of Science, Technology and Society, National Yang-Ming University and Researcher at the Risk Society and Policy Research Centre of National Taiwan University. Her research interests include environmental justice, deliberative democracy and governance. Fan's recent book chapters on environmental justice in East Asia and wind turbine construction in Taiwan appeared in the *Routledge Handbook of Environmental Justice* (2018) and *Energy Transition in East Asia* (2017).

Routledge Research on Taiwan Series
Series Editor: Dafydd Fell, SOAS, UK

The *Routledge Research on Taiwan Series* seeks to publish quality research on all aspects of Taiwan studies. Taking an interdisciplinary approach, the books will cover topics such as politics, economic development, culture, society, anthropology and history.

This new book series will include the best possible scholarship from the social sciences and the humanities and welcomes submissions from established authors in the field as well as from newer authors. In addition to research monographs and edited volumes, general works or textbooks with a broader appeal will be considered.

The Series is advised by an international Editorial Board and edited by *Dafydd Fell* of the Centre of Taiwan Studies at the School of Oriental and African Studies.

Positioning Taiwan in a Global Context
Being and becoming
Edited by Bi-yu Chang and Pei-yin Lin

Young Adults in Urban China and Taiwan
Aspirations, expectations, and life choices
Désirée Remmert

Taiwan Studies Revisited
Dafydd Fell and Hsin-Huang Michael Hsiao

Cross-Strait Relations Since 2016
The end of the illusion
J. Michael Cole

Deliberative Democracy in Taiwan
A deliberative systems perspective
Mei-Fang Fan

For more information about this series, please visit: www.routledge.com/Routledge-Research-on-Taiwan-Series/book-series/RRTAIWAN

Deliberative Democracy in Taiwan

A deliberative systems perspective

Mei-Fang Fan

Routledge
Taylor & Francis Group

LONDON AND NEW YORK

First published 2021
by Routledge
2 Park Square, Milton Park, Abingdon, Oxon OX14 4RN

and by Routledge
605 Third Avenue, New York, NY 10017

First issued in paperback 2022

Routledge is an imprint of the Taylor & Francis Group, an informa business

© 2021 Mei-Fang Fan

British Library Cataloguing-in-Publication Data
A catalogue record for this book is available from the British Library

Library of Congress Cataloging-in-Publication Data
Names: Fan, Mei-Fang, author.
Title: Deliberative democracy in Taiwan : a deliberative
systems perspective / Mei-Fang Fan.
Identifiers: LCCN 2020028400 | ISBN 9780367407377 (hardback) |
ISBN 9780367809607 (ebook)
Subjects: LCSH: Deliberative democracy–Taiwan.
Classification: LCC JQ1536 .F36 2020 | DDC 320.951249–dc23
LC record available at https://lccn.loc.gov/2020028400

ISBN: 978-0-367-62905-2 (pbk)
ISBN: 978-0-367-40737-7 (hbk)
ISBN: 978-0-367-80960-7 (ebk)

DOI: 10.4324/9780367809607

Typeset in Times new roman
by Newgen Publishing UK

Contents

List of figures   vii
List of tables   viii
Foreword   ix
Acknowledgements   xi

1 Introduction: democracy as deliberative systems   1

PART I
Complex interactions of micro- and macro-deliberative
systems   21

2 The public space   23

3 The empowered space   46

4 Transmission and accountability   67

PART II
Deliberative policy-making and democratic innovations   91

5 The democratisation of science in deliberative
   systems: the controversy over nuclear waste
   repository siting   93

6 Indigenous political participation and deliberative
   governance: the controversy over mining on
   traditional territories   122

7 Democratic innovations and participatory budgeting in
  deliberative systems   146

8 Conclusion   168

  Index   181

Figures

1.1   The deliberative system   8
3.1   The main structure of the Taiwanese political system   50
6.1   Location of the Truku tribe and the ACC   126
7.1   Organisation of Taipei City Government's PB partnership
      cooperation plan   150
7.2   The PB deliberative system   163
8.1   The co-evolution of deliberative systems   170

Tables

5.1 Modes of transmission and hybrid forms of governance   110
7.1 Functions of the PB process in deliberative systems   162

Foreword

Deliberative democracy is the main theme in recent democratic theory. Increasingly it is also applied to the empirical study of democracy and to the practicalities of institutional design. In the last decade or so, deliberative democracy has increasingly emphasized the idea of deliberative systems. For some time, exhortations to use the deliberative systems approach have been much more common than real applications of it; still fewer are real applications that are done well. That is beginning to change, but it is rare indeed that anyone takes on a whole country in deliberative system terms. Mei-Fang Fan undertakes here what I believe to be the first book-length treatment that interprets the whole political system of a country as a potentially deliberative system. That system extends from local civic practice to the formal institutions of national government, encompassing Parliament, civic organizations, indigenous peoples, social movements, local governments, designed citizen forums, experts and social media.

Deliberative Democracy in Taiwan is, then, a truly pioneering book. Of course it should interest scholars, students and others who care about Taiwanese politics, as it provides a fresh and insightful angle on this democratizing society. But it should also be read by people in the deliberative democracy field worldwide, as an exemplary (as well as pioneering) application of the deliberative systems approach, showing exactly how it can be brought to bear at a whole-country level.

Taiwan is a particularly interesting case given that, among Asian countries, it is at the forefront in both conventional liberal democratic terms and in deliberative innovations. Many of these innovations appear in the book. But, true to the systems frame, these innovations are treated in terms of how they influence and interact with larger deliberative systems. Some of the innovations, such as mini-publics and participatory budgeting, can be found in other countries too. Others, such as Citizens' Congress Watch (which monitors the performance of individual parliamentarians in deliberative terms) are Taiwan originals that deserve to be copied elsewhere. There is much that the world can and should learn from Taiwan when it comes to deliberative democratic possibilities. Of course, Taiwan is not perfect in deliberative terms, and Fan shows how its deliberative qualities could be deepened.

Mei-Fang Fan combines a sophisticated appreciation of deliberative democratic theory with in-depth empirical analysis (using multiple methods) of cases from Taiwan. The practices she covers range widely across, for example, e-participation, co-governance, citizen science, citizen forums, public consultation, rule-making and youth participation. The cases range from nuclear waste to participatory budgeting in Taipei (where an interesting alliance of academics and civic organizations proves pivotal). She provides special insight into the deliberative practices of indigenous peoples and how they constitute not just a deliberative system of their own but can be seen as joining larger deliberative systems. This is an important addition to the developing multinational literature on indigenous deliberation and how it relates to the governance of states.

In short, Mei-Fang Fan presents in this book a pioneering achievement that is a major advance in the deliberative democracy field and a powerful analysis of politics in Taiwan.

John S. Dryzek
Centenary Professor, ARC Laureate Fellow,
Centre for Deliberative Democracy and Global Governance,
University of Canberra

Acknowledgements

I am grateful to John Dryzek for giving me the opportunity to visit the Centre for Deliberative Democracy and Global Governance at the University of Canberra from July to December in 2018. I am most indebted to him for his intellectual support, inspiration and insightful comments on the book proposal and for writing the foreword for the book. Gratitude also goes to Kei Nishiyama, Davis Roger, Nicole Curato, Selen Ercan, Simon Niemeyer, Emerson Sancehz, Jensen Sass, Hannah Barrowman and Choi Heng for their insightful comments on my seminar, inspirations and friendly conversations during my visit to the Centre.

My sincere thanks go to Leslie Mabon, Chih-Yuan Yang and Kuan-Chiu Tseng for the invaluable comments and suggestions on numerous or particular chapters of the book. Several chapters were presented at the Annual Conference of the Taiwanese Political Science Association, the Annual Conference of the Taiwan Association for Schools of Public Administration and Affairs (TASPAA) and the book workshop held in 2019. Special thanks to Ching-Ping Tang, Kuo-Ming Lin, Tze-Luen Lin and Kai-Hung Fang for their helpful comments, and to those who raised intriguing questions in these discussion sessions.

I am also grateful to those who generously spent their time sharing their precious participatory and deliberative experiences, knowledge and viewpoints. This book is dedicated to deliberative democracy practitioners and initiators, members of civil society groups and the activists concerned with democracy, human rights, justice and the environment in Taiwan who have inspired my work. Special thanks to Chih-Ming, Miao-Lin, Yi-San and Rui-Xin for their diligent work in data collection and editing.

My gratitude also goes to the series editor at Routledge, Dafydd Fell, for his support; I appreciate the insightful comments provided by the anonymous reviewers. Special thanks to Stephanie Rogers, Emily Pickthall and the production team for their great editorial work throughout the publication process.

I am grateful for the support from my colleagues at the Institute of Science, Technology and Society at National Yang Ming University and the generous research funding provided by Taiwan's Ministry of Science and Technology (MOST). Finally, I would like to express my profound gratitude to my family for their love and support.

1 Introduction

Democracy as deliberative systems

Taiwan as a potentially deliberative system

Deliberative democracy scholars consider deliberation fundamental to our thoughts about democratic deepening in transition societies, and deliberative capacity can contribute to the analysis of the democratic quality of political systems. Deliberative theory has taken an institutional, empirical and systemic turn over the years. For Dryzek (2016), the various 'turns' are essential components of a productive dialogue about how democracy can and should be pursued in theory and practice. The recent shift towards a deliberative systems approach suggests understanding public deliberation as a broad system that encompasses a diversity of communicative practices, from debates in parliaments and participatory forums to more informal conversations and communicative activities. The concept of deliberative systems offers new ways of understanding deliberation as a communicative activity that occurs in multiple spaces, and of thinking about the deliberative qualities of the system as a whole, as well as the division of deliberative labour, functions and the connectivity of its particular components (Mansbridge et al., 2012; Dodge, 2014; Stevenson & Dryzek, 2014).

For theories on deliberative democracy, it is promising that 'democratic deliberation can narrow the range of political disagreements not only in contexts of moral and religious pluralism but also in contexts of cultural pluralism' (Weinstock & Kahane, 2010, p. 13). Deliberation might enable discovering analogies or parallels between cultures, thereby making shared moral reasoning possible (Weinstock & Kahane, 2010, pp. 13–14). Deliberative democracy is crucial for seeking transitional justice in transition processes. Dryzek (2013) argues that, in a world of plural justice claims, deliberative democracy is necessary to the pursuit of justice. The main need is for 'a deliberative system encompassing those affected by collective decisions, with places for non-partisan forums and discursive representatives, conditionally open to multiple forms of communication, and geared to the productions of workable agreements under normative and discursive meta-consensus' (p. 329).

Taiwan's democratisation and democratic deepening have been accompanied by burgeoning and zealous social movements, various forms of public participation, democratic reforms, deliberative practices and innovations. The Taiwanese political system transformed from an authoritarian dominant-party system to a democracy in the late 1980s. Kuomintang (KMT) initiated the democratic transition, leading to the first presidential national elections in 1996. In 2000, voters elected the Democratic Progressive Party's (DPP) candidate, Chen Shui-bian, as president, which resulted in the first transfer of power between parties in the central government. The second party turnover was completed in 2008, and the third power transfer was concluded in 2016. The incumbent president, Tsai Ing-wen of the DPP, won the 2020 presidential election.

The introduction of deliberative practices to Asia was influenced by deliberative democracy theory and practices in the West over the past few decades, and the diffusion of deliberative ideas and practices led to a 'deliberative turn' in East Asia. Similar to Japan, the liberal-democratic system in Taiwan has been shaped by a plurality of political cultures. Political culture influences the settings of political institutions and shapes the institutional design and practices of deliberative democracy (Tang et al., 2018). Concepts of deliberative democracy were introduced in Taiwan by Anglo-American-trained social scientists in the late 1990s. The DPP won the presidential election in 2000 due to a division of power within the KMT. With less than 40% of the electoral support and a minority in the legislature, the DPP attempted to adopt deliberative democracy to pursue democratic legitimacy. This has resulted in a growing emphasis on deliberative citizen engagement in policy-making in Taiwan.

The first consensus conferences in Taiwan were held in July 2002 on national health insurance (Lin & Chen, 2003). The Department of Health commissioned a second-generation health insurance planning team to hold the National Health Insurance Payment consensus conference – a move that set the precedent for joint promotion by the government and scholars. Since 2002, the rapid development of deliberative practices has been catalysed by scholars who advocate for and build partnerships with civil society. Citizen conferences have been conducted on various national and local issues, including surrogate motherhood, genetic testing, cable cars, urban gentrification, GM foods, water resource management and others (e.g. Lin & Chen, 2003; Lin, 2007; Fan, 2015a). By 2008, the central and local governments had commissioned over 20 consensus conferences. To date, over a hundred innovative deliberative forums have been conducted at the national, county–city and community levels in Taiwan. Most deliberative activities have been conducted by academic institutions and are commissioned by central and local governments, whereas some have been initiated by non-governmental organizations (e.g. Huang et al., 2007; Tu, 2007).

KMT's return to the central government in 2008 witnessed a decline in the practice of deliberative democracy. However, until then, the phenomenon of deliberative democracy had already diffused to different sectors of the society; in fact, several governmental departments and bureaus still rely on deliberative mechanisms to resolve policy disputes (Huang & Hsieh, 2013).

Since the Tsai government assumed office in 2016, government agencies have promoted institutional and innovative reforms. Additionally, they have encouraged national and online participation activities, such as mini-publics, e-participation for rule-making, public participation platforms, and youth participation. However, the existing literature on deliberative democracy does not encompass multi-faceted deliberative practices in Taiwan.

This book presents a pioneering whole-country application of the deliberative systems approach and deepens the understanding of Taiwan's democratic governance and institutional innovations. The book also strengthens the linkage between theoretical development and deliberative practices' multifaceted nature in Taiwan. It examines how democratic innovations operate and connect the sphere of micro-deliberative forums, empowered spaces and civic society in a multiple-level deliberative system. How democratic innovations and various components perform different functions, complement each other and contribute to the deliberative quality of the whole system, and the co-evolution of deliberative systems is also studied. As a front-runner of new democracies in Asia and with a relatively open society, Taiwan's deliberative democracy's unique features enrich the idea of deliberative systems and provide insights into deliberative governance to bring about polity-seeking transformation and improvement in the quality of democracy. In particular, scholars can contrast democratic deliberation in Taiwan with authoritarian deliberation in other Confucian societies.

Taiwan as a valuable case

Taiwanese deliberative practices and democratic innovations offer valuable insights into the rest of the world for the following reasons. First, Taiwan's history exemplifies the rapid transition to and emergence of a democratic polity, thus elucidating the global trend of democratisation. This is especially rare in Asia where there are many authoritarian (e.g. China and Vietnam) or strongly technocratic governance modes (e.g. Japan). The rise of social movements and a vibrant civil society have become constant forces that accelerate institutional reform and influence governance processes, thereby creating new spaces of public participation. Taiwan has integrated Western democratic values with those of Taiwan's many cultures, and institutional change and the promotion of democratic innovation in Taiwan continue to be flexibly adapted to emerging technologies and changes in the global environment.

Second, Taiwan shares many challenges with other actors around the globe, such as the need for energy transition, the problem of nuclear waste siting, scarcity of resources and the emergence of unprecedented risks (e.g. climate change, emergent technology risk). With particular respect to the democratisation of science, citizen activism and a revival in social movements have facilitated greater dialogue, deliberative practices and reflection on such democratisation; these have deepened institutional evolution and citizen participation in the policy-making process.

Third, Taiwan has many lessons to share with the world. These lessons have been gained from its experience with catastrophic events – involving pollution, natural disasters, technological problems and institutional failure. 'Deliberative learning' emphasises the building of civic-deliberation institutions in place of technocratic ones; it eschews institutions where policies change but dominant framing assumptions go unchallenged (Jasanoff, 2010, pp. 31–34). The many crises that Taiwan faced constitute opportunities for Taiwanese society (as opposed to only the Taiwanese state) to hone their ability to deal with uncertainty and ambiguity, evaluate policy frames and search for alternative explanations (Fan, 2015b). In the face of the present coronavirus 2019 (COVID-19) pandemic, the world has paid attention to Taiwan's effective response. Such effectiveness has been due not only to technical excellence and a robust public health infrastructure but also to a constructive and collaborative state–society relationship. Such a relationship has been honed through deliberative learning and through transparent and democratic governance processes. Taiwan learned the hard way, from its mistakes, during the 2003 SARS epidemic, where it then greatly strengthened its public health infrastructure in anticipation of the next public health crisis. The government also enhanced transparency and public communication to rebuild trust between citizens and government officials.

Fourth, young activists in Taiwan skilfully use digital technology to remake democracy to be more open and digital. This is exemplified in the Sunflower Movement in 2014. Furthermore, civic hackers and the open source community joined the Tsai government in 2016. They established the so-called Public Digital Innovation Space and institutionalised the use of online platforms to facilitate dialogue and integrate consensus-seeking into rule-making. In Taiwan, digital spaces for practicing deliberative democracy have emerged.

Framework for systemic analysis

Deliberative democracy, where citizens are to participate in normative debates, is considered the best method for remedying a lack of representativeness in institutions (Gutmann & Thompson, 1996, p. 5). Deliberative democracy emphasises the legitimacy of the collective decision-making process, encourages citizens to open-mindedly consider public interests, advocates respect for diversity in opinions and values and promotes rational communication and debate. According to Bächtiger et al. (2018), the ideals of deliberative democracy are always contested and evolving. Researchers and practitioners of deliberative democracy have introduced various types of deliberative experiments whose outcomes have influenced the evolution of deliberative democratic theory. The first-generation thinkers viewed deliberation as the give and take of reasons for and against various positions, and they combined this conception of deliberation with 'the ideals of high-quality argumentation or rational-critical debate, a focus on the common good, mutual respect, and the concept of a rationally motivated consensus to which all could agree' (Bächtiger et al., 2018, pp. 3–8). The second-generation thinkers expanded the ideals of their predecessors, being driven by the ideals of democratic inclusion and plurality. In general, the ideals constituting good deliberation are open to revision.

Bächtiger and Parkinson (2019) provide a new understanding of deliberation that emphasises contingency, performance and distribution of deliberative acts. First, contingency stresses that 'the various forms of deliberation depend on the particular goals of deliberation and the contexts in which deliberation takes place' (Bächtiger & Parkinson, 2019, pp. 48–49). Second, the performative aspect of deliberation entails 'a dynamic vision in that actors may shift communication over time' (Bächtiger & Parkinson, 2019, pp. 48–49). Third, the interplay of different deliberative virtues across time and space is crucial to understand the effects and functions of deliberation in a democracy. Thinking of deliberation as a dynamic process opens up new ways of seeing deliberation on a large scale as a sequence of events, and it allows for understanding deliberation in a micro-forum as performed and distributed, and to apply systemic views to small-scale events.

Although many scholars of deliberative democracy consider it to be a normative ideal, many original systems theorists – such as Mansbridge, Parkinson, and Chambers – think of it more as a description of democracy. Curato et al. (2019) view the 'systemic turn' of deliberative democracy as a normative, empirical and political project. They argue that power plays an ambiguous and sometimes contradictory role in the deliberative system and that it is crucial to critically examine the context in which these exercises of power take place.

This book stands in this systemic-descriptive tradition. It uses the methods of thick description to elucidate the contextual complexities and emergence of deliberative systems in practice. In doing so, this book contributes to making deliberative democracy more deliberative and more democratic.

Dryzek (2016) argues for three images of the theory of deliberative democracy that locate its essence in, respectively, 'a single forum, a deliberative system, and an encompassing polity featuring particular integrative norms' (p. 1). Theorists of deliberative democracy need to think about how practices that make sense in terms of each image connect to the other two, which helps solve internal disputes and respond to critics – such as Carole Pateman's (2012) concerns about broad participation and Iris Young's (2000) and Lynn Sanders's (1997) critiques of rationalistic forms of communication. As Dryzek (2016) highlights:

> Forums only make sense when linked in a system that can synthesize very different deliberative virtues (notably, justification, reflection, and inclusion). Any system's democratic qualities can only be evaluated in terms of the polity. While judgment in terms of conditions of normative integration in the polity is therefore primary, particular forums can promote

deliberative authenticity in a system, and systems enable inclusive application of deliberative ideals.

(p. 1)

Dryzek (2014, p. 106) indicates that we need to think about how interlinked forums (e.g. parliaments, legislatures, assemblies, citizen forums) relate to larger processes in the informal public sphere, and how all those things fit together. Also, any deliberative system should contain what Thompson (2009) has called 'meta-deliberation' as part of a deliberative system, that is, the capacity of the system to reflect on its own shortcomings and remedy them if necessary.

Dryzek (2009) suggested that a deliberative systems approach is suitable for analysing democratic transitions. The deliberative capacity of a country in transition is its ability to host structures for reasoned, inclusive and consequential discussion. Stevenson and Dryzek (2014) identify seven components of a deliberative system as follows:

1) *Private space* is made up of the political conversations and interactions between family and friends, with colleagues or in meeting places, such as restaurants.
2) *Public space* is where more open and accessible communication is found, including in civil society, among citizens and in the media.
3) *Empowered space* is where legitimate collective decisions are taken, including parliament, a policy-making council, an executive committee, courts, international negotiations and spaces such as stakeholder dialogues that have been given by the government the power to act and decide.
4) *Transmission* of influence from public space to empowered space. Such transmission can take place in a number of ways. Narratives developed in the public space can have direct impacts on the debate within the empowered space through political campaigns and protest. Transmission can also occur more subtly as a result of cultural change that begins in the public space but eventually changes the understandings and perspectives of those in the empowered space.
5) *Accountability* involves the empowered space being responsible to the public space. Elections are the most common and important accountability mechanism within liberal democratic states, and we have to consider other accountability mechanisms in deliberative systems.
6) *Meta-deliberation* is the capacity of a deliberative system to reflect on its own shortcomings and transform itself if necessary.
7) *Decisiveness* is the degree to which the previous six elements acting together actually determine collective outcomes.

Drawing on Dryzek's work on deliberative systems, Burall (2015, pp. 29–30) adds that other accountability mechanisms include parliamentary hearings, ombudsmen, courts and media. Burall argued that transmission from the empowered space to the public space is just as important if a system is to be truly deliberative. The spaces are interlinked and there are both positive and negative feedback loops between them. It will require mechanisms for collecting and evaluating information about who is participating in, and missing from, the system as a whole and how well the different components are interacting.

Dryzek (2009) argued in favour of the idea of deliberative capacity that is best suited for the comparative analysis of different systems. These features include deliberative authenticity, inclusiveness and consequentiality. Deliberative authenticity means that 'it is unaffected by coercion, induces reflection about preferences, reveals claims that are systemically connected to more general principles, and exhibits reciprocity' (Dryzek, 2010, pp. 136–137; see also Felicetti et al., 2016, p. 429). Inclusiveness refers to 'the range of interests and discourses present in a political setting' (Dryzek, 2009, p. 1385, as quoted in Felicetti et al., 2016, p. 15). The representativeness of arguments and views brought to the forum by the selection of invited speakers should be considered as well. Consequentiality means that a mini-public should have an effect or make a difference on collective decisions or outcomes (Dryzek, 2010; Felicetti et al., 2016, p. 431).

O'Flynn and Curato (2015) argue that 'free deliberation among equals' can be treated as an important indicator of democratic quality (p. 298). They outline a deliberative systems framework that might be used 'for *describing* or characterising the spaces where deliberation occurs and how they relate to each other, and for *evaluating* the extent to which inclusive and reasoned deliberation underpins the democratic trajectory of the transition process' (p. 299, emphasis in original). They consider deliberation fundamental to our thinking about democratic deepening in transition societies and that the fairness of an election must be premised upon deliberation. In line with Dryzek and O'Flynn and Curato (2015), this book puts further emphasis on the crucial role of digital innovations and connectivity in deliberative systems in the times of rapid development of information and communication technology (ICT) and emergent digital citizens and activism. Digital innovations allow connectivity and interconnection of multiple participation platforms, components of deliberative systems, and spaces across time, scales and borders (see Figure 1.1).

A relatively inclusive deliberative theory integrates all types of deliberation, from the micro to the macro. Public deliberation is best conceptualised as an activity that occurs in a range of discursive spheres that collectively engage a diversity of civil society actors (Hendriks, 2006). Theorising deliberation at a systemic level helps us think about how to scale deliberative forums up and out into an expanded political structure with a complex and dynamic division of deliberative labour (Karpowitz & Raphael, 2014).

Bächtiger and Parkinson (2019) take a problem-oriented approach to both micro- and macro-research on deliberation and provide a new understanding of deliberation and deliberativeness as contingent, performative and distributed.

The Deliberative System

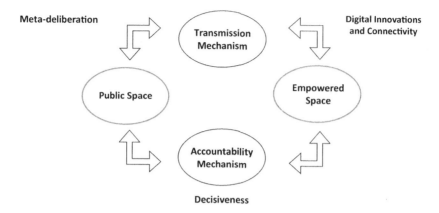

Figure 1.1 The deliberative system
Source: Modified from O'Flynn and Curato (2015, p. 304) and Burall (2015).

They link various forms of deliberation and democratic communication to five deliberative goals – epistemic, ethical, legitimacy-oriented, emancipatory and a combined transformation and clarification goal – as well as to different contexts, and provide six avenues for future research. Their development of the account of deliberative systems has been focused on three elements of sequencing – listening, structuration and deciding – that capture the dynamics of real-world political debate and provide empirical cues. As they highlight,

> One that starts with listening to and stimulating narratives and claims on the public from the public sphere; structuring the narratives and claims that emerge in an open, visible way; and making building collective decisions in a context of active listening, or representation as relationship building.
> (Bächtiger & Parkinson, 2019, p. 103)

They argue for considering six features of a deliberative system: the *agents* of deliberation; the *sites* of deliberation; the *entities* that are discussed and transmitted from site to site; the *transmission* processes themselves; the *transformation* processes that turn discussion entities into policy and law; and the *implementation* processes that see policy and law acted on and enforced (p. 17). They provide a framework of measuring deliberation and distinguish additive and summative views. An additive view tries to identify goal- and context-specific deliberative moments in various sites of a democratic system, and assumes that goal- and context-specific deliberativeness must have been present in some venues of a democratic system to make the later 'deliberative'.

A summative view takes a broader perspective on deliberativeness and focuses on 'complex transmissions and interplays that produce a deliberative timbre' (p. 18). They call for the need to broaden the analytical lens and study deliberative actions in a multisite and multistage democracy.

The various approaches disagree in various respects, such as in their different criteria used to evaluate deliberative democracy and their different views on the relative merits of using the additive versus summative approach to measuring deliberation. This book uses Dryzek's deliberative system approach because it is appropriate to the context and case studies for the following reasons. First, Dryzek's approach focuses on deliberative structure and its constituent components, with an eye towards process. According to Dryzek, a deliberative system must be evaluated with respect to how authentic, inclusive, and consequential it is. In particular, non-deliberative acts and practices can have positive systemic deliberative consequences and should thus be treated as part of the system. The deliberative-system framework is sensitive to context and to the multiplicity of deliberative practices within and between various parts of the system. Furthermore, the concept of a deliberative system foregrounds local activists and residents in their deliberative and epistemic practices, thereby recognising their contribution to policy-making and the wider body of deliberative systems. Likewise, (new) discourses may persist in the system even if some civil society organisations do not. This highlights a strength of the deliberative systems approach.

Moreover, elements of meta-deliberation and decisiveness are useful to empirical research that shows how civic organizations and the state have recognised their shortcomings, adapted and, to a degree, made systemic changes that increase the potential for greater equality for indigenous people. For example, President Tsai issued a formal apology to the nation's indigenous peoples on 1 August 2016, Indigenous Peoples' Day in Taiwan, pledging on behalf of the government to take comprehensive action to achieve transitional justice and promote social harmony and reconciliation. She also unveiled the Indigenous Historical Justice and Transitional Justice Commission. The current second committee comprises the president as the convener, one representative for each of the 16 groups of indigenous peoples, three representatives for all Pingpu ethnic groups, representatives of relevant government agencies, experts and scholars, and between 9 and 11 representatives of indigenous civic groups. It opened a new channel for dialogue, reflection and clarifying conflicts. According to the Indigenous Peoples Basic Act and the Council of Indigenous Peoples' current guidelines on traditional territories, any land development, wildlife conservation or anthropological projects in traditional tribal territories must be approved by the indigenous community. This facilitates ongoing plural conversations within tribal communities and interactions between indigenous peoples and non-indigenous residents. Furthermore, there are increasing numbers of new civic society organizations (e.g. Citizen Congress Watch, Congress Investigation Corps) setting up online platforms and forums to transmit information rapidly and help citizens to easily access information and participate in public affairs and deliberation, which encourage legislators and government officials to actively respond to public discourses and critiques.

This book locates deliberativeness in the democratic system of Taiwan and analyses the democratic innovations of Taiwan's governance architecture and deliberative practices and their interplay. It takes a dynamic view of deliberation and explores the connection of public space and empowered space, transmission and accountability mechanisms, how different components interact and complement each other, and a systemic relationship of the parts as a whole of Taiwan's democratic deepening processes.

Methodology

The interpretive approach could help to understand how deliberation occurs in practice and reflect on the theoretical implications for normative theory (Dryzek, 2007; Hendriks, 2006; Ercan et al., 2017). Although the deliberative systems approach is theoretically attractive, it raises methodological questions, such as how do we identify multiple communicative sites within a deliberative system and how do we study deliberative quality empirically (Ercan et al., 2017; Bächtiger, 2018)? Based on Habermasian discourse ethics on the intersubjective achievement of understanding and the process of decision-making, King (2009, p. 6) argues that evaluation of deliberative quality needs to assess how this is perceived by other participants. Ercan et al. (2017) also argues in favour of interpretive research methods that can play crucial roles in empirical studies of deliberative systems, including a) portraying the sites, agents and discursive elements that comprise a deliberative system; b) understanding connections and transmissions within a deliberative system; and c) appreciating the context of deliberative forums and systems.

This book adopts an interpretive approach, which helps to better understand the multiple meanings associated with contested policy issues and the different ideas and experiences of public deliberation. One of the strengths of interpretive research is that it is iterative, flexible and guided by practice and could provide insights into unforeseen problems and opportunities for deliberative democracy (Ercan et al., 2017).

Interpretative analysis views the phenomenon from the subjective perspectives of the participants, and understands the meaning of participants' experiences within a rich narrative story (Bhattacherjee, 2012). Also, interpretative analysis gives us the freedom to understand the complexities associated with an emerging area, such as deliberative democracy, where there may be a range of perspectives at play. This book uses interpretive analysis that focuses on language and meanings from the perspective of activists and participants involved in the social phenomenon; study values, ideas, frames and discourses that shape actions and institutions, and the ways in which they do so; and it particularly looks at how multiple actors interact, network and transmit ideas in a deliberative system.

In addition to an interpretive analysis of the evolving concepts and a variety of practices of deliberative democracy in Taiwan, this book uses three cases of democratic innovations to capture distributed deliberation, examines significant events and sites of dialogue and deliberative practices that connect and complete each other, and highlights the importance of strengthening linkages of the interconnected spheres of science and policy to enhance the deliberative capacity of governance. Research on deliberative systems with detailed discussions on the relationship between the dynamic interactions and connection of spheres of science and policy and the role of expertise in deliberative systems is limited.

My three case studies were on the revival of environmental movements, indigenous activism and democratic innovations in the system that is Taiwanese deliberative democracy. The interconnections between this system's components and subsystems facilitate a space for deliberation, contribute to countering exclusion, make deliberative systems exert more of a democratising effect, and expand the democratic imagination.

I use Mansbridge et al.'s (2012) concepts of the epistemic, ethical and democratic functions of deliberative systems to structure the analysis in the case study chapters. First, the epistemic function of a deliberative system is 'to produce preferences, opinions, and decisions that are appropriately informed by facts and logic and are the outcome of substantive and meaningful consideration of relevant reasons' (p. 11). Second, the ethical function of the system is to promote mutual respect among citizens. Mutual respect is *intrinsic* to deliberation: it keeps the deliberative system running. Being open to being moved by the words of another is to respect the other as a source of reasons, claims and perspectives (p. 11). Mutual respect also implies non-domination. Third, the democratic function entails the inclusion of a plurality of voices, interests, concerns and claims on the basis of feasible equality, which is the core of what makes deliberative democratic processes democratic. A well-functioning democratic deliberative system ought to actively promote and facilitate inclusion and equal opportunities to participate in the system (p. 12). The realisation of the three epistemic, ethical and democratic functions promotes the legitimacy of democratic decision-making. A systemic approach recognises potential conflicts between these functions and the fact that some will be more important than others in different parts of the system. Judging the quality of the whole system on the basis of the functions and goals specified for the system does not require that those functions be fully realised in all the parts (Mansbridge et al., 2012, p. 12).

Common to all three case studies are their divisions of labour, the multiplicity in their instantiations of democracy and deliberation, and the multiplicity in their transmission mechanisms that influence the performance of these multiple functions of deliberative systems. The cases of public deliberation on nuclear waste siting and indigenous grassroots participation in a mining controversy exemplify the interconnection between the functions of reason-giving deliberative interaction and of non-deliberative forms of citizen action, whereas the case of participatory budgeting (PB) in Taipei City elucidates how different PB processes can complement other components of the democratic system.

The first case – public deliberation on nuclear waste facility siting – was selected to examine, in deliberative systems, both the science–democracy relationship and how knowledge is produced and used. I explored the perspectives of those involved in environmental activism, deliberative forums and the knowledge-creation and discursive practices in various domains. The case study highlights the interactions, divisions of labour and interrelations between various communication activities among stakeholders and between elements that perform particular functions in the deliberative system. For example, the citizen conference on 'where should radioactive waste go?' in March 2010 functioned to enable citizen understanding of the complex issues, discourses, pieces of information and value propositions from various perspectives; it also enhanced the interactions between government agencies, Taipower (the state-owned utilities provider), civil society groups, experts and lay citizens. The deliberative forums undertaken by the national Stop Nukes Now organisation from March to October in 2016 strengthened public communication, improved citizen consciousness of nuclear waste issues and connected various public interests and groups in the community. The case study traces a variety of deliberative practices and their interplay in a democratic system, in addition to both their diffuse influences on the quality of deliberation on nuclear waste governance and their beneficial effects on the connections between the system's components.

The second case – indigenous political participation and governance of traditional territories – was selected to represent how Taiwan is seeking transitional justice and how civil society organisations can improve the integration of civic deliberation into deliberative systems and the wider landscape of political decision-making. Through a case study of natural resource exploitation in tribal lands in Taiwan, Chapter 6 explores the ongoing struggles for indigenous land rights and how collective activism has both shaped policy-making and led to ongoing dialogue and debate surrounding the Mining Act amendments. It explores how indigenous and environmental groups spearheaded discursive change and built coalitions in response to the state's long-standing policy. Such change in wider deliberative systems enhanced the deliberative capacity of environmental governance, in addition to occurring in multiple spaces – such as indigenous and environmental alliances, local and central government agencies, the judiciary, the Legislative Yuan (Taiwan's parliament) and the Control Yuan.

The third case, PB of Taipei City, was selected to exemplify democratic innovations in deliberative systems, illustrating city and neighbourhood as important sites of deliberative experiments. PB has been widely discussed and even institutionalised in many cities worldwide. However, no study has adopted a deliberative systems approach. Drawing on the practice of PB in Taipei City, Chapter 7 examines the unique government–academia alliance and the multiple roles that academic institutions and civil society organisations played as intermediary actors in facilitating deliberative practices, accelerating transmission and making institutional adjustments. This case analyses the dynamic connections between residents' assemblies and other components of PB, in addition to how ongoing communication between government officials, local elites, partnership schools and civic organisations serve interlocking functions in a democratic system.

This book builds on a rich set of empirical data. I have adopted the use of context-sensitive qualitative methods, including documentary analysis, interview research and participant observation.

Documentary analysis

I collected relevant books, journals, working papers, government publications, newspapers and statistical data, which helped to support, supplement and cross-check the correctness of my interpretations of situations and related arguments. Government publications comprise legislative issue documents, the relevant documents of legislative motion, proceedings from the Legislative Yuan's policy forums, parliamentary committee hearings, the Archives of the Minutes of the Deliberation, policy documents and the Control Yuan's report on policy controversy. I also examined non-governmental organisations' publications, especially Citizen Congress Watch's (CCW) evaluation report on legislators and *Legislative Weekly*. CCW, a specialised institute comprising 37 civil organisations, aims to oversee the parliament, conduct evaluations, identify and remove incapable legislators and promote congressional reforms. CCW conducts Civil Evaluation Conferences, in which hundreds of citizens participate as evaluators once a session. They facilitate dialogue and interaction between legislators and civic organisations (Chapter 3). This book builds on a rich set of data from numerous deliberation practices and activities, including minutes of meetings, citizen reports and preliminary reports. The documentary analysis involved examining relevant Taiwan news reports, films and documentaries, propaganda materials from environmental group campaigns, websites of non-governmental organisations, press releases and petition statements.

The material was used interpretatively; that is, the contents of documents and media reports were used as an interpretative tool to understand and assess the public discourses, debates and claims forwarded by different actors. I employed documentary analysis to support interviews and supplement their insufficiencies. Additionally, I was directed towards further relevant materials and interview questions. Documentary analysis and interviews alternated with each other in the collection, judgment and absorption of materials.

Interview research and informal conversations

Interviews with open-ended questions and snowball sampling were employed. Open-ended questions usually encourage unpredictable discourses to provide a new perspective for the research. Snowball sampling promotes the emergence of some relevant interviewees introduced by the other interviewees. It enables the researcher to locate the right people to talk to – people who might be willing to participate and will provide the researcher with some choices about whom to contact.

Interviewees comprised researchers and practitioners of deliberative democracy, members from non-governmental organisations and community colleges who promote deliberative democracy and participate in policy-making, and legislators and government officials. Interviews were semi-structured, covering the interviewees' views on policy issues, deliberative practices and innovations and citizen actions. How the interviewees viewed the government's ways of dealing with controversies and participation activities were explored. Attention was also paid to the challenges and issues deemed critical by the interviewees. I enquired about other relevant, interesting questions raised by other interviewees that needed to be re-proved or answered from different viewpoints.

Participant observation

Participant observation includes attending public meetings, citizen consensus conferences, and resident assembly and deliberative forums, where various actors and the public engage in communications and deliberation. I have been working on the nuclear waste controversy for over ten years. I and other members of the academic deliberative democracy research team conducted a citizen conference on nuclear waste facility siting in 2010. The main goals of the citizen conference were to provide a platform for dialogue on nuclear waste disposal issues and raise concerns on them. Participant observation was conducted to understand civic mobilisation, discursive practices, and participation processes across time and space in the deliberative systems. Additionally, dynamic connections between civic forums and hybrid forums of the alliance and effects of public deliberation were also explored.

I serve as a member of the steering committee of deliberative forums (for example, the national eID Card open policy workshop) and the Taipei City participatory budgeting government–academia alliance. Since 2016, I have also participated in Beitou District Office PB working teams to provide suggestions on deliberative practices and train graduate students to serve as facilitators in resident assemblies. I have participated in different communicative and deliberative events and analysed how deliberative practices interact and connect in the political context as well as the dynamics that played out. Insights from participant observation, documentary analysis and interviews are integrated into a detailed thick description of different components of deliberative systems.

The structure of the book

Chapter 1 provides the analytical framework and background on the case study of Taiwan. Chapters 2–4 constitute Part I, and the remaining chapters constitute Part II. Part I is about theorising Taiwanese politics as a deliberative system, specifically, examining how different forms of civic action in a deliberative democracy emerge contextually and how citizen action and crucial components interconnect to increase the deliberative capacity of the overall system. Chapter 2 analyses the deliberative capacity of the public sphere where reflection is facilitated and where people can deliberate on public issues. The public spaces involved include activist networks, social movements, ordinary citizens, mini-publics, online forums and the media. These public spaces lay out the main discourses that actors can contest and reflect on. The case study also examines the dynamics of discursive coalitions and discursive practices in policy debates, in addition to how social movements encourage deliberation. It examines the significance and democratic functions of deliberative forums at the national, local and grassroots level, in addition to specifying how information and communication technology can be appropriated by citizens, forum initiators and social movements in emerging domains, such as social media and citizen science.

Chapter 3 analyses the deliberative capacity of the empowered space, defined as that where legitimate collective decisions are taken, particularly the Legislative Yuan. It examines how civil society organisations promote parliamentary transparency. It also details these organisations' diffuse influences on the quality of deliberation within the empowered space and their positive contributions to connections between, and the deliberative nature of, the system's components. The emergence of third-force parties is also mentioned along with their inclusion of multiple and marginalised discourses in the empowered space during the policy-making process and their contribution to inclusiveness. I detail the role of emergent civil society groups in Legislative Yuan reform and their evaluation of the performance of legislators. I consider the increased use of mini-public and public hearings to represent both a plurality of voices in the empowered space and the contribution of online platforms to strengthening connections between the public and the empowered space.

Chapter 4 presents an analysis of transmission and accountability. It illustrates the importance of transmission mechanisms in deliberative systems, which are processes that transmit ideas and claims from the public space to the empowered space to influence the policy-making process. It analyses those mechanisms that have been rapidly developing where transmission is versatile; these include nationwide public consultative exercises, institutional innovations, deliberative forums and mini-publics on the Internet, networked governance and the election process. This chapter highlights the importance of transmission and accountability mechanisms and how civic society groups actively involved in transmission and accountability mechanisms advance the deliberative capacity of the whole system.

Part II comprises three cases studies on democratic innovations, various modes of interplay between the system's components, and various modes of transmission with their unique functions, effects and limitations; all these parts of the system work together to enhance deliberative capability and social learning. These three cases illustrate (1) how multiple sites of deliberation interact within the larger political system and (2) how systemic elements exercise their respective epistemic, ethical and democratic functions in the deliberative system.

Chapter 5 uses the case of deliberation on siting a nuclear waste facility to examine the dynamic interactions and connections between the policy and scientific spheres in deliberative systems. It analyses how knowledge is produced and used in deliberative systems by exploring the voices and perspectives of those involved in environmental activism, in deliberative forums and in the knowledge-creation and discursive practices in various domains. The chapter analyses the interactions, divisions of labour and interrelations between different communications events, processes and activities. It highlights the interplay between deliberative practices in deliberative systems and how civil society organisations democratise science while facilitating participatory initiatives that have accelerated the evolution of participatory institutions.

Chapter 6 discusses indigenous political participation and the co-evolution of deliberative systems; it considers indigenous activism and political communication as a part of the macro-deliberative system as well as a micro-deliberative system in itself. Examining the controversy surrounding mining in Truku indigenous lands, this chapter explores how indigenous participation enhanced the democratising power of deliberative systems, in addition to the co-evolution of tribal deliberative systems and their interaction with the state. Specifically, indigenous activists and environmental groups mobilised to facilitate deliberation on indigenous lands and mining regulations, including campaigning, by employing various means such as petitioning, lobbying and litigation. Activists mobilised and utilised resources to seek public attention and support from outsiders in wider society. This chapter, with regard to the process of tribal political participation and social negotiation, elucidates both the contributions of indigenous political participation in deliberative systems and the dynamic interactions between indigenous activism and the state.

Chapter 7 examines PB in deliberative systems. This chapter illustrates the dynamics of deliberative practices in multiple spaces, noting how social expectations and the democratic imagination of civic organisations are key to enlisting the participation of organisation members as well as reshaping the practice, features and development of PB. The dynamic connections of various discussions and deliberations in various spaces and at different stages of the PB cycle enhance the deliberative quality of local governance and deliberative systems.

Chapter 8 highlights the idea that perceiving deliberative democracy in terms of a deliberative systems approach helps increase the visibility of emergent spaces for claims-making and justification. This approach provides a pathway to understand the relational interdependence of participatory practices, ICT utilisation, and spaces of communications across time and scales. This chapter discusses the unique and emergent participation, innovative practices and institutional evolution in Taiwan – lessons from Taiwan's deliberative democracy that other countries could benefit from, new challenges and opportunities raised for deliberative democracy, and argues for inclusiveness and meta-deliberation in times of disaster and uncertainty.

References

Bächtiger, A. (2018). A preface to studying deliberation empirically. In A. Bächtiger, J. Dryzek, J. Mansbridge, & M. Warren (Eds.), *Handbook of deliberative democracy* (pp. 657–662). Oxford: Oxford University Press.

Bächtiger, A., & Parkinson, J. (2019). *Mapping and measuring deliberation: Towards a new deliberative quality*. Oxford: Oxford University Press.

Bächtiger, A., Dryzek, J., Mansbridge, J., & Warren, M. (2018). Deliberative democracy: An introduction. In A. Bächtiger, J. Dryzek, J. Mansbridge, & M. Warren (Eds.), *Handbook of deliberative democracy* (pp. 1–31). Oxford: Oxford University Press.

Bhattacharjee, A. (2012). *Social science research: Principles, methods, and practices.* Tampa: University of South Florida.

Burall, S. (2015). *Room for a view: Democracy as a deliberative system.* London: Involve.

Curato, N., Hammond, M., & Min, J. (2019). *Power in deliberative democracy: Norms, forums and systems.* Basingstoke: Palgrave Macmillan

Dodge, J. (2014). Civil society organizations and deliberative policy making: Interpreting environmental controversies in the deliberative system. *Policy Sciences, 47*(2), 161–185.

Dryzek, J. S. (2007). Theory, evidence and the tasks of deliberation. In S. W. Rosenberg (Ed.), *Deliberation, participation and democracy: Can the people govern?* (pp. 237–250). Basingstoke: Palgrave Macmillan.

Dryzek, J. S. (2009). Democratization as a deliberative capacity building. *Comparative Political Studies, 42*, 1379–1402.

Dryzek, J. S. (2010). *Foundations and frontiers of deliberative governance.* Oxford: Oxford University Press.

Dryzek, J. S. (2013). The deliberative democrat's idea of justice. *European Journal of Political Theory, 12*, 329–346.

Dryzek, J. S. (2014). Twists of democratic governance. In J. P. Gagnon (Ed.), *Democratic theorists in conversation: Turns in contemporary thought,* (pp. 101–116). Basingstoke: Palgrave Macmillan.

Dryzek, J. S. (2016). The forum, the system and the polity: Three varieties of democratic theory. *Political Theory, 45*, 1–27.

Ercan, S. A., Hendriks, C., & Boswell, J. (2017). Studying public deliberation after the systemic turn: The crucial role for interpretive research. *Policy and Politics, 45*(2), 195–212.

Fan, M.-F. (2015a). Evaluating the 2008 Consensus Conference on GM Foods in Taiwan. *Public Understanding of Science, 24*(5), 533–546.

Fan, M.-F. (2015b). Disaster governance and community resilience: Reflections on Typhoon Morakot in Taiwan. *Journal of Environmental Planning and Management, 58*(1), 24–38.

Felicetti, A., Niemeyer, S., & Curato, N. (2016). Improving deliberative participation: Connecting mini-publics to deliberative systems. *European Political Science Review, 8*(3), 427–448.

Gutmann, A., & Thompson, D. (1996). *Democracy and disagreement*. Boston: Harvard University Press.

Hendriks, C. M. (2006). Integrated deliberation: Reconciling civil society's dual role in deliberative democracy. *Political Studies, 54*(3), 486–503.

Huang, T.-Y., & Hsieh, C.-A. (2013). Practicing deliberative democracy in Taiwan: Processes, impacts and challenges, *Taiwan Journal of Democracy, 9*(2), 79–104.

Huang, T.-Y., Shih, C.-L., & Fu, K.-J. (2007). The reasoning process in local public deliberation: The case of consensus conference held by Yi-lan Community College in 2005. *Journal of Public Administration, 24*, 71–102.

Jasanoff, S. 2010. Beyond calculation: A democratic response to risk. In A. Lakoff (Ed.), *Disaster and the politics of intervention* (pp. 14–40). New York: Columbia University Press.

Karpowitz, C. & Raphael, C. (2014). *Deliberation, democracy, and civic forums: Improving equality and publicity*. Cambridge: Cambridge University Press.

King, M. (2009). A critical assessment of Steenbergen et al.'s discourse quality index. *Roundhouse, 1*, 1–8.

Lin, K.-M., & Chen, D.-S. (2003). Consensus conferences and deliberative democracy: Citizen participation in Taiwan's national health insurance policies. *Taiwanese Sociology, 6*, 61–118.

Lin, Y.-S. (2007). No difference between us: The relationship between experts and lay persons in the surrogate motherhood consensus conference in Taiwan. *Taiwan Journal of Democracy, 4*(3), 1–32.

Mansbridge, J., Bohman, J., Chambers, S., Christiano, T., Fung, A., Parkinson, J., Thompson, D. F., & Warren, M. E. (2012). A systemic approach to deliberative democracy. In J. Parkinson & J. Mansbridge (Eds.), *Deliberative systems: Deliberative democracy at the large scale* (1–26). Cambridge: Cambridge University Press.

O'Flynn, I., & Curato, N. (2015). Deliberative democratization: A framework for systemic analysis. *Policy Studies, 36*(3), 298–313.

Pateman, C. (2012). Participatory democracy revisited. *Perspectives on Politics, 10*(1), 7–19.

Sanders, L. (1997). Against deliberation. *Political Theory, 25*, 347–376.

Stevenson, H., & Dryzek, J. S. (2014). *Democratizing global climate governance*. Cambridge: Cambridge University Press.

Tang, B., Tamura, T., & He, B. (2018). Deliberative democracy in East Asia: Japan and China. In A. Bächtiger, J. Dryzek, J. Mansbridge, & M. Warren (Eds.), *Handbook of deliberative democracy* (pp. 791–804). Oxford: Oxford University Press.

Thompson, D. (2009). Deliberative democratic theory and empirical political science. *Annual Review of Political Science, 11*, 497–520.

Tu, W. L. (2007). Deliberative democracy and social movement: An inspiration from the local-initiative consensus conference of Hsinchu science-based industrial park at Ilan. *Journal of Public Administration, 23*, 67–93.

Weinstock, D., & Kahane, D. (2010). Introduction. In D. Kahane, D. Weinstock, & D. Leydet (Eds.), *Deliberative democracy in practice* (pp. 1–18). Vancouver, Canada: University of British Columbia Press.

Young, I. (2000). *Inclusion and democracy*. Oxford: Oxford University Press.

Part I
Complex interactions of micro- and macro-deliberative systems

2 The public space

Discourses as a guiding thread

Public space is where more open, accessible communication and wide-ranging discourses are found. It contains activists, social movements, the academe, commercial actors, independent journalists, community organisations, bloggers, citizens as they gather either virtually or physically, and even politicians. Locations include formal meetings of activists and advocates, occasions when activists and advocates from different sides get together, mini-publics, public hearings, informal meetings in cafés and virtual internet forums. Public space can involve face-to-face gatherings and media activities (Dryzek, 2010, p. 11; 2014, p. 28).

Dryzek (2006) defines discourse as 'a shared set of concepts, categories and ideas that provide its adherents with a framework for making sense of situations, embody judgments, assumptions, capabilities, dispositions, and intentions' (p. 1). The discourse approach maps public space in terms of the more prominent discourses that pervade it rather than actors or interest groups because political actors' interests and preferences are not fixed. It emphasises that actors can contest, reflect on and subscribe to different discourses depending on the issue. Discourses can change in their content, therefore, discourses are much more enduring than the ever-changing cast of actors and forums. Discourses as a distinct analytical category perform a coordinating function in that citizens do not need to directly communicate with each other to inform their actions. Discourses organise people's views and consequently affect their decisions and actions (Curato, 2015; Stevenson & Dryzek, 2012, pp. 31, 191).

Four discourse types emerged from my interpretative analysis, and these categories are key to understanding the issues in the Taiwanese context. The basic four categories are reform and transitional justice, the cross-strait relationship and Taiwanese subjectivity, market-oriented neoliberal discourse, and sustainable development and low-carbon energy transition. This section identifies the content of these discourses and the subcategories within them, and key actors and advocates of each discourse, while the discourses remain at the centre as the guiding thread.

Reform and transformation towards social justice

The first discourse type is reform and transformation towards social justice discourse that advocates institutional reform and democracy deepening. Taiwan has been regarded as having a vibrant civil society, and non-governmental organisations (NGOs) have become constant forces pushing for change of the polity and effecting change from within extant governance processes. After three instances of power transfer and the democratisation process, freedom, democracy, human rights and justice have become the core values and main discourses in public space. The public space has been the site for imagining democracy, with some civil society organisations engaged in advancing democracy and promoting human rights and egalitarian society. The Taiwan Association for Human Rights (TAHR), founded in 1984, advocates 'democratic reforms to ensure civil and political rights' as the main campaign topic in its initial years and has extended its engagement to a variety of human rights issues, including assisting with investigations and offering litigation support for individuals where authorities violate basic human rights, engaging in a policy watch, and advocating monitoring according to the latest agenda from international human rights organisations (Taiwan Association for Human Rights, n.d.). TAHR frame their struggles for democratic reform to rectify injustice and fight against power.

The Act on Promoting Transitional Justice was passed by the Legislative Yuan on 5 December 2017 to rectify injustices committed by the authoritarian KMT government. The Transitional Justice Commission was established by the Executive Yuan in May 2018 to increase the availability of political archives, remove authoritarian symbols, redress judicial injustice and produce a report on the history of the period that delineates steps to further promote transitional justice. Furthermore, an emergent social enterprise, termed Watchout, dedicated to lowering the threshold of civic participation was commissioned by the Ministry of Culture to conduct a series of scenario workshops concerning the transformation of Chiang Kai-shek Memorial Hall to facilitate deliberation and reflection on historic and transitional justice topics.

These discourses are also reflected among grassroots movements with activist networks. For example, the Kanke Indigenous Sustainable Development Association in Datong Township, Yilan County, invited various civic groups that provide multiple care services to share experiences regarding their work, tell stories about policy problems and alternatives and increase networking among indigenous communities. They also encouraged collaboration between scholars and multiple actors to establish the Alliance for Amending the Indigenous Long-Term Care Service Law, build a coalition, and propose alternatives that respect the needs of indigenous people and their own care service methods, advocating 'the return of elderly care autonomy'. Indigenous activism and advocates highlight the questions 'Who needs to be cared for?' and 'Who assesses the allocation of recipients for care services?'

However, the answers are not limited to physical health and the field of bio-medicine but also encompass mental and spiritual health, social relationship and cultural meaning (Fan & Sung, 2020).

The cross-strait relationship and Taiwanese subjectivity

The second discourse type is the peaceful cross-strait relationship and Taiwanese subjectivity discourse. Social movements and civil society organisations challenge the rationale and discourses behind the bureaucratic rules and regulations of governance. This discourse is reflected among political parties, but people can reflect on competing discourses depending on the issue. An iconic case is the Sunflower Movement, which started when 200 students occupied the national legislature on the evening of 18 March 2014 to protest the ruling party's passing of a free-trade agreement with China without clause-by-clause review. The Sunflower Movement, named after the floral gift sent to protesters as a symbol of hope, gained widespread public support and launched a rally of half a million participants. The Sunflower activists become a political trigger to counter the KMT government's push for trade liberalisation with China for big corporations' benefits at the expense of individuals. People voiced their worry that close economic integration with China would compromise Taiwan's political autonomy and self-governing status. The Sunflower Movement ended peacefully after Legislative Speaker Jin-Pyng Wang visited the occupied parliament chamber and promised to postpone a review of the trade pact until legislation monitoring all cross-strait agreements was implemented. The protestors prevented the immediate ratification of the trade pact and facilitated ongoing deliberation in the public space and empowered space. The Sunflower Movement was an electoral setback for the KMT because of their failure to respond to public discourse and the political crisis. Therefore, the DPP won the presidency and the legislative majority in 2016 (Ho, 2019). During Sunflower Movement protests, responses to students' appeals to overturn the trade pact varied. In March 2019, the Taiwan Citizen Front was formed by civic society activists and academics because of their concerns regarding a conservative force counterattack and the threat of Mainland China harming Taiwanese democracy after the KMT won a majority in the 2018 local elections. The Taiwan Citizen Front has proposed a citizen charter and aims to facilitate social dialogue, cultivate Taiwan's democracy, affect public policy to prevent the degradation of democracy and constantly promote reform engineering in pursuit of a better Taiwan.

Competing discourses are also reflected in debates regarding adjustments to high school civics curriculum guidelines and in the Anti-Black-Box Curriculum Movement, which is the first movement to be primarily organised by high school students. The Ministry of Education hosted a public hearing and announced adjustments to high school textbooks and guidelines in 2014, which engendered a teachers' alliance and student and grassroots civic group protests of the KMT government's push towards Sinocentric textbook revisions. High school activists used social media to connect with other students and launch the Occupy the Ministry of Education protest, claiming that the Ministry of Education's plan to modify the guidelines of a Chinese language and social studies textbook violated administrative procedures, and calling for the withdrawal of the adjusted curriculum and the codification of the curriculum adjustment process. The student activists learnt to align with other groups, to cooperate and negotiate with people with diverse opinions, and to develop their citizen capacity, all of which led to the government ceasing the adjustment process (Wang, 2017). The conflicts and actions engendered by this curriculum adjustment sparked dialogue between people with different opinions and reflection on the subjectivity of Taiwanese individuals.

Market-oriented discourse

The third discourse type is market-oriented discourse, which emphasises economic development and technological innovation. This discourse is associated with the business community, politicians and think tanks. It has the aim of raising industry interests, increasing job opportunities and improving the minimum wage and benefits. The DPP's think tank, New Frontier Foundation, proposes people-oriented economic development that emphasises innovation, job opportunities and equal distribution of economic performance. Democratisation and liberal labour law reforms provide a political opportunity for labour activists and movements to employ institutional tactics in the form of parliamentary lobbying and tripartite negotiation as a mainstream strategy (Ho, 2017). The Taiwan Labour Front, founded in 1984, was the first labour activist organisation. It aims to 'build a society without exploitation, where people respect and tolerate each other and share resources equally' (Taiwan Labour Front, n.d.). The Taiwan Labour Front objects to the sacrifice of people's rights in exchange for capitalist short-term profits, and it strives for an economic democracy that includes 'the right of co-determination and humanization of the workplace' (Taiwan Labour Front, n.d.).

Advocates for an egalitarian economy and labour rights have shaped the process of labour, social and financial policy reform. The manifestation of market-oriented discourses in government policy indicates that this discourse affects the empowered space. The labour policy reform in 2016, called the 'one mandatory day off and one flexible rest day', allowed Tsai's government to safeguard the working hours of Taiwanese workers and implement the 'two-days-a-week of holidays' transitional bill. However, this legal reform caused controversy regarding labour rights and triggered conflict between workers and employers. In 2017, a second amendment was pushed through that conditionally added more flexibility to working hours; however, the amendment failed to resolve the dispute and workers were dissatisfied with the amendment. The reform process led to numerous rounds of mediation and bargaining; the voices and concerns of labourers were heard and a deliberative negotiation space was created.

Sustainable development discourse

The fourth discourse type is sustainable development discourse, which strives to reduce greenhouse gas emissions and seeks industry-structure transition, electricity reform and low-carbon energy transition. Government officials remain supportive of industry and economic growth, tend to adopt the modernisation discourse, and have a strong belief in the objectivity of science to guide environmental decision-making at the risk of neglecting the social and cultural dimensions of sustainability. Contrary to the mainstream media, the Public Television Services created the Our Island Program to emphasise environmental justice and land concerns. The program featured a special report concerning environmental problems in which environmental information was provided to raise public concern regarding conservation. This broadcast has further affected the report orientation of other media (Wang & Liaw, 2006).

Scholars and environmental NGOs (ENGOs) are paying increased attention to the social effects engendered by environmental concerns and have advocated for strong sustainability and environmental and land justice. The anti-nuclear movement is the emblematic case. A series of protests organised by anti-nuclear organisations have been held since the 1990s. Tens of thousands took to the streets of Taipei on 9 March 2014 in an anti-nuclear protest organised by the National Nuclear Abolition Action Platform (NNAAP). Protesters wore yellow ribbons that read 'Stop the Fourth Nuclear Power Plant. Give Power Back to the People'. Citizen activism has forced the government to stop the construction of the fourth nuclear power plant and to declare a non-nuclear goal for 2025. ENGOs facilitated eight citizen forums based on the concept of deliberative democracy from March to October 2016. Activism contributes to the democratising quality of deliberative systems. This topic is further discussed in Chapter 5. Anti-nuclear movements and civic activism facilitate the construction of local discourses and the shaping of policy-making towards a transition to renewable energy.

The controversy of Kuokuang Petrochemical's attempt to build its eighth naphtha-cracking plant highlights the power of discourse on environmental sustainability and intergenerational justice. A social movement successfully stopped the expansion of the petrochemical industry. The entire complex was expected to span 2,700 hectares of wetlands in Changhua County, which would have incurred problems with land procurement. The government listed the project as a 'major national investment plan' and the plan appeared to be unstoppable when it was entered in the June 2009 environmental effect review process. Opponents have deployed strategies to counter the official discourse that asserted that the development project was economically beneficial and necessary. Activists used various methods to voice their opinions and stimulate public deliberation and mobilisation, including organising marches and performances, buying wetland stocks, petitioning, conducting debates on health risks compared with economic benefits, and revealing significant problems caused by air pollution, high water consumption and agricultural pollution. Finally, President Ma Ying-jeou publicly declared his opposition to the Kuokuang Petrochemical plants on Earth Day, 22 April 2011 (Tu, 2012). Another example is the government's plan to expand the Shenao coal-fired power plant in New Taipei by mid-2025 as nuclear power is phased out. However, the project faces strong criticism, and environmental groups have expressed concern that the Shenao coal-fired plant will have an irreversible effect on the health of people living in northern Taiwan. Considering public concerns regarding air pollution, the government decided to abandon the Shenao plant project and sought an alternative plant for a third liquefied natural gas terminal.

Discourses from the perspective of marginalised groups have been articulated in the public space concerning various public problems. Various avenues and sites are available for articulation and contestation, which reflects the vibrant, dynamic and inclusive nature of the public space. The following section discusses the connectivity of multiple spaces of deliberation and highlights the dynamic connectivity of arenas in the public space, with a particular focus on the linkage of mini-publics and social movements, the crucial role of social media and online platforms and referendums in facilitating debates and dialogues, and the mobilisation to reshape policy discourse and the policy-making process and related effects.

Rapid and large-scale development of mini-publics

This section analyses how mini-publics are developing rapidly and how they are linked to social movements and civic society organisations; it also provides several principal examples of mini-publics and the innovations they heralded. Since 2002, over 100 innovative deliberative mini-publics have gathered at the national, county–city and community level. Most deliberative activities have been conducted by academic institutions commissioned by central and local governments, whereas others have been initiated by non-governmental organisations and community colleges. Taiwan also participates in global deliberative governance processes, such as World Wide Views on Global Warming in 2009 and World Wide Views on Climate and Energy in 2015. In addition to using original and modified forms of the Danish model of consensus conferences, scholars and civic groups have attempted to combine and adjust multiple deliberative models according to local contexts and issues, such as the Open Space on Ethnic Reconciliation in 2004 that emphasised storytelling and narratives to allow mutual understanding and reconciliation (Fan, 2010). Other such instances include the Scenario Workshop of Tamsui River Remediation in 2006 and the Citizen Jury on New Development Projects in Qiyan Community in 2007.

Lin and Chen (2003) researched the institutional configuration of state–society relations from the perspective of political structures and argued that people's discontent with the functioning of representative institutions and governmental decision-making structures shaped the development and operation of consensus conferences in Taiwan. Scholars in the fields of sociology, political science and public administration are crucial proponents of deliberative democracy. Professor Kuo-Ming Lin and Professor Dong-Seng Chen from the Department of Sociology of the National Taiwan University are two key pioneers of deliberative democracy. Through their collaboration with community colleges and civic society organisations, they conduct consensus conferences commissioned by government agencies. Consensus conferences, which were introduced by the aforementioned scholars, represent the first form of deliberative democracy employed to include citizens' views concerning complex issues in the policy-making process. Since the first consensus conference on national health insurance conducted in 2002, consensus conferences have stimulated discussion and further experimentations and trials by proponents of deliberative democracy. Women's groups called for the Department of Health to commission the establishment of deliberation procedures or conferences and led two state-sponsored national consensus conferences on surrogate motherhood in 2004 and 2012, conducted by Professor Kuo-Ming Lin's deliberative team.

Civic society organisations also play a valuable role in promoting deliberative practices and in organising activities and sites for deliberations and reimagining democracy. Beitou Community College is run by Beitou Cultural Foundation, which was established in 2003, and has promoted deliberative democracy, cultivated citizens' democratic awareness and conducted experimental deliberative practices. Beitou Cultural Foundation drafted the Beitou Charter through contentious discussions to obtain community consensus in order to create a local learning platform that combined lifelong learning and action. With the assistance of Professor Kuo-Ming Lin's Technology, Democracy and Society team, Beitou Community College and Beitou Cultural Foundation conducted consensus conferences in 2004 on the future of the Beitou Hot Spring Museum and Beitou Old Street; for this, they recruited and trained deliberative volunteers. This was the first time that online deliberation was included in addition to deliberations in person. Beitou Community College and the Youth Platform Foundation initiated the first experimental participatory budgeting model, which was then implemented by grassroots groups in Taiwan in 2015. Beitou Community College joined the government–academia alliance of participatory budgeting in 2015 and collaborates with Taipei City Government to promote PB and deliberative democracy in the local community, provide training courses, and conduct PB practices in high schools and at Beitou Community College, which cultivates meaningful deliberation amongst local communities (see Chapter 7).

The Youth Platform Foundation has promoted youth participation and deliberative democracy since 2010. The foundation aims to collaborate with non-governmental organisations and social enterprises to assist youth organisations in taking action, stimulate social reform and work on policy reform and social empowerment. They held a series of forums on 'Our Budget Deliberated by Ourselves' in 2014 and have been involved in the participatory budgeting of six cities since 2015. They also initiated the 'Turn around! Citizens Participation in Participatory Budgeting Together' project, which involved visits to and analysis of multiple sites of PB activity in six cities. Furthermore, they invited executives and actors of PB to participate in forums with the aim of creating spaces for dialogue on experiences of PB and to engage in democratic innovations that could change the power relationship and distribution between civic servants and the public. The Youth Platform Foundation seems to regard deliberative practices and PB as the reform movements required to change Taiwanese society.

Deliberative democracy and movement and advocacy organisations seem to have a symbiotic relationship that involves both mutual influence and mutual benefit. Different from most citizen conferences in Taiwan led or supported by the public sector, the citizen conference of the Hsinchu Science-based Industrial Park at Ilan (HSIP, Ilan) was held independently by civic groups, led by Ilan Community College. Ilan Community College collaborated with deliberative democracy scholars to introduce the citizen conference and encourage local people to participate in discussions of the SIP development and its possible impacts. Civic groups may strengthen their mobilisation network and accumulate their local knowledge through running a citizen conference (Tu, 2007). Besides, the NNAAP organised by the anti-nuclear and civic society organisation with assistance by scholars conducted eight citizen forums in 2016 to facilitate public deliberation on nuclear waste controversy (see Chapter 5).

Advocacy organisations employ the mini-public model to collect citizen opinions to communicate them to government agencies. This also increases public awareness and knowledge regarding policy-making. Tainan Community College has been actively involved in environmental protection issues in southern Taiwan for decades and conducted an 'anti-air pollution citizen conference' in front of the community temple to obtain residents' opinions, perceptions and policy suggestions. They also invited the Environmental Protection Bureau, Bureau of Health and Bureau of Education to participate in the conference to talk to residents, disclose relevant information and respond to citizen questions. Government officials acknowledged that data indicated that air quality in the Annan area was substandard and stated that they would add monitoring infrastructure to regulate the total air pollution emissions of industrial zones, encourage citizens to use public transportation to reduce emissions, and recognise citizen action and the citizen conference as effective methods of promoting community health education (Tsai, 2015).

Furthermore, the Taiwan Alliance to End the Death Penalty, a coalition of abolitionist NGOs and research institutes promoting the reform of Taiwan's penal system in addition to advocating for the abolition of the death penalty, hosted approximately 20 citizen deliberative forums and 10 expert and stakeholder deliberative forums from May 2018 to May 2019 to facilitate deliberation on alternatives to the death penalty. The Taiwan Alliance to End the Death Penalty argues that the government and legislators simplify complex problems by stating that public opinion supports the death penalty. The alliance aims to create an open forum for public discussion on various issues surrounding the death penalty's abolition and calls for victims' rights to be taken into account in penal reforms.

Facing legislative battles from opposition parties and increasing pressures of protests and participation from civic society organisations, the DPP government strategically utilised state-sponsored consensus conferences to deal with governance dilemmas and controversies (Lin, 2009). To create spaces for policy discussions that are rational, equal and geared towards public interest, the Youth Development Administration of the Ministry of Education invited Professor Kuo-Ming Lin to introduce deliberative democracy and published a consensus conference manual. The Research, Development, and Evaluation Commission also commissioned Professor Kuo-Ming Lin to introduce different deliberative democracy practices in Taiwan and publish an operation manual for employing deliberative practices to promote deliberative democracy in national, city, and community settings (e.g. Lin, 2008).

Key DDP politicians play important roles in promoting deliberative democracy. When Cheng Li-chun served as the Minister of the National Youth Commission (which has been transformed into the Youth Development Administration, Ministry of Education) from 20 May 2004 to 21 February 2008, she was involved in promoting youth participation and deliberative democracy and conducted the Youth State Affairs Consensus Conference to provide a platform for young people to voice their concerns regarding state affairs, democratic processes and public policy. Youth deliberative practices combine models of consensus conferences, national issues forums and learning circles. The first Youth State Affairs Consensus Conferences were held in 2004. The Youth Development Administration and the planning group selected eight topics for youth deliberation based on public suggestions and online voting. The topics related to actions such as reducing university tuition fees, balancing property rights protection and youth learning rights, reducing the gap between school education and job opportunities, promoting constitutional reform and young citizens' rights, improving the international participation of Taiwanese youths, ameliorating national finance, addressing the disparity in opportunity between urban and rural areas, and publicising land development and ecological conservation. Regional consensus conferences where held in the north, middle, south and east of Taiwan from September 4 to 12, and national consensus conferences were subsequently held on September 18 and 19 in Taipei, with 160 representatives attending from the regional conferences. On the final day of the conference, the Premier responded to the report from the youth citizen conference and promised to hold youth conferences every year to acknowledge young people's suggestions. The Youth Development Administration responded positively to the report from the 2005 Youth Conference, which addressed conducting more citizen conferences, transmitting deliberative democracy concepts, holding youth consensus conferences regularly, and promoting deliberative democracy in counties, communities and online platforms. The main topic of the 2006 Youth Consensus Conference was the institutionalisation of the Conference. Participants reached an agreement that the Youth Development Administration should establish a Consulting Committee for the Youth Consensus Conference as a promotional institution.

In 2008, the Youth State Affairs Consensus Conference became the Youth Policy Alliance Online Platform; it integrated relevant promotional measures and mechanisms. The Youth Development Administration established the Youth Good Governance Alliance, which provided a platform for young people to participate in public affairs, including policy forums, policy proposals, agencies meetings and visits, and action plans for youth participation in the community. It also provided training courses for young people to become facilitators in deliberative forums. By constructing youth policy dialogue platforms and promoting deliberative democracy, the Youth Development Administration stimulated youth involvement in policy issues; this provided inspiration for student social movements, such as the Sunflower Movement. The role of the deliberation model on the Sunflower Movement will be addressed further.

The Youth Development Administration also promotes 'deliberative class meetings' to encourage students to discuss school and public affairs in class meetings in a deliberative way to enhance junior high school students' democratic practical abilities. Research found that deliberative class meetings positively affected democratic behaviour. Students' abilities to communicate with each other and express themselves rationally, respecting others and participating in discussions, are improved significantly, which helps to make democracy in Taiwan continue to be cultivated and grounded (Chang, 2008; Huang, 2009). Concepts of deliberative democracy have been incorporated into high school textbooks, and schools have become important sites for learning, practicing and imaging deliberative democracy.

Owing to Taiwan's exclusion from the United Nations, its participation in World Wide Views (WWViews) on Global Warming is among the few examples of scaled-out public deliberation in which Taiwanese voices are heard. The WWViews on global warming organiser in Taiwan is professor Tze-Luen Lin, Faculty of Social Science of National Taiwan University and the Taiwan Sustainable Energy Research Foundation. WWViews on Climate and Energy is organised by Professor Lin and the Risk Society and Policy Research Centre, National Taiwan University, with the support of the Taiwan Environmental Protection Administration. WWViews on Climate and Energy in Taiwan adopted the 21st Century Town Meeting conducted in Taipei, Taichung and Tainan City with 305 participants deliberating on environmental issues of global importance on 6 June, with 106 forums held in cities in 88 countries simultaneously (Fang, 2015). Taiwanese citizens' reports – and those from other countries – were submitted to the relevant UN Convention. In addition to citizen reports, policy recommendations provided by forums earned positive responses from city mayors. It facilitates citizen deliberation, reflection on climate and energy issues and our duties as global citizens, and raises public awareness.

Various mini-publics combined in Public Television programs and online deliberation across time and space have interlinked with other deliberations sites. Mini-publics and online deliberation can complement each other. By using two citizen conferences on urban-planning projects operated in the Beitou district – one is online and the other is face-to-face; they discuss the same issues, use the same procedure, and deliberate on the same readable materials – Chen et al. (2008) found that the application of ICT could improve the effectiveness of the citizen conference. The online citizen conference delivered more policy knowledge to participants than the face-to-face one. In addition, participants in the online model were more 'rational' and more likely to express their opinions compared to those who met in person.

Deliberative democracy practices allow diverse voices to be heard and create spaces for deliberation and justification between ordinary citizens, experts, commissioned deliberative research teams, government agencies, members of steering committees composed of experts from various disciplines and members of civic organisations. Based on the Taiwanese experience of public forums, Lin (2016) observed that civic groups' attitudes to and opinions on deliberative practices were influenced by the organisational characteristics of the civic groups as well as by their relationships with other groups and the state.

The above mini-publics practices have some drawbacks and face criticisms, notably in relation to experts dominating the discussion and a lack of evidence that deliberative forums are linked to policy decisions being made (Chen, 2006; Huang, 2008). One might also doubt the quality of mini-publics held by advocacy organisations because they seem to have held clear, pre-set positions. Curato et al. (2019, pp. 174–175) considered that deliberative democracy is caught between two critiques. One is that deliberative forums do little to correct information asymmetries and epistemic injustice, and the second is that deliberation becomes problematic when it is too powerful and when practitioners seek to empower deliberative forums. They rightly argue that mini-publics are 'one of many ways a political system can uphold norms of inclusiveness, respect, and reason-giving'; 'deliberation's power should be proportional to its goal', and it should be responsive to public scrutiny.

Civic society organisations' continuous involvement in promoting citizen participation, deliberation, education and empowerment could complement inadequacies and improve the quality of deliberative processes. As Lin (2016) suggested, civic discussions and social capital are crucial factors for constructing a civic cultural basis to encourage deliberation. However, gender and education have a mediating effect on civic mindedness, political efficacy, political knowledge and communication skills; women and people with low educational attainment are more reluctant to participate in deliberation. The following section discusses how civic organisations could play a principal role in developing citizen capabilities and reducing inequality. They could also complement mini-publics in facilitating ongoing conversations between citizens and actors, and encourage interactions that allow marginalised voices to be heard and shape policy discourses in the public sphere.

Deliberation within social movements

Social movements and their critical public spaces as arenas for the formulation of dissent and scrutinising of representative democratic institutions are important for deliberative democracy. Recent social movements have facilitated deliberative democracy and participation 'from below' to address crises of representative democracy and liberal political institutions. Social movements created open public spaces, social forums and camps for citizen deliberations at the local, national and transnational levels, and represent important experiments of democratic innovations in settings of inequality and diversity (Della Porta & Doerr, 2018). I illustrate three cases to echo Mansbridge's (1996) argument for social movements as key sites for imagining democratic innovations, and I highlight how social movements contribute to linking discourses and networks across scales of knowledge production, and facilitate deliberations on science and policy.

The Sunflower Movement is an iconic case. Although, at first, the Sunflower activists' occupation of parliament appeared to be a nondeliberative act, the occupy action and discursive practice had positive systemic deliberative consequences. Sunflower activists initiated 'Street Deliberation' (DStreet, 2014) and advocated that everyone should have the opportunity to become involved in open spaces and group forums to review the free trade agreement. Students and academics acted as facilitators in the deliberative forums on the street. Indigenous youth groups also actively participated in the activities. In addition to the controversy concerning the free trade agreement, a 'Citizen Constitutional Meeting on the Street' was held, and thousands of citizens met to deliberate on the objectives of constitutional reforms. Sunflower activists declared their objective and vision of a Citizen Constitutional Meeting to respond to the government's refusal of a constitutional reform request. The Sunflower Movement established alliances with over 20 civil society organisations to initiate the Citizen Constitutional Promotion Alliance. The alliance holds a nationwide grassroots forum to encourage participation in the bottom-up political reform movement. The Citizen Constitutional Promotion Alliance was formally created in 2014 and held grassroots forums and youth constitutional forums nationwide to call for participation in a constitutional reform movement (DStreet, 2014).

The Sunflower Movement and DStreet facilitated the implementation of further deliberative practices, forums and training courses for facilitators in deliberation on campuses. For instance, several community colleges hold a Democracy Classroom on the Street – Citizen Deliberation symposium that provides participants with spaces to deliberate on free trade controversies.

After the protests, numerous Sunflower activists entered various areas of politics. Some activists shifted their attention to institutional forms of politics by joining or establishing political parties or running for public office, whereas others joined advocacy groups, civil society organisations and social enterprises (Ho, 2019). Sunflower activists have become politically engaged and participate in creating political forces that influence the government and shape policy discourses. They are crucial organizers of the Citizen Constitutional Promotion Alliance and other emerging organisations and deliberation activities. The key initiator of DStreet, who has extensive experience assisting in holding deliberative practices funded by the government and civic society, created the Taiwan Youth Citizen's Forum (TYCF) and joined a political party to assist in policy dialogues. These cases indicate that even if a social movement or civil society organisation declines, the discourse that was created may continue to influence society (e.g. membership of a different organisation), highlighting the strength of the deliberative system approach.

The second case is deliberation in local protests against inappropriate wind turbine development, regulations defects and procedural injustice. Local opposition to wind turbine construction projects evinces the gap between green energy policies and local perceptions and social values as well as competing knowledge claims among policy actors. Local activism against the wind turbine construction project in Yuanli Township, Miaoli County caused great public attention and got students' support. Local residents and activists were concerned with the proximity of the turbines to their homes, worrying that low-frequency noise produced by the machines may negatively affect their health and quality of life. The grassroots organisation stated that they welcome the government promoting alternative clean sources of energy, but that it should develop a mechanism for residents to participate in projects, rather than supporting large enterprises. Environmental protection groups think that the government's promotion of renewable energy should emphasise small electric power stations distributed among the community rather than large-scale electric power equipment that might cause negative environmental impacts. Members of the Wild at Heart Legal Defense Association attempted to restrict wind turbine construction in a peaceful and nonviolent manner but have been in conflict with the police on several occasions. During the trials, duty lawyers, students and residents all advocated for safeguarding their hometown and freedom of speech, considering themselves as fighters for justice. The Taiwan High Court finally gave a final verdict of acquittal. Local activists continued to promote the Yuanli Grassroots People's Forum at the protest site, and residents freely discussed local public issues and the imagined 'energy democracy'. The Grassroots People's Forum helped to strengthen local communication, enhance citizens' identity and consciousness, and attempted to link wider communities and public interests (Fan, 2017, p. 190).

The grassroots organisation and the wind power company negotiated to reach an agreement of 'keeping two and tearing down two wind turbines' in 2014. Local activism has adjusted the company's development project, the government's research and review of safe distance regulations, and local politics. Local activists promoted solidarity during local protests and deliberated on how to encourage collective forces of participation in public affairs. The activists chose to set up the Yuanli Coast Association to continue to monitor the amendment of safe-distance regulations and to promote citizen participation in local development (Li, 2015). Local protests and action link networks cross the existing administrative boundaries of villages. Some local activists have become key members of community associations engaged in community building, promotion of participation in local affairs, and promoting organic farming and community eating together. A few activists have successfully run for public office to challenge the dominant local political power structure and seek local change.

There has been increasing grassroots movements to engage in legal mobilisations as an important way of seeking justice, which creates a space for deliberation and dialogues on science and policy among citizens and experts. Lin (2018) argues that *Former RCA Employees' Mutual Aid Association v. Radio Corporation of America (RCA)* created a space for deliberation about the causal effects of chronic exposure to organic solvents on human health. Victims, industry, legal professionals and other experts created and contested knowledge related to the effects of groundwater pollution. Workers, lawyers, social science academe and student volunteers held hundreds of meetings to engage in communication and collaboration on the translation of employees' working and disease experiences and conducting research for court hearings to affect the verdict favouring the workers.

Wang (2014) indicated that several factors that have facilitated the new trend of Taiwanese environmental movements have used litigation to achieve their goals, such as during the crisis related to the legality of an Environmental Impact Assessment, the decline in the mobilisation of social movements, the fight for judicial independence and the appearance of environmental lawyers. Collaboration between environmental lawyers and social movement activists has led to favourable outcomes in several lawsuits, such as the landfill development projects. However, use of the judiciary as a vehicle for social reform is impeded by resistance from executives. Although environmental activists' victories in courts do not necessarily affect policy, news media could attract public attention and encourage dialogue and reflection, which might shape policy discourses. Environmental activists tend to consider that winning lawsuits does not necessarily stop the environmental harms to residents; thus, such activists encourage residents to join them in environmental activism.

Alternative media, online platforms and social media as deliberation interfaces

Innovative information technology, alternative media, online platforms and social media play a crucial role in facilitating political participation and deliberation and have increasing influence on politics. Citizen media and online platforms provide instant information for online communities, attract the attention of ordinary citizens, and create spaces for people to voice their concerns and communicate with others with competing perspectives, which contributes to ongoing dialogues and interactions among members of the visual community. For example, Civilmedia@Taiwan, established in 2007, is an independent and alternative media that reports on social movements that are ignored by the mass media; in doing so, they highlight citizen values and movement claims and call for change on issues related to human rights, environment, culture, migrant workers, social welfare, gender, aboriginals and others. Online platforms and social media are deliberation interfaces that stimulate constant discussions and dialogues. They provide the basis for increased civic involvement, including through workshops and advocacy. Social movements and mini-publics usually employ social media and other online platforms to attract attention and stimulate discourse surrounding pertinent issues.

Researchers have reported the vital function of the media in policy-making, such as by providing information, framing issues and facilitating dialogue. Exploring the performance of the media in their deliberative reporting on the public policy of 'One Fixed Day Off and One Flexible Rest Day', Chien (2019) found that the overall deliberative performance of the mainstream media was not as good as that of alternative media because the former mostly rely on corporations as one of their main sources of information, and they neglect the labour situation in Taiwan. Alternative media performed the best in the areas of 'deep contextualization' and 'discourse basis' and retained the anti-discourse characteristic of speaking for the workers and supporting labour groups. One source, @Coolloud, made labour groups' demands more visible.

Internet platforms have become common spaces for citizens to voice their concerns to the public. Platforms such as Yahoo Live, YouTube and Facebook have become a place to obtain political and civic information and to discuss opinions. Some online programs use *kuso* culture, semi-entertainment or common parlance to make policy issues more accessible to average citizens. Such information is disseminated through talk shows and shared in other media. The following section illustrates the actions of the main online platform and community and how they are connected to the deliberative sites of other social movements and civil society organisations.

G0V.tw is an online community and platform formed at the end of 2012 that aims to find ways to make technology work for stakeholders and to create meaningful conversations among NGOs, government, and the general public. Its mission is to use 'technology in the interest of the public good, allowing citizens easy access to vital information and power to shape the civil society'. Based on the open source culture, participants can join free, create their own projects and make the best use of government data. G0V.tw creates new ways for citizens to participate in government and public affairs, and its successful projects include Government Budget Visualisation, Campaign

Finance Crowdsourcing, Legislator Voting Guide, and others. It contributes to improving information transparency and people's access to data and makes it easy for ordinary citizens to participate in public affairs. In its early days, g0v's participants were predominantly coders. But now non-tech participants, such as NGO workers, civil servants and everyday citizens, make up more than half of the 4,000 participants. G0v.tw holds bi-monthly onsite hackathons, and its users collaborate via virtual channels (Fan et al., 2019).

Core members of g0V.tw have also actively participated in the Sunflower Movement and used information technology and related platforms to inform the public and encourage communication and deliberation on this controversial topic (Fan et al., 2019). Audrey Tang, the Minister Without Portfolio and leader of the digital government of Tsai since 2016, has employed different tools and platforms to assist the digital community in constructing a communication platform connecting the visual and physical world to remodel democracy and create meaningful conversations among NGOs, government and ordinary citizens. During the Sunflower Movement's occupation of parliament, Audrey Tang focused on debate, deliberation and action on the street and joined the g0v.today website hack team, engaging in broadcasted talks and citizen activities at various sites to allow people to understand different opinions and facilitate communication between people who held different positions (O'Flaherty, 2018). To promote open data and public–private collaboration, the Digital Ministry has been promoting the Presidential Hackathon since 2018. The topic of the second Presidential Hackathon is Intelligent State; government officials, civil servants and the public are invited to present proposals and participate in hacking. This event aims to encourage innovations and public service. To broaden public participation, the general public can propose ideas and let the hacker team engage in hacking. The Hackathon activities organised by the government can strengthen cooperation among government agencies, civic tech groups and the public. It facilitates ongoing equal dialogues, justification and reflection during the processes of idea proposal, hacking and the implementation of the proposal, which could improve the democratising quality of the deliberative system.

Voice Square, a public commentary forum, provides an online platform for the public to question government agencies, legislators and related groups, and communicate with other citizens. It also invites actors and government officials to join workshops to discuss various public issues (Fan, 2019). Take the controversy surrounding the Taiwanese government's attempts to lift the ban on food imports from Japan's radiation-affected Fukushima region, for example; the online forum emphasises the deliberative principle described as follows:

> Use questions and attachment to contribute your own power and voice. When you disagree with someone, remember what he or she said instead of responding aggressively. If the question is justified, an answer is required. The public raise questions and further questions and hope that

legislators and parliamentarians are willing to accept citizens' demands and promote change. When you differ in opinion with someone, question them instead of scolding them. Public affairs should be transparent.

(Voice Square, n.d.)

This shows that online civic forums have the potential to facilitate citizens to respect and listen to others' opinions, reflecting on the problems of substantive issues and engaging in justifying their arguments.

Voice Square strives to make information transparent, clarify current problems and conduct questionnaires and surveys to highlight public attitudes and preferences regarding food safety topics. The platform also facilitates discussion and scientific communication between experts and nonexperts. Before the public hearing, people raised questions on Voice Square to attract the attention of government agencies; the Taiwan Food and Drug Administration and the Atomic Energy Council responded to these questions. In addition, an expert on food safety joined the platform and replied to questions related to compound packaged foods. Voice Square has facilitated mutual understanding and dialogue. Furthermore, those who opposed the proposal to lift the ban on food imports from the nuclear disaster area took action in the form of political consumerism. For example, activists appealed for the boycotting of Japanese goods on Facebook and refused to purchase potentially contaminated foods. Political campaigners expressed the importance that online members share relevant information, and that the opposing sides may share a common ground. The online platform mediators asked participants to share their perspectives and offer opinions on others' views to better understand public views on this topic and to explore possibilities.

When you click 'Share your opinion . . .' to type your comments, please start with 'I think . . .' Please give your honest opinion so that you appear decisive and please do not enter questions. Submit one opinion at a time; if you have multiple points to make, please submit them separately.

Facebook and visual communities could play an important role in attracting public attention to marginal groups' situations and discourses and facilitate advocacy and action to press the government to address the controversy.

The controversy on flooding and wild creek remediation on Orchid Island is a significant case that shows how indigenous activism integrated with visual community mobilisation facilitated space for deliberation and improved the defects and democratising quality of deliberative systems. Tao tribesmen transcended their original boundaries to engage in communication and activate plural deliberative spaces when facing conflicting new challenges and the government's dominant policy positions with limited discursive space. Tao activists used the virtual community as both an internal and external communication platform and engaged in transmitting and visualising Tao traditional knowledge systems and practices. Indigenous grassroots participation facilitated knowledge coproduction and social learning and reshaped tribal political subjectivities. Civic activism led to policy program adjustment to integrate local ideas and materials, although the government was unable to totally adopt traditional practices due to considerations of feasibility (Fan, 2018).

Referendum facilitates public debate and ongoing dialogues

Referendum has been regarded as the direct method of enabling the public to have a say regarding controversial issues. A multi-question referendum was held on 24 November 2018 alongside local elections. The referendum was the first since the December 2017 reform to the Referendum Act, which reduced the threshold for submitting questions. Ballots with signatures from 1.5% of the electorate (approximately 280,000 people) were required to successfully include a question on the ballot. Seven of the ten referendums were approved: reducing output from thermal power plants, ceasing expansion of coal power plants, prohibition of food imports from Fukushima, restricting marriage under Civil Code to one man and one woman, not implementing homosexual aspects of the Gender Equality Education Act, protecting the rights of same-sex couples outside of the Civil Code, and repealing the planned end of nuclear power stations. The three referendums that were rejected were: same-sex couples marrying under the civil code, gender equity education in the national curriculum, and changing the name of the country's Olympic team from 'Chinese Taipei' to 'Taiwan'. However, several referendum questions relating to the same problem complicated matters considerably and risked confusing voters. Critics argued that citizens should face a single question on a single topic and should have the opportunity to hear the arguments from both sides. This would reduce the risk of crucial topics becoming conflated with wider political disagreements (Spencer, 2018).

Referendum has consequentiality in deliberative systems. Take the referendum against nuclear foods, for example. Hau Lung-pin, the initiator of the referendum against importing foods from the nuclear disaster zone, previously served as a professor of food technology and is now Vice Chairman of the KMT. He stated that people wanted to use the referendums to tell the government, 'we do not want nuclear foods; do not burn coal and do not pollute the air'. The KMT emphasised their stance against 'nuclear foods' and the importance of 'saving the children', indicating that the DPP government intended to deregulate policies related to food imports, which would mean deviating from public opinion and neglecting public health. The KMT launched activities in multiple counties to gain support for the referendum. The mayor of Nantou County took the lead in supporting the referendum. KMT booths were set up in public areas, such as tourist street food markets. Housewives and mothers were particularly concerned about health and food safety issues. In addition to their signatures, they attached stickers to their bodies to express their strong opposition to imports of radiation-contaminated foods. A few DPP legislators also indicated that the public had the right to vote in a referendum.

Those who supported lifting the ban on food imports set up a counter office for the referendum. The representative of the office was Huang Shih-hsiu, founder of the Nuclear Energy Rumour Terminator. Other major representatives included Taiwanese representatives in Japan and Japanese representatives in Taiwan. Facebook members issued a statement expressing their opposition to the nuclear food referendum and argued in favour of giving the public more information, acquiring a better understanding of radiation and avoiding rumours that spread fear.

The referendum against importing food products from Japan's nuclear disaster area was ultimately approved by 7.79 million voters (77.74%) and rejected by 2.23 million voters. Hau Lung-pin believed that the rejection of nuclear-contaminated foods was a manifestation of the will of the people, and that it showed that most people were worried about foods imported from Japan's nuclear disaster area and indicated that the government should maintain a policy to prohibit imports of said foods. President Tsai indicated that the result of the referendum would be legally binding for the next few years and hoped to follow World Trade Organisation (WTO) principles to arrive at a proposal that would be acceptable to both Taiwan and Japan (Fan, 2019).

Referendums are increasingly becoming the battleground for actors with competing political opinions. Actors have employed social media and linked activist networks to inform and mobilise individuals to vote on particular topics. However, some people have criticised the rules of referendums, suggesting that they may become a political tool in elections and can disadvantage minorities. The amended Referendum Act passed by the Legislative Yuan in June 2019 stipulates that a referendum will be held every two years, starting in 2021, which separates referenda from general elections. The referendum day is the fourth Saturday in August. The amendments in the Referendum Act facilitate further discussions and reflection regarding the democratic implication of referendums, such as the problems or topics suitable for a referendum, whether everyone can have the opportunity to participate in discussion and deliberation on ballot questions, and the supervision mechanisms.

Discussion and conclusion

Democratic deepening is not only about the peaceful transfer of power through the electoral process or building political parties and effective institutions. It is also about creating inclusive spaces where citizens can engage with different discourses and influence the outcome of collective decisions in a non-coercive manner (Curato, 2015). Taiwan has autonomous non-governmental organisations and a vibrant civil society, and political democratisation has been formed simultaneously (Hsiao, 2019). The public space has considerable deliberative capacity regarding inclusivity and authenticity in the contestation of discourses. Discourses in the public space are free and wide-ranging; even the views of marginalised groups can be articulated, contested, revised and reconsidered, such as workers' welfare and indigenous long-term care services. Civic society groups' alliance-building with scholars and academic institutions has enabled these organisations to drive policy change and achieve substantial public policy outcomes, as illustrated in the reform on electric liberalisation as a strategy for a nuclear-free country.

Various forms of deliberative practices in public spaces contribute to functions of deliberative systems, including epistemic, ethical and democratic functions identified by Mansbridge et al. (2012). First, the epistemic function of a deliberative system, such as networks of civic society organisations and alliances between academia and civil society organisations, are crucial to promoting and conducting mini-publics, which are vital for epistemic, educational and social learning functions in the public space. The consensus conference on GM food in Taiwan facilitated multiparty dialogues, enhanced citizens' knowledge and affected their attitudes and preferences (Fan, 2015). Civic activism has pressured the government to adopt labelling regulations and ask candidates for mayor to support the use of non-GMO ingredients in school lunches, to raise related public awareness and avoid potential risks to children. Furthermore, social movements and anti-nuclear experts have played a crucial role in informing the public by translating highly technical ideas regarding nuclear power into understandable language, challenging nuclear officials' claims about safety and necessity, organising anti-nuclear protests, coordinating activist networks with national and transnational reach and shaping public discourse regarding a nuclear-free homeland since the 1980s.

Second, the ethical function of the system is to promote mutual respect among citizens. Mini-publics enlarge the space of ongoing deliberations and increase mutual respect not only among citizens but also between citizens and experts. Besides, sustained participation in volunteer groups enables people to gain knowledge, relationships and mutual trust that are necessary for participation in democratic life (Kimura & Kinchy, 2016). Emergent citizen science projects have been shown to promote mutual respect and build social capital. The Taiwan Roadkill Observation Network is a social-media-based community with the mission to reduce roadkill by recording and analysing roadkill incidents. Voluntary participants reached a consensus to observe not only reptile roadkill but all deaths of terrestrial vertebrates in accessible wild fields, which turned the Roadkill Society into a project capable of detecting more general environmental problems and provided an opportunity for collaboration on certified researched (Chiou, 2019). The voluntary society contributes to raising public concern and educating the public, and the data have become a basis for further policy advocacy regulations and a reference for Environmental Impact Assessments.

Third, the democratic function is to promote an inclusive political process in terms of equality. The deliberations process in the public space can make underrepresented voices be heard equally and make issues of access central.

Environmental movements and activist networks against the Kuo-Kuang Petrochemical Corp development project illustrates that ordinary citizens offer powerful counter-narratives to the development of the petrochemical industry and should not be excluded from public domain technological decision-making. As Chiou (2019, p. 268) argues, 'lay citizens' propositional claims were no less useful than those of experts, who also relied mostly on ordinary reasoning to answer the technical question under the state of non-knowledge'.

The increasing mini-publics' practices, civic activism and civic society organisations encourage deliberative democracy in peoples' daily lives in formal and informal settings, in turn influencing those around them to engage in deliberation and have diffuse impacts.

References

Chang, C.-Y. (2008). *The impact evaluation of deliberative class meeting on democratic behavior* (Unpublished master's thesis). Department of Public Policy and Management, Shih Hisn University, Taipei City, Taiwan.

Chen, D.-S. (2006). Limits of deliberative democracy: The experience of citizen conferences in Taiwan. *Taiwan Democracy Quarterly, 3*(1), 77–104.

Chen, D.-Y., Huang, T.-Y., Lee, C.-P., Hsian, N., and Lin, T.-L. (2008). Deliberative democracy under ICTs in Taiwan: A comparison between on-line and face-to-face citizen conference. *Public Administration & Policy, 46*, 49–106.

Chien, Y.-H. (2019). *Deliberative reporting by the alternative media and mainstream media: The example of 'one fixed day off and one flexible rest day'* (Unpublished master's thesis). National Taiwan University, Taipei City, Taiwan.

Chiou, W.-T. (2019). What roles can lay citizens play in the making of public knowledge? *East Asian Science, Technology and Society: An International Journal, 13*, 257–277.

Curato, N. (2015). Deliberative capacity as indicator of democratic quality: The case of the Philippines. *International Political Science Review, 36*(1), 99–116.

Curato, N., Hammond, M., & Min, J. (2019). *Power in deliberative democracy: Norms, forums and systems*. Basingstoke, UK: Palgrave Macmillan.

Della Porta, D., & Doerr, N. (2018). Deliberation in protests and social movements. In A. Bächtiger, J. Dryzek, J. Mansbridge, & M. Warren (Eds.), *Handbook of deliberative democracy* (pp. 392–406). Oxford: Oxford University Press.

Dryzek, J. (2006). *Deliberative global politics: Discourse and democracy in a divided world*. Cambridge: Polity Press.

Dryzek, J. (2010). *Foundations and frontiers of deliberative governance*. Oxford: Oxford University Press.

Dryzek, J. S. (2014). Twists of democratic governance. In J. P. Gagnon (Ed.), *Democratic theorists in conversation: Turns in contemporary thought*, (pp. 101–116). Basingstoke: Palgrave Macmillan.

DStreet. (2014). *DStreet Facebook page*. www.facebook.com/twdstreet/posts/5352970 39906293?__tn__=K-R

Fan, F.-T., Chen, S.-L., Kao, C.-L., Murphy, M., Price, M., & Barry, L. (2019). Citizens, politics, and civic technology: A conversation with g0v and EDGI. *East Asian Science, Technology and Society: An International Journal, 13*, 279–297.

Fan, M.-F. (2015). Evaluating the 2008 Consensus Conference on GM Foods in Taiwan. *Public Understanding of Science*, *24*(5), 533–546.

Fan, M.-F. (2017). Nimby or civil disobedience? Conflicting framing and discourses of knowledge: Wind turbine construction in Taiwan. In K.-T. Chou (Ed.), *Energy transition in East Asia: A social science perspective* (pp. 179–193). Abingdon, UK: Routledge.

Fan, M.-F. (2018, November). Indigenous grassroots participation and the co-evolution of deliberative systems. Paper presented at the Political Studies Association Conference, Wellington, New Zealand.

Fan, M.-F. (2019, July). Democratizing food governance and deliberative policy-making. Paper presented at the 2nd Food Governance Conference, University of Sydney, Sydney, Australia.

Fan, M.-F. & Sung, S.-C.(2020) Indigenous Political Participation in Deliberative Systems: the Long-Term Care Service Controversy in Taiwan. *Policy Studies*. Published online first https://doi.org/10.1080/01442872.2020.1760233.

Fan, Y. (2010). Story-telling and democratic discussion: An analysis of ethnic dialogue workshop in civil society. *Taiwan Democracy Quarterly*, *7*(1), 65–105.

Fang, S.-Z. (2015). The threat of climate change and the general public: Worldwide view on climate and energy in 2015. Retrieved from the *Risk Society Policy Research Centre, National Taiwan University website*: https://rsprc.ntu.edu.tw/zh-tw/m01-3/climate-change/265-wwviews-review-article.html

Ho, M-S. (2017). Between protests and negotiation: Economic and social implications of the Labour movement in Taiwan. In A. Sakamoto, K. Momoko, & J. H. Wang, (Eds.), *Unfinished miracle: Taiwan's economy and society in transition* (pp. 125–158). Taipei: Institute of Sociology, Academia Sinica.

Ho, M-S. (2019). The road to mainstream politics: How Taiwan's Sunflower Movement activists became politicians. In R. Youngs (Ed.), *After protests: Pathways beyond mass mobilization* (pp. 61–68). Brussels: Carnegie Europe.

Hsiao, M. H.-H. (2019, November 16). Keynote speech. *Taiwan Association of Third Sector Research* [Conference keynote address] The Asia Youth, Third Sector, and Social Movement Conference, Taipei, Taiwan.

Huang, L.-Y. (2009). *Action research on a deliberative class meeting for improving junior high school students' democratic practical abilities: An example of one ninth-grade class in Keelung* (Unpublished master's thesis). Institute of Education, National Taiwan Ocean University, Keelung City, Taiwan.

Huang, T. Y. (2008). After deliberation: Exploring the policy connection of consensus conference from public sectors' perspectives. *Soochow Journal of Political Science*, *26*(4), 59–96.

Kimura, A. & Kinchy, A. (2016). Citizen science: Probing the virtues and contexts of participatory research. *Engaging Science Technology, and Society*, *2*: 331–361.

Lin, K.-M. (2008). *The practice of administrative democracy: Deliberative democracy and citizen partition in national issues*. Taipei: The Research, Development, and Evaluation Commission, Executive Yuan.

Lin, K.-M. (2009). State, civil society, and deliberative democracy: The practices of consensus conferences in Taiwan. *Taiwanese Sociology*, *17*, 161–217.

Lin, Yi-Ping. (2018). Reconstructing Genba: RCA groundwater pollution, research, and lawsuit in Taiwan, 1970–2014. *Positions: Asia Critique*, *26*(2), 305–341.

Li, Yun. (2015, August 27). What changes after protest? Peaceful revolution: Anti-wind turbine youth activists cherish land and deep plowing in Yuanli. *PeoPo Citizen News.* www.peopo.org/news/285443

Mansbridge, J. (1996). Using power/fighting power: The polity. In S. Benhabib (Ed.), *Democracy and difference: Contesting the boundaries of the political* (pp. 44–66). Princeton, NJ: Princeton University Press.

Mansbridge, J., Bohman, J., Chambers, S., Christiano, T., Fung, A., Parkinson, J., Thompson, D. F., & Warren, M. E. (2012). A systemic approach to deliberative democracy. In J. Parkinson & J. Mansbridge (Eds.), *Deliberative systems: Deliberative democracy at the large scale* (1–26). Cambridge: Cambridge University Press.

O'Flaherty, K. (2018, May 4). Taiwan's revolutionary hackers are forking the government. *WIRED.* www.wired.co.uk/article/taiwan-sunflower-revolution-audrey-tang-g0v

Spencer, D. (2018, December 1). Lessons from Taiwan's recent referendums and why e-voting is the way forward. *Taiwan News.* www.taiwannews.com.tw/en/news/3585946

Stevenson, H., & Dryzek, J. (2012). The discursive democratization of global climate governance. *Environmental Politics, 21,* 189–210.

Taiwan Association for Human Rights. n.d. *Home page.* www.tahr.org.tw/

Taiwan Labour Front. n.d. *Home page.* http://labor.ngo.tw/about-labour-en/introduction-en

Tsai, W.-C. (2015, June 27). Citizen conference in front of the community temple: Teachers and students of Tainan Community College voiced anti-pollution. *Tainan Community College Newsletter.* http://tncomu.tw/modules/tadnews/index.php?nsn=2962

Tu, W.-L. (2007). Deliberative democracy and social movement: An inspiration from the local-initiative citizen conference of Hisinchu Science-based Industrial Park at Ilan. *Public Administration, 23,* 67–93.

Tu, W.-L. (2012). Book review: Wetlands, petrochemicals, and imagining an island. *East Asian Science, Technology and Society: An International Journal, 6*(1), 143–145.

Voice Square. n.d. *Voice Square [Facebook page].* www.facebook.com/vsquare.tw/

Wang, C.-S. (2014). The legal mobilization of Taiwanese environmental movements. *Taiwanese Political Science Review, 18*(1), 1–72.

Wang, J.-P., & Liaw, S.-C. (2006). Analysis of environmental justice and media's sense of place in the 'Our Island' program of the public television services: A case study of the film 'Is this Place Safe?' *Journal of Geographical Research, 44,* 1–22.

Wang, Y.-C. (2017). *The subjectivity of social actors of new media social movement- the case of anti-black box curriculum* (Unpublished master's thesis). National Taiwan University, Taipei City, Taiwan.

3   The empowered space

Introduction

The *empowered space* is where legitimate collective decisions are taken. Some examples of empowered spaces include a parliament, a policy-making council, an executive committee, a court of law, a round of international negotiations and a space (such as a stakeholder dialogue) that has been given executive and decision-making authority by the government (Stevenson & Dryzek, 2014). In particular, the quality and democratic representativeness of parliamentary debate are crucial determinants of the entire deliberative system's capacity (Burall, 2015).

The reform of election rules, the transfer of power from KMT to DPP in 2016 and the emergence of Third Force parties in the 2016 legislative election have improved the inclusiveness by encouraging reflection on and consideration of public discourses during collective decision-making. In June 2005, a constitutional amendment was implemented to reform the electoral system from a combination of multimember district, single non-transferable vote (SNTV) and closed-listed proportional representation into a combination of single-member district majority with closed-listed proportional representation. After reforms, the Seventh Legislative Yuan included 113 legislative seats, with legislators required to seek re-election after 4-year terms. These seats included 73 plurality seats for regions, municipalities and counties; three seats each for plain and mountain aboriginals; and 34 at-large seats. Each party's list of at-large candidates must contain nationals living in Taiwan, and at least half of these candidates must be women. Regional legislative seats are assigned according to the population distribution of municipalities and counties. The previously used SNTV system caused the formation of local factions, increased political corruption and bribery, and affected the quality and efficiency of procedures in the Legislative Yuan (Chen, 2015). Proportional representation (PR) under a mixed-member majoritarian system (MMM) is more likely to provide voters with a clear mechanism of electoral accountability than single-member districts under an MMM system (Yu & Fan, 2014). Moreover, at least half of the non-divisional list of political party candidates were required to be women. This institutional adjustment of

gender quotas has improved the participation of women in political affairs and has resulted in political parties encouraging female members to actively participate in political and public affairs.

Electoral system reform influences how legislators behave and interact with their constituents. By examining the bills introduced by legislators from the Fifth to Seventh Legislative Yuan (from February 2002 to January 2012), Sheng (2014a) found that legislators under a new electoral system introduce more bills than those under the old system. They attributed this to the greater incentive to introduce general interest bills from legislators benefitting from garnering more than 50% of the vote. Specifically, in a two-competitor race in a single member district under the new plurality system, competitors have an incentive to take the position of the median voter. Legislators under new rules have invested more into constituency services, listened more closely to public opinion in their constituency, and campaigned harder for their constituents than those operating under the old rules (Sheng, 2014b). When public opinion in their constituency diverged from the position of their political party, legislators tended to play the role of mediator, reconciling the two. Legislators whose districts were expanded focused more on acquiring funds for development, thus taking roles resembling those of a district delegate. For legislators whose districts decreased in size, they focused on service tasks, the content of their tasks varied more widely, and they were more active in attending funerals, weddings and ceremonies in their districts (Zhang, 2013). Electoral system reforms forced legislative candidates to engage with their constituents for enhanced communication and interaction to understand public concerns and win voters' support.

The emergence of Third Force parties seeking to provide an alternative in Taiwanese politics has promoted inclusiveness and enlarged the deliberative space in the policy-making process. The New Power Party (NPP) emerged from the Sunflower Student Movement and was founded in early 2015. The NPP won five seats in the Legislative Yuan during the 2016 legislative election,[1] making it the third largest party. The NPP, who have advocated for universal human rights, civil and political liberties and Taiwan nationalism, won the support of 30 civic groups and called for voters to support Third Force parties with ideals and civic consciousness in the 2016 election (Gerber, 2016). The NPP have emphasised transparency and new politics in which people can make decisions, including the proposal of a People's Legislative Yuan through which people can participate in constitutional reform. Their pro-independence position narrowed the distance between the NPP and the DPP (Ho, 2017). The NPP made efforts to contest dominant ideas and advocate for the interests of marginalised groups, thus affecting the policy-making process and influencing party and faction negotiations in the Legislative Yuan, as well as the content of bills. For example, NPP legislators have argued that the decision-making process for the selection of textbook content should be open and transparent; moreover, they have issued support for same-sex marriage legalisation, ending the construction of the fourth nuclear power

plant, transitional justice, judicial reform and amendments to the Referendum
Act and Civil Servants Election and Recall Act. The NPP have occasionally
been able to highlight and justify its ideas and have achieved goals in the
face of discord between the DPP and KMT. However, the NPP opposed the
DPP's labour reform policy in 2016, considering it to be bad for workers and
employers (BBC News, 2018). Recently, the NPP have faced internal tensions
and some members have left to join the DPP because of discontent with a
leadership that dominates party decisions and operation (Up Media, 2019).

The increasing proportion of female legislators has contributed to inclusiveness and equal opportunities in the legislative process. In 2016, Tsai Ing-
wen was elected as the first female President of Taiwan, and Tsai won a second
term in 2020. The emergence of female power, rise in gender consciousness
and increasing participation of women in political affairs provide the opportunity to introduce a marginalised voice into the empowered space. The proportion of female legislators increased from 20.2% in 2000 to 38.1% in 2016,
which is higher than the international average of 22%. Civil society groups
tend to state that female political participation can improve the promotion of
women's rights and facilitate the passage of bills that are beneficial to women,
such as those improving day care services and maternity leave (Hsiao, 2016).

Female politicians can provide gender-sensitive perspectives based on
different social experiences and facilitate considerations of the situations,
experiences and knowledge of marginalised groups in decision-making
processes. According to Tang (2018), although some women enter the political stage to fill a male vacancy in a family, faction or party, once they have the
opportunity to display their ability, they may provide a progressive and positive driving force for social transformation. Female politicians do not focus
only on women's policies but are also concerned with oppressed minorities
and promote policies of gender equality and social justice. For example, the
number of female mayors in Taiwan has increased from two in 2014 to seven
in 2018. This has encouraged more women to participate in politics. Gender
differences in political communication and deliberation in the empowered
space warrant attention.

Politicians who joined the legislature in 2016 through proportional
representation have more diverse backgrounds and social experiences;
they include a rock star, an aboriginal activist, environmental activists and
scholars. A record 19 parties ran candidates in the 2020 legislative election.
The Taiwan People's Party (TPP) obtained enough party votes to cross the
5% threshold and won five at-large legislative seats to become the third largest
party in the Legislative Yuan, followed by the NPP with three at-large seats.
The TPP was established in August 2019 by Taipei Mayor Ko Wen-je, who
was elected its founding chairman. Ko stated that the TPP provides another
choice in addition to the KMT and DPP. The party favours an open and
transparent government and aims to gain sufficient legislative seats to become
a critical minority party that can provide a check on the two major parties.
The NPP's list of at-large legislative nominees included an environmental

activist, a human rights lawyer and the mother of a 4-year-old girl who was murdered on a street in Taipei in 2016 (Lee, 2020).

Besides, many parties, including the DPP's at-large legislative nominations, are becoming younger. Parties' youth orientation reflects the value of intergenerational justice emphasised by the Taiwanese society at present, and different age groups need to have someone to speak in the Legislative Yuan (Interview with a legislator, January 2020). Socioeconomic diversity in the body of legislators results in policy deliberations that better reflect the experiences of ordinary citizens in general and underrepresented voices in particular; this contributes to greater inclusiveness and respect for difference, which strengthen linkages between the public space and the empowered space of deliberative systems. Figure 3.1 presents the main structure of the Taiwanese political system. The Legislative Yuan is one of the five branches of government.

Oversight and influence of civil society organisations on legislative deliberation quality

Civil society organisations initiated legislator evaluation campaign activities as early as 1989. In 2007, many NGOs were affiliated with an alliance called Citizen Congress Watch (CCW). Since the Seventh Legislative Yuan, legislator evaluations have been published regularly by CCW after the end of each session. The aim of CCW is to draw attention to excellent legislators and poor quality legislators, as well as to promote legislative reform and transparency through supervision.

CCW has undertaken legislator evaluation once every 6 months since 2008 (the Seventh Legislative Yuan) and published *Legislative Weekly*. CCW asks all legislators to sign a document committing them to legislative reform to realise their promise to be responsible for citizens. CCW has won the support of legislators for their aim to increase the transparency of the Legislative Yuan. A task force comprised of seven legislators from various parties reached a consensus on 30 January 2009 to implement a video on demand (VOD) system for the public. Since February 2009, the Legislative Yuan has enabled the public to access its VOD system to watch live broadcasts of the eight standing committee meetings and plenary sessions without registering any personal information (see IVOD, n.d.). This system enables the public to scrutinise lawmakers' conduct and has contributed to improving the transparency of legislative debates (Wang, 2009).

CCW also facilitates dialogues on reform between legislators. Legislators, experts and civil society groups have been invited to dialogues on parliamentary reform and reviews of legislative performance. At a forum for the review of the ninth Legislative Yuan, the three participating legislators emphasised 'rational negotiations, deliberative discussion, and multiple balance'. CCW expressed hope that legislators can promote reform together (Citizen Congress Watch, 2020).

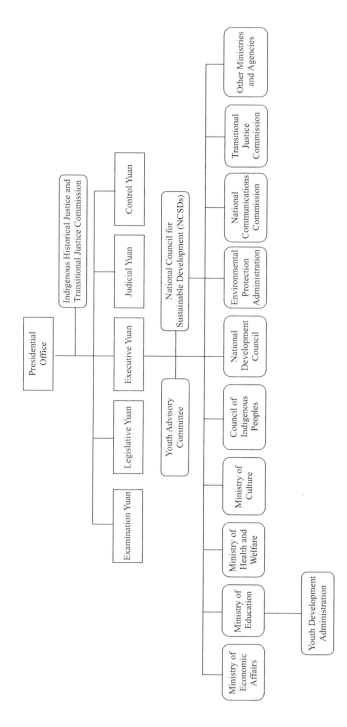

Figure 3.1 The main structure of the Taiwanese political system

CCW's evaluation facilitates more deliberation

CCW employs quantitative and qualitative criteria for evaluation. Some qualitative criteria measure deliberation quality, which contributes to legislators' overall questioning quality. According to CCW, quantitative criteria include attendance rate, questioning rate, bill proposal rate, budget review rate, citizen evaluation based on the VOD system and information disclosure. Additional points are provided for bills, budgets and special deeds. Qualitative criteria are divided into four types. First, *professional questioning* includes document preparedness, rigorous content research, professional opinion, familiarity with duties and the authority of officials under questioning, and adherence to meeting regulations. Second, *positional value* includes concerns of public interest, an emphasis on minority rights, the absence of favouritism for members of the same party, clear positions on meeting topics, courage in opposing the powerful and independence from commercial interests. Third, *problem solving* includes matching questions to the subject matter, clear and consistent questioning, presentation of specific problems, proposal of concrete solutions and independence from commercial interests. Fourth, *attitude and techniques* include following meeting rules, absence of discriminatory or provocative questioning, explanation of reasons, not interrupting, and providing officials with sufficient time to answer questions. Attitude and techniques correspond to respect, authenticity and sincerity, and positional value reflects an emphasis on public interests and the common good.

Deliberations on improving evaluation and broadening public participation are ongoing. CCW constantly evaluates these criteria and their methods are evolving, thus providing deliberative space and platforms for citizens to participate in legislative oversight. CCW collaborates with schools and civil society groups to provide opportunities for university students, ordinary citizens and voluntary legislative overseers to participate in legislative evaluation. Questioning is a crucial criterion for the evaluation of legislative performance. Citizens nationwide can evaluate legislators by watching legislator questioning on the VOD system, which is a notable feature of CCW's legislative evaluation process. Since the fourth session of the Seventh Legislative Yuan in 2009, CCW has organised VOD citizen evaluations by using computer classrooms on campuses nationwide. Citizens and students watch the questioning of two or three legislators and complete evaluation forms. Questions include whether their impression of the legislator changed during questioning and which parts of the performance were best and worst. Then, citizens who participated in the same VOD evaluation form a discussion group to discuss their opinions and comments regarding the legislators' performance (Liao, 2013).

The process of legislator evaluation increases the deliberative space and promotes positive interaction. The process is divided into two stages: preliminary review and review. The preliminary review comprises five evaluation teams: basic performance and citizen evaluation panel; speech and action evaluation panel; bill evaluation panel; budget evaluation panel; and dean, vice-dean and party cadre evaluation panel. CCW organises three meetings to discuss evaluation rules, a focus group and consultation meeting for legislative assistants, and 16 meetings to discuss preliminary review results. A total of 2,456 citizens participated in legislative evaluation using the VOD system in 2019. Based on the results of a preliminary review, lists of outstanding and poorly performing legislators are finalised at a review meeting. The aim of these lists is to encourage outstanding legislators and gradually remove unqualified legislators to build a robust legislature.

Facilitation of rational discussion and improvement of legislative image

The CCW legislator evaluation based on the VOD system contributes to the overall questioning of performance and transparency in the Legislative Yuan. Transparency and instant public oversight have facilitated rational discussions on policy issues in contrast to the exaggeration, exhibitionism and verbal attacks on opponents that can attract media attention. In a study of 170 citizens who participated in the VOD legislator evaluation, Wang (2011) found that trust in the Legislative Yuan was significantly enhanced after watching 4 hours of VOD, and participants tended to report that dominant media reporting is fragmented and incomplete. Before the introduction of the VOD system, the public received some partial reports of Legislative Yuan activities from mass media. Dominant media organisations tend to broadcast speeches of popular legislators or focus on fighting and verbal attacks; thus, some legislators without a particular questioning style are less widely covered. Live broadcasting enables the public to observe questioning and legislative deliberation and understand the legislative context and dialogues between legislators and officials. This promotion of legislative transparency improves the public impression of the quality of legislative deliberation.

CCW evaluation has influenced legislative performance and political communication. Studies have indicated that most legislators are concerned about the public's evaluation of them. According to statistics reported by the Legislative Yuan, many citizens are increasingly engaged with and understand the process of legislative inquiry because of the VOD system. During 2016, the first and second sessions of the Ninth Legislative Yuan, live video of Legislative Yuan proceedings received more than 10.6 million visits, a more than 12-fold increase compared with the seventh and eighth sessions of the Eighth Legislative Yuan in 2015 (829,000 visits). Legislators are generally concerned about the results of CCW evaluation, including the lists of outstanding and underperforming legislators. Regardless of their personal characteristics, constituency, party and duration of tenure, legislators tend to hold positive attitudes towards CCW evaluation. Questioning and bill proposal are two influential criteria that have a significant impact on their behaviour during legislative inquiries. According to CCW evaluation reports, legislative performance is improving, including in the items of attendance, questioning and bill proposal. A high proportion of legislative assistants, especially those of legislators elected for the first time in 2016, attend the pre-evaluation briefing meeting organised by CCW, which demonstrates that legislators value the evaluation (Liao, 2015).

Both CCW and legislators recognise the importance of civic oversight. For the Ninth Legislative Yuan, CCW rated 32 legislators as outstanding. CCW organised a news conference, published legislator evaluation reports and invited legislators rated as excellent to attend an awards ceremony to share their thoughts. The founding chairman of CCW noted that the proportion of legislators rated as outstanding is increasing and that legislative performance is improving. He mentioned that 'oversight of legislators by CCW has indirectly enhanced questioning quality and improved the image of the Legislative Yuan'. The former chairman expressed his hope that this excellence will be spread across all legislators in the Legislative Yuan. Award-winning legislators have recognised the positive influence of CCW oversight. One legislator noted that,

> some legislators in the Eighth Legislative Yuan considered the CCW evaluation somewhat harsh. However, the performance of the Eighth Legislative Yuan was not outstanding. Regardless of their party, legislators in the Ninth Legislative Yuan have conducted themselves with more caution, especially since the introduction of a live broadcast. This has proved that oversight has a positive effect on performance.
> (Citizen Congress Watch, 2019)

Another legislator and former member of a civil society organisation claimed that civil society groups should have the opportunity to express their concerns in legislative committees and voiced a desire for more connections with civil society groups (Citizen Congress Watch, 2020).

Promotion of legislative reform and citizen evaluation by CCW have strengthened the connections between the public and empowered spaces and have contributed to an increase in the deliberative quality of the empowered space. Evaluation of its operations and processes is shaping the nature of the legislative sphere. Some legislators have used CCW evaluation results as campaigning tools during elections, and others have accepted the influence of live broadcasting into daily interactions and discussions with voters. People use legislator evaluation results as reference for conversation with friends and relatives in their private spaces to assess their legislator and local councillor and decide whom to support during an election.[2]

Nationwide networking of local CCWs

CCW also promotes transparency in local politics and has called for civil society organisations overseeing local governments and local councils to promote transparency and remove unqualified councillors. CCW has established a network of local organisations to form the National Congress Watch Alliance

(NCWA). Since 2014, the NCWA has examined the transparency of local councils every 2 years. In 2018, the alliance announced that 19 of 22 local councils failed to meet transparency standards, and they commented that the less transparent a local council is, the less stringent it is during budget review and the worse its fiscal discipline is. The Alliance uses 26 indicators to evaluate the transparency of a local council, with results assigning councils to one of three classes: passable, to be strengthened and extremely poor. Only councils in Keelung City, Taipei City and Chiayi City were evaluated as passable. Based on on-site observations, a member of the NCWA branch for Yilan County indicated that some councillors leave after signing in or leave after questioning. The activities of local council committees are difficult to determine because they do not provide live broadcasting, recorded video, meeting records or verbatim speech records, and visitors are not permitted to take photographs in the auditorium. According to the executive director of the NCWA branch for Taoyuan County, the main problem faced by the Taoyuan County Council is that council committees are not open. Councillors have previously argued for budget proposals to be changed; nevertheless, these proposals have passed. Lack of access to council committees negatively affects the well-being of local citizens. Kaohsiung Civil Servant Citizen Watch claimed that 'transparent information is required to oversee the Kaohsiung City council' and that the council should proactively formulate budgets to improve transparency and publish minutes of the proceedings. They also indicated that 'excellent councillors must promote transparency' (Kaohsiung Civil Servant Citizen Watch).

In a study of how Tainan City councillors behaved differently when a live parliamentary broadcast was implemented, Chao (2013) noted the convenience of watching parliamentary proceedings at home or at the representative's service centre as opposed to having to go to the city council building in person, and that Chao (2013) revealed that, in addition to considerably increasing information participation, the expanded use of information technology mitigates the damage that negative media reports can have on representative politics. In addition to promoting transparency, the NCWA evaluates councillors' performance to remove unqualified councillors. In September 2018, Kaohsiung Civil Servant Citizen Watch held press conference to announce councillor evaluations for the third term of the Kaohsiung City Council. Approximately 100 volunteers participated in the evaluation. Volunteers watched videos of interpellation sessions in which councillors questioned city government officials and completed an online questionnaire. The questionnaire included the following six indicators of interpellation quality: 1) The councillors did not use personal attacks or inappropriate speech, such as antidemocratic or anti-human rights remarks, during the interpellation; 2) The topic of the interpellation was clear, the interpellation was well organised and key points were easy to understand; 3) The interpellation included innovative methods for holding the city government to account; 4) The interpellation focused on important issues of concern to citizens' interests; 5) The interpellation was based on data and analysis, key points were highlighted and recommendations were provided; and 6) The interpellation exhibited a broad perspective, progressive ideas and deep understanding of issues, as well as a holistic view of municipal administration. These indicators were rated on a 5-point Likert scale. Results demonstrated that the overall council performance failed to meet the standard. Among the councillors, 10 were rated as excellent and 12 were placed on the watchlist. Excellent councillors exhibit diligence in their interpellation, questioning and reviewing; they speak actively and ask questions with thoughtful content. Those on the watchlist exhibited serious negligence, made indiscreet remarks and, when acting as the speaker, violated the basic principles of fairly chairing meetings. Kaohsiung Civil Servant Citizen Watch critiqued this improper conduct and urged councillors to improve (Kaohsiung Civil Servant Citizen Watch).

These evaluation indicators included deliberative characteristics, such as mutual respect, sincerity, reasoning, orientation to the common good and equal opportunities. Standards for good deliberation could be more thoroughly incorporated into the design of council evaluation. Civil society organisation oversight combined with digital technology has contributed to providing citizens with access to council information and enabled them to oversee councillors. Thus, such organisations have a diffuse influence on the deliberative quality of the political system.

Utilising mini-public and public hearings to incorporate the plurality of voices in the empowered space

When collective decision-making incorporates the perspectives of stakeholders, the empowered space includes a wider range of inputs and thus gains public legitimacy (Dryzek, 2010). Hendriks and Kay (2019) noted that most participatory practices in parliaments have been focused on informing the public about the existing functions and activities of legislatures rather than on strengthening ties between citizens and elected representatives. Hendriks and Kay (2019) argued that deeper and more inclusive forms of public engagement in committees will improve the committee's representative capacity, deliberative capacity and epistemic and public scrutiny functions. In general, broader and deeper citizen involvement in agenda-setting outside partisan politics enhances the deliberative capacity of committees and mitigates the outsized influence of political parties, powerful interest groups, and the government on the committees' perspectives.

Seeking and constructing transitional justice through mini-publics

Since President Tsai won the 2016 presidential election, the government and Legislative Yuan have suggested adopting deliberative democracy practices to address controversial broad-impact policy issues and to encourage compromise between parties. According to the Legislative Yuan meeting record, citizen conferences were mentioned more frequently during discussions of policy issues compared with the previous KMT-controlled legislature. Some legislators supported the facilitation of social dialogue and mini-public hearings to legitimise institutional decisions, and others asked administrative agencies to conduct citizen conferences during interpellation. An interpellation of the Education and Culture Committee was organised to discuss responses to transitional justice rules in 2017. The adoption of a bottom-up approach by the Ministry of Culture received a positive response from legislators (Legislative Yuan, 2017a):

MINISTER OF CULTURE: We want to initiate transitional justice, but we know that there are competing opinions in society, and we aim to adopt a bottom-up approach. Most importantly, people must have the right to discuss and determine whether to maintain or reform Chiang Kai-shek Memorial Hall. Instead of commemorating an authoritarian ruler with the national resources and budget, Taipei, the capital, should be given new possibilities, and people should be given a new space. This issue should be discussed so that all citizens can deliberate and decide . . . We will announce a collective discussion project to be held in July, which will include four scenario workshops, followed by a citizen conference in February. This process will result in multiple alternatives, which will be discussed in a public hearing.

LEGISLATOR: We expect this approach will be successful. However, the DPP previously tried to remove symbols of authoritarianism and implement transitional justice without making new laws, and this resulted in some problems. I remember that people have different opinions and some tried to reframe Chiang Kai-shek Memorial Hall as an historic site according to the Cultural Heritage Preservation Act to avoid destroying Chiang Kai-shek Memorial Hall. Now that the rules promoting transitional justice have passed, will people considering Chiang Kai-shek Memorial Hall as an historic site after collective discussion be an obstacle?

MINISTER OF CULTURE: . . . no matter whether we adopt the output of collective discussion, the draft or the rules promoting transitional justice, if a historic site is involved, we can follow the deliberation mechanism for cultural assets.

The exchange reveals a clarification of problems and an effort to increase understanding of possible solutions. The Minister of Culture emphasised deliberative forms of public participation and promoted public deliberation and social dialogues on transitional justice.

Deliberative process of legalising same-sex marriage

The Tsai government and legislative committee promoted various deliberative forms of public participation to facilitate more communication between stakeholders. In the CCW Forum of Review and Evaluation for the Ninth

Legislative Yuan, Lee Chun-yi, who was a DPP legislator in the Seventh Legislative Yuan, indicated that the Legislative Yuan is designed to allow the plurality of voices to be heard, although the outcome may not be satisfactory for all stakeholders. He claimed that the special bill legalising same-sex marriage is an example of the Legislative Yuan aiming to find a balance rather than hastily passing a draft.

In a 2016 study commissioned by the Ministry of Justice, four citizen conferences were conducted in Taichung, Hualien, Kaohsiung and Taipei to encourage social dialogue on civil partnership, and a website and a Facebook fan page were created to facilitate public participation and measure public opinion. The researchers also conducted two focus group sessions, with the groups comprising 12 experts, including family court judges and attorneys as well as advocates from social groups specialising in LGBT rights and children's rights. The Taiwan Civil Partnership Act was drafted under consideration of the potential social impact. However, according to the Ministry of Justice, some people claimed that the civil partnership law could not meet the needs of their LGBT friends and proposed a same-sex marriage law. During an interpellation of the Judiciary and Organic Laws and Statutes Committee in 2017, one legislator requested the Ministry of Justice to explain their position regarding the legalisation of same-sex marriage. The Vice Ministry of Justice emphasised public deliberation and collective dialogue to find solutions:

> There have been many discussions about whether the civil law should be amended or a special law should be written . . . The opinions of these two sides have diverged substantially. The Judiciary and Organic laws and Statutes Committee of the Legislative Yuan held a number of public hearings during the last session . . . Relevant government agencies and the President have attached great importance to this issue. At this stage, the Minister of Justice has invited different groups to engage in dialogue to determine if compromises are possible. Therefore, the Ministry of Justice has not proposed a solution.
>
> (Legislative Yuan, 2017b)

Legislators recognised that the issue of same-sex marriage involves considerable social-value conflicts, different notions of marriage and family composition, and social and cultural influences. Thus, they have tended to promote dialogue between competing social groups and have held public hearings to attempt to reach a compromise. Most DPP and NPP legislators support same-sex marriage rights, whereas most KMT legislators tend to favour restricting marriage under the Civil Code to that between a man and woman. Despite the conflicts, misunderstandings, emotional language and dissatisfaction of competing social groups during this contested policy process, people have tended to expect more dialogue to increase mutual understanding, enable compromise to be reached and mitigate the oversimplification of issues. Legislators appear to have consensus on the value of social dialogue, communication and deliberative democracy. The legislative chairman of the public hearing on the same-sex marriage legislation held by the Judiciary and Organic Laws and Statutes Committee recognised the contributions of social groups and experts and emphasised consideration of different voices:

> This is the second public hearing. The first public hearing was convened by the committee last Thursday. Scholars and experts have discussed whether same-sex marriage and same-sex adoption should be legalised. We have heard different voices and diverse opinions on whether to amend the Civil Code or formulate a special law. The outline of the public hearing today differs from the previous one. We hope to focus on the core values of the problem from different angles. To listen to a wider range of voices, different experts and scholars were invited to the second public hearing. When lawmakers face the challenging issue of same-sex marriage, they must be more open-minded, think cautiously, and listen carefully to the opinions of all parties. The valuable opinions you provide today will become an important reference for future consideration of related bills in the Legislative Yuan.
>
> (Legislative Yuan, 2016)

The public hearing was broadcast live, and approximately 20,000 people from competing groups expressed their concerns outside the Legislative Yuan. Some indicated that several public hearings are insufficient and that more communication and deliberation is required to reach a resolution.

On 24 May 2017, the Constitutional Court of Taiwan declared that prohibiting same-sex marriage infringes on the freedom and equality of marriage and that the government must address this problem within 2 years. Groups with competing positions have expressed their opinions by networking and have mobilised to influence policy processes. Christian groups opposed to the legalisation of same-sex marriage established the Alliance for the Happiness of the Next Generation, which proposed holding a referendum on the issue in an attempt to overturn the Constitutional Court's ruling. They proposed two referendum questions related to same-sex marriage, which were approved by the Central Election Committee: Do you agree that marriage defined in the Civil Code should be restricted to the union between one man and one woman? Do you agree to the protection of the rights of same-sex couples in co-habitation on a permanent basis in ways other than changing of the Civil Code? Social groups in favour of same-sex marriage also proposed referendum questions advocating for legalising same-sex marriage. The referendum results revealed that 72.48% of voters approved of 'restricting marriage under the Civil Code to one man and one woman', and 61.12% of voters approved of 'protecting the rights of same-sex couples outside of the Civil Code' (Central Election Commission, 2018). LGBT rights campaigners expressed their dissatisfaction with the referendum proposals and procedures. Social groups in favour of same-sex marriage criticised the combination of the referendum with local elections, which allowed referendum choices to be orientated with party preference and enabled parties to mobilise their supporters to vote in the referendum according to the party position. Moreover, people criticised the Central Election Committee for approving the referendum proposals too quickly and with an insufficient period of debate between the two sides before the referendum.

Nishiyama (2019) argued that schools as a 'mediating space' can become a meaningful part of deliberative systems. Schools can 'serve as a bridge between children's everyday practices and deliberative actions in the public space' (p. 473). The mock referendum on high school campuses connects various sites of communication in deliberative systems. The 2018 referendum was the first opportunity for adults aged 18 and 19 years to vote in referendums.[3] To encourage more young people to vote in the referendum, 23 high school student organisations simulated a mock referendum that was based on the voting procedures of the Central Election Commission. The two referendum questions advocating for marriage equality were strongly approved, indicating that most high school students support the advancement of LGBT rights (Taipei Times, 2018). Based on activism and reading-group networks, student activists from Taipei First Girls' High School used social media to connect with high school student organisations nationwide to organise a mock referendum to raise citizenship consciousness among students. In a Facebook post, student organisers stressed that,

> we are high school students who believe students have an actual influence on society and policy. We hope to raise the willingness of young people to participate in public affairs through mock referendums on campuses nationwide. In addition to encouraging students aged 18 years to vote in referendum, we expect the referendum results to demonstrate the opinions of this generation.
>
> (Referendum for 18, 2018)

This mock referendum succeeded in attracting media attention and demonstrating the potential influence of high school students.

To comply with the Constitutional Court ruling, the Legislative Yuan passed a special law protecting same-sex marriage outside the Civil Code on 17 May 2019. Supporters of same-sex marriage used various methods to make their voice heard and speak to legislators and government elites (e.g. public hearings, social movements, marches, campaigns, petitions and lobbying), thus shaping policy-making processes. Legislators received a wide range of input on the public discourse concerning same-sex marriage through social dialogues, consultation and deliberation. This input may have influenced the legislators' voting behaviour and encouraged them to represent the views of stakeholders and constituency supporters. Most KMT legislators have defended traditional core family values or represented the positions of Christian groups. Despite the opposition of the KMT caucus, seven KMT legislators supported the compromise of a special law after listening to opinions from their constituents. However, legislators who disobey the party whip may risk party disciplinary action and the loss of party support.

This dynamic policy-making process highlights the communicative freedom that minority and marginalised groups, including the younger generation, require to express their opinions. Activists and groups that favoured the legalisation supporting same-sex marriage have criticised their social and economic disadvantages and the inequality of resources during the referendum. However, younger people who are more open and tolerate differences can often effectively use digital technology to fully utilise their limited resources and thus encourage youth participation in the empowered space and its subsystems. Such emerging public groups have actively participated in various forms of communication (e.g. storytelling) and have urged the inclusion of relevant considerations and an orientation towards compromise in the empowered space.

Enhancement of connections between publics and legislative committees through an online platform

Hendriks and Kay (2019) argued that parliamentary committees represent important deliberative spaces where policy problems are identified and framed and where public input is vital. She suggested some institutional and extra-institutional means of connecting publics more meaningfully with legislative committees. These means included innovating existing procedures for public hearings, providing new spaces for public engagement, coupling citizen deliberation with parliamentary-committee deliberation, taking committees to where publics meet and seeking out and connecting committees to informal publics. Some useful empirical insights are available from the Social Welfare and Environment Legislative Committee through which netizens can deliberate directly with members of the Legislative Yuan. The DPP convener of the Social Welfare and Environment Legislative Committee held a food management public hearing titled 'French Fries and Chips and Other Fried Foods Cause Cancer' in March 2015. An online broadcast was arranged with the time provided on the agenda for netizens to offer their opinions. Legislative committee assistants collected these opinions from the discussion forum of the live broadcast and presented them at the public hearing for administrative agencies, legislators and stakeholders to hear. This approach can enhance communication between citizens and their elected representatives.

Digital technology and online platforms can be used to improve citizen participation in decision-making. Public hearings in the Legislative Yuan have tended to feature the limited participation of invited members of the public. Digital technology enables experiments with new forms of decision-making and encourages citizens to participate in Legislative Yuan hearings. With the emergence of netizens' participation, legislators should investigate new methods for decision-making. For example, the conveners of legislative committees could hold online votes on policy issues and incorporate policy issues related to most people's concerns into the agenda. Moreover, legislators could upload abstracts of their questions for government officials to Facebook and enable netizens to provide additional information and opinions. Thus, netizens experience a sense of participation and legislators can obtain more complete information, which will increase the quality of the decision-making process and develop Taiwan's democracy. An online platform for legislative committees and public hearings could provide a quota of seats for observers and online speakers (Chao, 2015). Adjustments to the procedures for public hearings could create new spaces for citizen participation and improve inclusiveness in the empowered space.

Parliaments around the world have been experimenting with new forms of public communication and engagement. In particular, legislators have been actively communicating with the public through websites, blogs, YouTube and social media platforms, such as Twitter and Facebook (Hendricks, 2019). In addition to the use of social media to provide instant policy information and live broadcasting of the Legislative Yuan, civic groups have actively utilised online platforms and social media to facilitate social dialogue and citizen participation. This has urged legislators to consider public concerns and discourses. An increasing number of new civil society organisations have established online platforms and forums for the rapid dissemination of information. Such platforms enable citizens to easily access information and participate in public affairs. The civil society organisation WatchOut provides an online platform for information sharing and communication related to controversial policy issues as well as commentary by government and politicians. This group also created a platform titled 'Ask a politician a question', which emphasises direct, open dialogue between politicians and citizens. WatchOut encouraged legislators and government officials to actively respond to public discourses, questions and critiques. Moreover, an issues laboratory project was conducted through which citizens were provided facts and data to learn to diagnose and understand problems directly from government reports.

Congress Investigation Corps, a virtual community founded in 2014, aims to establish a database of legislators' words and deeds as a form of oversight that will raise citizens' awareness of concerning policy issues, providing a method for legislator supervision. This online platform enables the rapid dissemination of policy information and provides an instant questioning function for the Legislative Yuan. This facilitates public participation and deliberation and encourages legislators and government officials to actively respond to public discourses and critiques. Approximately 300 members have supported and collaborated on this platform by uploading video of legislator questioning, providing news and records related to questioning, and maintaining the database. Users can search for particular legislators and monitor their performance in the legislature. Congress Investigation Corps has gained influence through community networks by asking supporters to expand its network and promote the platform. In addition to completing real-time video and audio records of the Legislative Yuan, Congress Investigation Corps has attempted to facilitate public participation and enable ordinary citizens to understand policy issues and bills. This has been achieved by using humour to promote legislative concerns in the Internet generation.

Conclusion: challenges and prospects

The empowered space faces the challenge of managing the practical demands of working within representative institutions and integrating different discourses to reach a legitimate intersubjective outcome through deliberative ethics and democratic norms (Curato, 2015). Although civil society organisations have successfully promoted legislative transparency, achieved real influence on legislator performance and pressured legislators to work harder, physical conflict still occurs between legislators of different parties. Structural problems and defects of the Legislative Yuan require improvement. Since 2004, the ideas of deliberative democracy and citizen conferences have been mentioned with increasing frequency in the Legislative Yuan. However, highly complex policy issues may require suppression of the deliberative space. For example, the deregulation of imports of American beef involves concerns about the risks of mad cow disease and is influenced by Taiwan–USA relations. Moreover, the positions of the political parties on this issue have changed with their roles in the legislature.

Furthermore, the function of legislative committees can be influenced by party caucus negotiation mechanisms in cases of dispute. Sheng and Huang (2017) found that the party negotiation mechanism has been recognised by parties and legislators as a major pathway to resolve disputes within the Legislative Yuan, where it is applied much more frequently than voting. A considerable portion of political actors within the Legislative Yuan, including those from the majority party, the minority party and small parties, approve of the utility of negotiation. However, the practice of this mechanism has not completely adhered to the rules, and the Speaker of the Legislative Yuan also has the discretion to determine the operation and the outcomes of party negotiation meetings. In the Forum of Review and Evaluation of the Ninth Legislative Yuan and the Forum of Expectations of the Tenth Legislative Yuan, held by the CCW, scholars and legislators expressed their concerns regarding the functions of the party negotiation mechanisms. Although the party negotiation process has been open and publicly broadcast, legislators from small parties have criticised this as a formality because the disparity in the numbers of seats held by different parties limits the influence of small parties. Small parties could create more opportunities for reform if the seats of two main parties are added together, more than half can be obtained. CCW have stated that more seats for small parties adheres with the principle of democracy; however, the party negotiation mechanism should not be abolished before alternatives are found because it does provide the opportunity for small parties to discuss and seek compromises. The performance evaluation of the Ninth Legislative Yuan conducted by CCW indicated that the party caucus negotiation mechanisms were ineffective for alleviating conflicts and enabling rational discussion. Therefore, CCW has urged party caucuses to improve their negotiation mechanisms (Citizen Congress Watch, 2019, October 4; Citizen Congress Watch, 2019, November 14).

The actors in party negotiations should consider the opinions of small parties and follow the principles of deliberative democracy, especially inclusion and equal opportunity of influence. In a successful deliberation, deliberators should change their minds when presented with a convincing argument (Bächtiger et al., 2018, p. 6). The Speaker of the Legislative Yuan plays a crucial role in facilitating compromise and consensus between parties, and legislative transparency may improve the democratic functions of these negotiation mechanisms.

Many legislators have recognised and valued the performance evaluation conducted by CCW. However, studies have revealed that legislators are faced with the challenge of serving well both their constituency and the Legislative Yuan. This structural problem might be attributed to political culture in which some people pay little attention to performance in the legislature and regard participation in constituency events and activities as more important. This affects legislators' willingness to attend meetings of the Legislative Yuan (Citizen Congress Watch, 2019, November 14).

Young people and the Internet generation are increasingly concerned about the quality of the legislature. The inspection of the Legislative Yuan by emerging civil society organisations is a critical driving force for legislative reform and a bridge between the legislature and citizens. Civil society organisations have increasingly utilised information technology to help people access policy information and enable the public to express views on policies. The civic groups that evaluate legislators' performance and monitor the legislature have provided live broadcasting of questioning sessions in legislative committees to notify the public about controversial public issues. They have also improved access to information on policies and individual legislators' questioning and performance record and have created deliberative spaces for participation in representative democracy. Emerging civil society groups have advocated for open data, promoted access to council records and engaged in supervision of the Legislative Yuan. They have thus provided the latest news and commentary regarding the legislature, broadcast live video, organised public forums, published e-bulletins and enhanced knowledge about legislative processes. The actions of these civil society organisations have epistemic and educational functions, and they encourage citizens to pay attention to the legislature and legislators' questioning. The spaces for citizens to participate in deliberation and oversight of the legislature are increasing. This encourages legislators to respect administrative officials when questioning, consider public concerns and discourses, and improve the deliberative quality of the empowered space.

Social media and online platforms that provide instant and dynamic information on policy issues and facilitate rapid communication are increasingly crucial in deliberative systems. Netizens who were previously uninterested in politics and public affairs can now receive relevant policy information from friends and family through online communities and may take an interest in these issues. Online platforms provide instant information and competing positions and encourage citizens to perform various types of participation and communication, such as writing comments regarding particular policy issues and facilitating other discussions through clarifying questions. Sometimes, legislators may respond to citizens' opinions by joining online discussions. The issues of gender equality have encouraged dialogue and discussion not only between citizens but also with legislators. Legislators have become more considerate of public opinions and discourses and more cautious with the content of their questioning. This has resulted in a rethinking of the connection between deliberative forms of public engagement and the institutions of representative democracy.

Notes

1 Three of the legislators gained constituency seats and two were elected from party lists.
2 Information obtained through an interview with a member of a youth civic organisation.
3 The legal voting age for referendums has been lowered to 18 in the 2017 amendments to the Referendum Act.

References

Bächtiger, A., Dryzek, J., Mansbridge, J., & Warreen, M. (2018). Deliberative democracy: An introduction. In A. Bächtiger, J. Dryzek, J. Mansbridge, & M. Warren (Eds.), *Handbook of deliberative democracy* (pp. 1–31). Oxford: Oxford University Press.

BBC News. (2018, January 10). Does NPP have a future after the dispute with DPP because of labor policy reform? *BBC News.* www.bbc.com/zhongwen/trad/chinese-news-42628002

Burall, S. (2015). *Room for a view: Democracy as a deliberative system.* London: Involve.

Central Election Commission. (2018). Referendum Results. web.archive.org/web/20181124220825/http://referendum.2018.nat.gov.tw/pc/en/00/m00000000000000000.html

Chao, C.-H. (2013). The Live-Broadcasted Influence on the Performance of Elected Representatives - A Case Study of the Interpellation of Tainan City Council. *Policy and Personnel Management, 4*(1), 37–68.

Chao, T.-L. (2015). How to solve the problem of undemocratic parliament? Let netizens go to parliament! *Website of the Legislative Yuan.* www.ly.gov.tw/Pages/Detail.aspx?nodeid=5003&pid=31821

Chen, C.-W. (2015). System discussion about Legislators in two-vote system of single constituency. *Yu Da Academic Journal, 41,* 221–244.

Citizen Congress Watch. (2019). Results of the nationwide investigation of local congress transparency. https://ccw.org.tw/organization/transparency/2018-3

Citizen Congress Watch. (2019, October 4). The latest news: The awards ceremony of outstanding legislators. *Citizen Congress Watch.* http://ccw.org.tw/news/-73

Citizen Congress Watch. (2019, November 14). Press release on the Forum of Review and Evaluation of the 9th term of the Legislative Yuan held by the CCW in 2019. *Citizen Congress Watch.* http://ccw.org.tw/news/-103

Citizen Congress Watch. (2020). *Home page.* http://ccw.org.tw/

Curato, N. (2015). Deliberative capacity as indicator of democratic quality: The case of the Philippines. *International Political Science Review, 36*(1), 99–116.

Dryzek, J. (2010). *Foundations and frontiers of deliberative governance.* Oxford: Oxford University Press.

Gerber, A. (2016, January 8). Civic groups voice support for 'Third Force'. *Taipei Times.* www.taipeitimes.com/News/taiwan/archives/2016/01/08/2003636709

Hendriks, C. M., & Kay, A. (2019). From 'opening up' to democratic renewal: Deepening public engagement in legislative committees. *Government and Opposition, 54*(1), 25–51.

Ho, M.-S. (2017). The Third Force and umbrella soldiers: Comparing the elections of Taiwan after the Sunflower Movement and Hong Kong after the Umbrella Movement. *Mainland China Studies, 60*(1), 59–86.

Hsiao, A.-C. (2016, May 19). Taiwan: A nice place for women's political participation. *BBC News.* www.bbc.com/zhongwen/trad/china/2016/05/160519_tw_suit_for_femail_leaders

IVOD. n.d. IVOD. The Legislative Yuan. ivod.ly.gov.tw

Kaohsiung Civil Servant Citizen Watch. (2019, September 24). The third session of the third term of city council failed in its overall performance. *Kaohsiung Civil Servant Citizen Watch.* www.kcscw.org/2019/09/108-9-24.html

Lee, I.-C. (2020, January 12). Taiwan People's Party top among 'Third Force' parties. Special report of legislative election. *Taipei Times.* www.taipeitimes.com/News/front/archives/2020/01/12/2003729111

Legislative Yuan. (2016). Meeting information, legalising same-sex marriage. 105(93). The second session of the ninth Legislative Yuan. Taipei: The Judiciary and Organic Laws and Statutes Committee. https://lci.ly.gov.tw/LyLCEW/communique1/final/pdf//105/93/LCIDC01_1059301_00002.pdf

Legislative Yuan. (2017a). Meeting records of responses to transitional justice rules. The fourth session of the ninth Legislative Yuan. Taipei: The Education and Culture Committee. https://lci.ly.gov.tw/LyLCEW/communique1/final/pdf/107/05/LCIDC01_1070501.pdf x

Legislative Yuan. (2017b). An interpellation. Taipei: The Judiciary and Organic Laws and Statutes Committee.

Liao, Y.-C. (2013). *Citizen Congress Watch and legislative politics.* Taipei: National Chengchi University.

Liao, Y.-C. (2015). The effect of 'legislator-evaluation' on legislative behaviors: An exploratory analysis. *Taiwan Democracy Quarterly, 12*(1), 1–59.

Nishiyama, K. (2019). Enabling children's deliberation in deliberative systems: Schools as a mediating space. *Journal of Youth Studies, 22*(4), 473–488.

Referendum for 18. (2018, November 3). A first lesson in democracy: Mock referendums in high schools across the nation. https://zh-tw.facebook.com/ReferendumFor18/

Sheng, S.-Y. (2014a). Change and continuity in legislators' bill-introduction before and after the reform of the electoral system: An exploratory analysis. *Taiwan Political Science Review, 18*(1), 73–127.

Sheng, S.-Y. (2014b). Revisiting constituency service and legislative work of Taiwan's legislators: A comparison before and after the reform of the electoral system. *Soochow of Journal of Political Science, 32*(2), 65–116.

Sheng, S.-Y., & Huang, S.-H. (2017). Party negotiation mechanism: An analysis through the lens of institutionalization. *Soochow Journal of Political Science, 35*(1), 37–92.

Stevenson, H., & Dryzek, J. S. (2014). *Democratizing global climate governance.* Cambridge: Cambridge University Press.

Taipei Times. (2018, November 23). 2018 elections: Schools hold mock referendum polls. *Taipei Times.* www.taipeitimes.com/News/taiwan/archives/2018/11/23/2003700477204772

Tang, W. H. (2018). Women power? The emptiness and reality behind women's participation in politics. *Street Corner Society.* https://twstreetcorner.org/2018/11/30/tangwenhui-2/

Up Media. (2019, November 11). Why did NPP come to this step? *UP Media.* www.upmedia.mg/news_info.php?SerialNo=75125

Wang, A. H. (2011). Providing information for citizen's political trust to congress: An exploratory study through IVOD. *Taiwan Democracy Quarterly, 8*(3), 161–197.

Wang, F. (2009, February 20). Legislative Yuan to broadcast its sessions online. *Taipei Times.* www.taipeitimes.com/News/taiwan/archives/2009/02/20/2003436553

Yu, C.-H., & Fan, T.-W. (2014). An exploratory study of electoral accountability under different legislative electoral systems. *Journal of Democracy and Governance, 1*(1), 111–141.

Zhang, Z.-C. (2013). *The continuity and change of the legislators' constituency service: The analysis of the Third to the Seventh Legislative Yuan* (Unpublished master's thesis). Department of Political Science, National Chengchi University, Taipei, Taiwan.

4 Transmission and accountability

Introduction

The transmission of influence from the public space to the empowered space is vital to the overall deliberative capacity of the democratic system. The content of such communication involves rhetoric, performance, argumentation and the provision of information. Transmission occurs through various means, including lobbying; regular meetings between constituents and members of parliament; public meetings, where parliamentarians bring findings from the meeting back to parliament; media and civic society campaigns aimed at influencing the legislature; and deliberative mini-publics that bring the narratives and debates between ordinary citizens into the decision-making process. Narratives developed in the public space either directly influence the debate within the empowered space or exert their influence in more subtle ways – such as through cultural change that begins in the public space before affecting the perspectives of those in the empowered space (Stevenson & Dryzek, 2014; Burall, 2015). Boswell et al. (2016) argued that transmission is the key enabler of inclusion at a system level. However, little research has been conducted on the mechanisms of transmission in deliberative systems regarding how, and to what effect, transmission is facilitated in practice. Boswell et al. (2016) discussed three promising mechanisms of deliberative transmission: institutional, innovative and discursive. They suggested that the systemic turn in deliberative democracy should be accompanied by a nuanced understanding of how transmission occurs across sites.

Accountability involves an empowered space being responsible to public space. It is exercised when politicians who fail to respond to their constituents' demands in decision-making are either removed from office through an election (the most common and important accountability mechanism within liberal democratic states) or through recall. Although electoral processes are free and competitive, campaigns involve adversarial rhetoric, which serves to limit the development of deliberative competencies; the contestation of discourses lapses into communication modes, such as black propaganda, misinformation and rumours (Curato, 2015). In addition to elections, accountability mechanisms include parliamentary hearings, ombudsmen investigations, commissioner evaluations, court hearings and judicial reviews. Media investigations can also serve as an accountability mechanism. Ensuring media independence is critical for maintaining and strengthening the capacity of this accountability mechanism and the deliberative system as a whole (Burall, 2015). The National Communications Commission (NCC) is an independent statutory agency of the Executive Yuan that is responsible for regulating the development of the telecommunications and broadcasting industries, promoting competition and ensuring consumer protection. To enhance the credibility of the media, the commission has implemented a series of measures for curbing the dissemination of fake news by the broadcast media, including requiring the broadcast media to incorporate fact-checking mechanisms into their business plans. The NCC's content review committee, which comprises independent experts from different academic disciplines, convenes frequently to address disputed broadcast content.

Debates and deliberations on the constitutional system and institutional arrangements of accountability mechanisms and a division of labour in deliberative systems have been ongoing. In Taiwan, investigative power is exercised separately by two parallel institutions: the Legislative Yuan and the Control Yuan. The Legislative Yuan has the power to implement the impeachment of the president, whereas the Control Yuan has other investigative and impeachment powers. The functions and powers of the Control Yuan are controversial. The members of the Control Yuan are nominated and appointed by the president with the approval of the Legislative Yuan. The Control Yuan receives people's written complaints and is authorised to exercise the powers of impeachment, censure and corrective measures. For the effective implementation of these powers, the Control Yuan is given the authority to conduct investigations. The Control Yuan's investigations can be divided into three categories: commissioned, assigned and self-initiated investigations. Its other functions include circuit supervision and inspection, invigilation, auditing and the development and implementation of Sunshine Acts. Many people have argued that because it is impossible to expect the Control Yuan to be completely independent, its powers should be returned to the Legislative Yuan, thereby allowing citizens to supervise the Legislative Yuan, and the Legislative Yuan to supervise the government. However, others believe that the quality of legislators varies, and that transferring all the rights of investigation to the Legislative Yuan is not appropriate. They believe that the Legislative Yuan might monopolise the right of investigation, endangering the stability of the state. Although the Control Yuan announces how public sentiment cases have been handled, it does not explain the detailed investigation process, and the public does not have adequate access to their judgements. The influence of the Control Yuan does not appear to be significant.

Independent commissions play a critical role in the accountability framework. For example, the Transitional Justice Commission is an independent government agency that was established by the Executive Yuan on 31 May 2018 for investigating the actions taken by KMT between 15

August 1945 and 6 November 1992, including the 228 Incident and White Terror. The committee is responsible for providing rulings and performing regulatory and investigative public tasks. Its tasks include making political archives more readily available, removing authoritarian symbols, redressing judicial injustice and promoting transitional justice. The commission's recommendations have resulted in the implementation of legislation or administrative measures.[1]

The transmission mechanism between the public space and the empowered space is rapidly developing and versatile. The Tsai government and the Digital Minister Audrey Tang have made efforts to use digital technology to boost civic dialogue. These efforts have infused the government with the spirit of social innovation through new initiatives, such as vTaiwan (virtual Taiwan – v is for virtual, vote, voice, verb; see vTaiwan, 2020), which enables various online communities to debate policy solutions and problems in the digital economy; Join Platform (Public Policy Participation Network Platform, 2020), which is an e-petition and civic engagement platform that uses a real-time machine to analyse online voting and to generate an interactive map to group different-minded users; and Public Digital Innovation Space, which promotes open government, youth participation, administration digitalisation and visualisation, and participatory government.

Moreover, an increasing number of civic society groups are actively involved in transmission and accountability mechanisms; this has contributed to the development of advanced democratic deliberative systems. Civic society organisations play a crucial role in creating more spaces for deliberative practices, reasoned arguments and conversations on policy issues and programmes. For example, civic society organisations' collaborative fact-checking projects, governance performance evaluations and policy proposal evaluations facilitate reasoned conversations. The following section highlights the main transmission mechanisms, map sites and spaces where deliberative practices occur, and the role of civic society organisations that connect these moments and spaces.

Institutionalising democratic innovations

E-rule-making and open consultation: vTaiwan

The government and members of the open source community collaboratively developed the vTaiwan platform in 2015. The platform connects government officials, members of the public and stakeholders in large-scale policy deliberation; it makes government action more decisive and online democracy more robust. Specifically, relevant government agencies are required to collect stakeholder opinions and proposals from vTaiwan and incorporate them into their policy decisions. They must also detail, to the public, how they intend to respond to deliberations on the vTaiwan platform. This new deliberative platform broadens participation in public affairs (Fan et al., 2019).

The creators of vTaiwan drew from the work of the Regulation Room (RegR) – which was operated by the Cornell E-Rulemaking Initiative to broaden participation and improve quality in rule-making through technology – and extended the RegR to be a recursive public space that is open to transformation and reformulation. vTaiwan empowers the public to define the topic of discussion, the agenda for the discussion and the tools used to facilitate the conversation. vTaiwan is run by the so-called coherent blended volition of participants and contributors, an approach that emphasises the 'conceptual blend' of diverse views by incorporating the most essential elements of the different perspectives into a coherent whole. The vTaiwan process comprises four successive stages: proposal, opinion, reflection and legislation. The transitions between stages are decided by consensus from the vTaiwan community. This open-format principle enables meaningful deliberation when all stakeholders are ready and willing to collaborate and iterate on solutions (Hsiao et al., 2018).

vTaiwan has numerous successes in solving complex problems on political issues, and its first experiment was the regulation of Uber. vTaiwan invited groups from across the debate spectrum to join its online space and ensured that the essential elements of the views of each stakeholder – such as members of the public, taxi drivers, Uber drivers and Uber Inc. – would not be ignored in the rule-making process. In response to the deliberative process during rule-making, Uber transformed its business model in Taiwan to become a legal app-dispatch company. However, not all cases on vTaiwan have resulted in regulation reform.

Although each citizen can submit a topic to vTaiwan, very few cases are proposed by citizens. In vTaiwan, as an ongoing institutionalised process funded by the government, maintaining autonomy in the selection of discussion topics is challenging. If a government authority refuses to discuss a public issue, the sensitive topic will not go through the vTaiwan process. Despite the challenges associated with it, the vTaiwan process has been operated within the principle of adhocracy and continues to be crafted by the community with the support of open source technologies. vTaiwan has the potential to address political polarisation and stand as a feasible model of decentralised consultation for society, having fostered a collaborative culture between civil society and the government (Hsiao et al., 2018). Research indicates that most participants of vTaiwan are familiar with the Internet and have a positive evaluation of Audrey Tang, a minister without a portfolio, because she was responsible for the establishment of vTaiwan. They generally have a high willingness to participate in discussions and can reach a consensus easily. vTaiwan represents a prospective experimental model for Taiwan's e-participation in public policy (Chen, 2016). By adopting focus group discussions, vTaiwan facilitates interactive and two-way communication and deliberation among policy stakeholders and encourages listening and justification to reach an acceptable consensus. The participants in the vTaiwan community explain professional terms and legal concepts in a manner that laypeople can understand. These efforts increase the mutual understanding between government officials and citizens. vTaiwan serves as an innovative transmission mechanism of the voices of the relevant public.

E-participation platform: e-petition

With the rapid evolution of ICTs and the constant emergence of new social problems, the Taiwanese e-government project promotes e-participation, open data and partnerships between the government and the people. E-participation can transcend spatiotemporal limitations to facilitate broad and equal participation. Information on the processes of e-participation platforms can be accumulated and utilised easily. Thus, the enrichment and availability of information in the process of online citizen participation are enhanced. Moreover, the anonymous nature of online participation encourages citizens to freely express their personal opinions regardless of their status, ethnic background and other factors; thus, citizens' psychological obstacles can be eliminated (Huang & Chen, 2004). The 'Public Policy Participation Network Platform', also called the Join Platform, is a popular platform for online participation developed by the National Development Council in 2015. The Join Platform allows citizens to offer policy recommendations and facilitates communication among government agencies and between the government and public on policy regulations. The platform emphasises focused discussion as well as two-way communication between the government and the public, in particular, and on the ideals of deliberative democracy, in general – including reasoned deliberation and respect. As mentioned in its official website:

> The pros and cons of a policy as well as the goals of different ethnic groups must be considered in policy discussions. We are convinced that any form of discussion on pros and cons will improve the policy. Depending on whether you agree or disagree with an issue, you can press yes or no to express your opinion. This sacred move lets us know that someone is paying attention to an issue. We welcome you to write down specific and feasible comments that can be amended, so that more opinions can be obtained in policy discussions. You can add your thoughts or supplementary information to the comments of other people or administrative agencies, so that the topics can be discussed comprehensively through different angles and levels of discussion. If you do not agree with the comments made by others or administrative agencies, please respect their comments and do not criticise or ridicule them. We deeply hope that in addition to avoiding emotional responses, you provide reasons for your point of view because this makes it easier for us to clarify the problem.
>
> (Public Policy Participation Network Platform, 2020)

The Join Platform enhances positive interaction and communication between the government and citizens, and government agencies must be responsive to public concerns and conversations. The design of the platform helps agencies highlight issues important to the public, and the agencies must respond to the policy proposals.

The Join Platform provides four modes for citizen participation in public affairs: 'Idea Proposal', 'Public Speaking', 'Let's Supervise', and 'Talking to the Heads of Agencies'. 'Idea Proposal' allows the general public to submit policy proposals. For deliberation, a proposal requires the support of 5,000 people. The relevant ministries then formally respond to the proposal. The aforementioned mechanism is the first e-petition innovation in Taiwan. Since 2016, a collaborative feature has been added to the platform, which allows others to provide comments on the original proposal to refine it. Moreover, people can now add their viewpoints as secondary opinions. The 'Public Speaking' mode is aimed at consulting the public on planning policy issues promoted by government agencies. It functions as a type of electronic public consultation. People can leave a message, access public information, click 'Agree' or 'Disagree', and use the 'Follow' function to subscribe. All online discussions and responses are transparent. The length of open discussions on different topics varies (e.g. 10 days, 1 month or a maximum of 3 months).

The 'Let's Supervise' function provides the public with a channel to monitor governance performance. It provides information on progress in the implementation of the conclusions of meetings and major government policy plans. The Join Platform enables the collection of discussion and feedback during the implementation of policies. People can leave comments, access public information, rate the platform and subscribe to the platform. The 'Talking to the Heads of Agencies' function is similar to the head mailbox of the official website, and it integrates the head mailbox of all executive ministries. The Join Platform makes good use of social media and operates Facebook fan pages. Each page under the four modes also has Facebook and Google sharing links to broaden participation and facilitate discussions.

The Join Platform has contributed to the institutionalisation of the mechanism of e-participation in policy deliberations. This platform provides policy proposals and public opinions to ministries. In contrast to vTaiwan's function of rule-making, the Join Platform does not bring participants' opinions into the process of decision-making; thus, it has less influence on policy-making than vTaiwan does (Chen, 2016). In a content analysis of proposals made by people and responses by the government, Tsao (2018) found that citizen policy proposal preferences could become a driving force in the development of policy programmes initiated by the government to solve problems. When citizens' policy proposals are based on a specific event that attracts the attention of the public in a short period, and the proposals then quickly pass the supporter threshold, the administrative agency will assess the external environment. If overall public opinion is consistent with the agency's position, the government's willingness to adopt the proposal will increase.

In an analysis of the hosting and co-organising agencies' perceptions and experience of the Join Platform, Chen et al. (2017) found that the Join

Platform has a meaningful impact, including enhancing the effectiveness of communications between government agencies and citizens, increasing the government's listening and understanding of public opinion, facilitating trans-agency collaboration and cooperation between the government and citizens, and broadening public participation. However, it faces three challenges. First, the platform affects the agencies' communication culture. Netizens expect the government to communicate directly and in real time, which would affect the government's external communication model in which multiple layers of approval are required before speaking. Executives are unfamiliar with online communication models, which creates the fear of mistakes. Second, it would reduce the support of the chief executive for responding to public opinions and increase the difficulty of coordination and response by administrative staff when public opinions differ from the value or ideology of the heads of the agencies. If the public's proposal involves the amendment of the law or if public opinions are considerably different from the legislator's pro-posal, tension will be caused between the agencies and the Legislative Yuan. Third, the mechanisms increase administrative costs for responding to public concerns. When a policy proposal cannot be fully integrated with existing administrative processes, additional coordination efforts are required. In the absence of resources and personnel, this requirement increases the burden on agencies. When a public proposal involves coordination between multiple min-istries, difficulties are caused in the division of labour within the government.

The Join Platform's online participation facilitates positive interaction and increased communication between government officials and citizens as well as increased communication and cooperation between agencies. Online par-ticipation and communications on policy proposals and programmes serve an epistemic function that clarifies the policy problem and helps citizens to understand policy issues and the government's response and considerations. These processes also facilitate ongoing face-to-face communication and links to deliberations in other areas of deliberative systems. In the case of social policy issues, participants in public hearings or meetings can express their opinions and invite friends to voice and respond to opinions on the Join Platform. Despite the aforementioned challenges, other transmission mechanisms can complement the operation of the Join Platform to encourage increased dialogue and reflection.

Public consultations

Since the Tsai government took office in 2016, government agencies have grad-ually merged the forms of national participation and online virtual participa-tion activities. These agencies have engaged in large-scale consultations on issues to facilitate institutional reform and policy promotion. Several public consultations were conducted in Taiwan during 2017–2018, including the National Cultural Meeting, National Agricultural Meeting, Energy Transition White Paper and Judicial Reform National Meeting. The common feature of these programmes is that the relevant government agencies conducted large-scale consultations in the early stages of the policy-making process. Most Taiwanese government agencies have a fixed framework on basic issues; however, they are willing to be flexible for other issues. In contrast to other national public consultations, a preparatory committee was established for the Judicial Reform National Meeting conducted by the president's office to collect opinions from various stakeholders and the public to establish the topic framework for discussion. The advantage of this approach is that, through open-ended consultations, the topic framework is not limited to the government's preference on judicial reform issues. Thus, people are more willing to provide suggestions (Lin, 2019).

The aforementioned four meetings differ in the degree of topic convergence, openness of the materials and other factors. In the National Agricultural Conference, 18 local grassroots forums as well as expert focus discussions and online proposals were simultaneously conducted. Then, eight meetings were held to converge the issues. Follow-up discussions were held to form policy proposals and programmes through focus discussions and think tank research. The other three national consultation meetings were more transparent at different stages of discussions and formal meetings, and the public has open access to most of the meeting records and videos. Thematic consultation and working groups were set up to conduct multiple rounds of discussions and provide a tracking mechanism, making it easy to understand how topics and opinion flows have been handled.

The transparency of the entire process and the friendly tracking mechanism can enhance the trust of participants and the public. Furthermore, the aforementioned three national consultations provided online proposal platforms. Similar to the e-petition function of the Join Platform, the National Cultural Meeting and National Agricultural Consultation set the threshold of the second motion. The advantage of this strategy is that the relevant ministries can understand the issues that are of high concern to the public, avoid excessive proposals and have a basis for discussion at the consultation meeting. In the Energy Transition White Paper and Judicial Reform National Consultation, experts or delegations (group members or preparatory committee members) judged and selected important policy issues for discussion from professional perspectives. In addition to issues of public concern, other important issues can be determined from the perspective of national benefits or the overall industrial and social development (Lin, 2019).

The Energy Transition White Paper was the first policy to be drafted through large-scale, long-term citizen participation. After taking office in 2016, the Tsai government aimed to move towards the vision of a non-nuclear homeland and promote energy transition. Therefore, the government was aware that promoting citizen participation in the early stages of the formation of policies and measures was crucial. Moreover, the government realised that they could collaborate with the public for promoting energy transition. The public participation mechanism design was divided into three stages, and multiple channels were provided for citizen dialogue. The first stage of public consultation activities focused on topic and issue exploration as well as policy recommendations. This stage included early discussions; online communities; group advice; opinions provided through the Internet, email and fax; and four preparatory meetings organised in northern, central, southern and eastern Taiwan to consult the public on improving the exploration of issues and topics related to energy transition. The second stage involved the design of policy programmes through five multidisciplinary expert working groups.[2]

After collaboration between various ministries, experts and social groups, the Ministry of Economic Affairs announced the key plan and draft contents of the Energy Transition White Paper on 23 March 2018. Moreover, citizen dialogue was launched to seek valuable opinions from different parties for improving the development planning for energy transition. The third stage aimed to broaden citizen dialogue to obtain feedback from stakeholders on the first draft of the white paper through meetings with social and industrial groups, online opinion solicitation at the National Development Council's Join Platform, and written opinion solicitation specially designed for research and academic groups. Two 'face-to-face' meetings were conducted for the general public to expand and deepen the dialogue and to create a new model for public discussion on energy policy. After considering the relevant opinions of the multidisciplinary expert working groups, the white paper was finalised.

The Energy and Carbon Reduction Office of the Executive Yuan serves as the integration and coordination unit to resolve disputes. The availability of live broadcasts and recordings made the participation process transparent. Moreover, data exploration and visualisation software tools were used to display issues and the opinion processing flow, which made it easy for people to track the flow of follow-up policy implementation. After more than 40 meetings with more than 2,000 participants, the first draft of the Energy Transformation White Paper was finally completed in July 2018 (Ministry of Economic Affairs, 2020). According to the Energy and Carbon Reduction Office of the Executive Yuan, the content of the Energy Transition White Paper was developed through a consensus between the people and the government. A long-term planning and regular adjustment review mechanism already existed at the time of planning. The aforementioned white paper included a large amount of public opinion and was developed through a bottom-up approach. The Executive Yuan is still confirming the implementation details before formally announcing the plan (Taiwan Environment Information Centre, 2019).

The public consultation process for the Energy Transition White Paper, which facilitated public dialogue, received recognition from civic society organisations. Citizen of the Earth commented on the website of the consultation process, and the opinions collected during the initial preparatory meeting were aggregated into 20 key plans. The working group wrote the first draft of the white paper. The plans titled Citizen Power Plant and Energy Conservation Goals and Path Planning were completely proposed by civic society. The most significant feature of the Energy Transition White Paper is the transparent and open information and extensive social participation. As indicated by Citizen of the Earth,

> Every large and small meeting and related document and material in the process is all uploaded verbatim to the website. This is a pioneering initiative in Taiwan. For the first time, information on major government meetings has been completely transparent and made public on the Internet.
>
> (Citizen of the Earth, 2019)

The deliberative participation mechanisms for energy transition have epistemic functions and have been consequential in incorporating public advocacy and proposals into policy. These mechanisms represent the processes of co-designing and seeking consensus, which enhance interaction between the empowered space and the public space.

Mini-publics and open policy-making

Mini-publics have been used to engage citizens on a range of issues in policy-making processes. Although academic groups, communities and non-profit organisations have played important roles in promoting deliberative democracy in Taiwan, past trends indicate that the government was the primary motivator of deliberative democracy during 2002–2011. The intentions of the government directly or indirectly affect other sectors. The National Health Insurance Payment consensus conference promoted by the Department of Health of the Executive Yuan and the Youth National Affairs Conference conducted by the National Youth Commission (Chapter 2) were pioneering conferences in Taiwan. The Environmental Protection Administration of the Executive Yuan was the first to use the World Café model for a national deliberative conference in 2012. The agency stated that the World Café model, with its deliberative spirit, is a suitable tool for resolving controversies in policies. Various sectors have become interested in holding World Café conferences (Huang & Hsieh, 2013, pp. 92–94).

The procedures of different deliberative forums models practised in Taiwan vary in terms of their roles in the policy process, participant recruitment and number, discussion format and length and effects on policy. Moreover, these models differ from traditional public meetings in three aspects. First, the recruitment of the participants in deliberative forums models is relatively open, which reflects the principle of fairness. The number of participants varies from hundreds, such as in deliberative polling, to as few as a dozen, such as in consensus conferences and citizen juries. Second, participants in deliberative forums are better prepared because the organisers of these forums offer readable materials or hold expert sessions to equip participants with the necessary knowledge to engage in meaningful discussions on equal footing. Third, the forums are well-structured so that the diversified values and knowledge of stakeholders are incorporated into the deliberation process. Experienced facilitators make efforts to maintain a sense of equality and meaningful dialogue and to realise the ideal of reciprocity. Some problems have been resolved using deliberative forums (e.g. national health insurance and tax reforms), whereas other problems are still in dispute (e.g. nuclear waste site selection and surrogate mothering; see Huang & Hsieh, 2013, pp. 92–94).

Various public deliberation techniques have been used, modified and combined with other consultation platforms initiated by the government to broaden public participation and reduce its time and space constraints. For example, the 'eID card' open policy-making workshop was conducted in 2017 to facilitate dialogues among the government, stakeholders and citizens. The policy-planning process included the face-to-face deliberation workshop (broadcast online), an online consultation platform and a conference. A total of 50 citizens were randomly selected from a stratified sample and participated in the open policy-making workshop. The concept of deliberative democracy and the process of the workshop were first introduced. Then, the director of the Home Affairs Department of the Ministry of the Interior introduced the eID card policy so that the participants could understand the purpose of the workshop and the background of the chip national identity card replacement programme. Subsequent discussions were divided into five stages: comprehensive discussions, first-stage group discussions, expert discussions, second-stage group discussions and overall discussion and sharing.

In the comprehensive stage, two experts discussed issues related to the chip national identity card from legal and application aspects, and questions and responses were allowed. In the first-stage group discussions, participants were divided into six groups, each of which was assisted by one facilitator. The members of the group stated their opinions, views and issues of concern. During the expert discussions, four experts and scholars discussed the pros and cons of the policy, including aspects such as legal feasibility, information security and human rights. After listening to the experts and scholars, the participants asked the experts questions and obtained responses. In the second-stage group discussions, each group formed an opinion on the three major issues of the chip national identity card. In the overall discussion, the representatives of each group reported the main discussion results of their group to all the participants. After the completion of the six group reports, the facilitator summarised the reports of each group. The facilitator then sorted out the common views or suggestions and differing views on implicit or explicit ID card data as well as meaningful public opinions that could be explored further (Huang, 2017).

The aforementioned open policy-making process increased spaces for citizen deliberations and facilitated dialogues among stakeholders. The Ministry of the Interior recognised public opinions, which were incorporated into the decision-making process. However, the Taiwan Association for

Human Rights expressed their concerns regarding the potential risks to privacy rights in the expert testimony forum of the workshop and in other arenas in the public space. They called for the postponement of the eID card policy. Disputes in policy-making attract public and media attention and facilitate further communications and reflection on controversial policy issues.

County-level deliberation mainly focuses on environmental concerns, including river pollution and traffic control, as well as casino gambling. Such deliberation includes general discussions on city or county development with candidates for county governor or city mayor. Community deliberation is closely related to spatial planning for specific areas (Huang & Hsieh, 2013, p. 94). A trend has emerged in which local governments are creating additional spaces to enable citizens to participate in policy-making for collaborative problem solving and achieving the good of the community. For example, the number of people with dementia in Taiwan has increased sharply. Approximately 90% of Taiwanese elderly individuals with dementia live in a community, therefore, establishing dementia-friendly communities is important. The Bureau of Public Health of the New Taipei City Government has attempted to listen to and understand the needs of elderly individuals with dementia and their families for establishing a comprehensive network to assist them. The bureau creates multiple localised dementia-friendly community models. In 2016, the Bureau of Public Health held forums with community leaders, family caregivers and physicians to explore the elements and vision of the construction of dementia-friendly communities for reflecting on current development in Taiwan. This initiative caused people to focus increased attention on dementia-friendly communities and activated the public imagination of people with dementia by facilitating deliberation with the younger generation.

The Bureau of Public Health adopted the Open Space Technology model to invite participants from different backgrounds to communicate and talk freely. Brainstorming was performed to explore various possibilities for the future development of dementia-friendly communities in New Taipei City and for the design of future dementia-friendly community action plans. The bureau established a platform and made efforts to connect the resources of the public and private sectors after conducting many discussions and meetings as well as listening to the needs of the community though open spaces, forums and other activities. These steps empowered community members to become supporters of families that include individuals with dementia and to collaborate on the development of dementia-friendly communities. Furthermore, the aforementioned forums and open-space workshops link to other communication spaces and activities initiated by dementia patient groups and care providers or families for collaboration on policy advocacy and the transmission of policy ideas. Online groups for patients with dementia and their care providers offer online platforms for these individuals to narrate their life experiences and make their voices heard.

Citizen action, campaigns and civic forums

Grassroots organising, campaigning and petitioning have been widely recognised and valued as key transmission mechanisms linking empowered spaces in the deliberative system. Citizen action has been taken against air pollution, and calls have been made for good air quality. A series of campaigns, citizen actions and citizen initiatives for community air monitoring (Tu, 2019) as well as various forums and dialogues in the last decade have forced the government to set the PM2.5 air quality standard and implement air pollution control programmes for improving air quality.

Since 2015, citizen campaigns have asked for the right to breathe clean air. Later civic action has asked the government to take air pollution control seriously, as reflected by the slogan, 'Go for the next generation, save health, save the planet and save children'. Due to the continuous civil demand for solving air pollution issues, the Taiwanese government has initiated policy planning and programmes, such as the 2015 Clean Air Action Plan and the 2016 Clean Air Action Plan Amendment Plan. Thus, the government's policy-making has been driven by civic actions. Furthermore, the large-scale anti-air-pollution campaign in February 2017 forced the Executive Yuan to hold a meeting on air pollution prevention strategy planning and promotion tracking. On 13 April, the EPA reported 'the specific objectives of air pollution prevention strategies action measures', which reflected the government's commitment to air pollution control (Liu, 2018). On 28 April, the EPA held a public hearing with the Ministry of Transportation and Communications and the Ministry of Economic Affairs on the '14+N Air Pollution Control Strategies Focus'. The EPA proposed policy goals and schedules that incorporated civil appeals and advocates. The number '14' refers to the air pollution prevention strategy that the government planned to implement, and 'N' is an additional solution path and plan that responded to civil demands. The '14+N Focus Forum on Air Pollution Control Strategies' explained the funding requirements of 14 detailed regulatory categories. The government explained that policy responses focused on civic appeals related to several important improvement measures for the two major pollution sources. Controlling the fixed pollution source involves 'electricity facility control' and 'boiler control' (Liu, 2018).

Government schedules for air pollution improvement policy programmes are evolving, as citizen groups continue to oversee, advocate and take action. The Legislative Yuan approved draft amendments to the Air Pollution Control Act in June 2018. These amendments granted local governments the right to set up air quality conservation zones. Two-stroke scooters and diesel-fuelled vehicles would have limited access to these zones at designated times. On 29 December 2019, numerous environmental groups organised anti-air-pollution demonstrations and called for reductions in coal consumption, reductions in greenhouse gas emissions and equal rights for breathing clean air. The EPA stated that policies, such as air pollution prevention and carbon reduction in power plants, have been effective, and the EPA supports the government's energy transformation plan. Since September 2019, more than 22 municipalities and counties (i.e. cities) have submitted the Greenhouse Gas Control Implementation Plan tailored to local conditions, which is in line with the national contribution of the UNFCCC (United Nations Framework Convention on Climate Change) for openness and transparency. The EPA initiates a review and amendment of the law and recognises the importance of public participation and joint participation from all sectors in air quality improvement and the energy transition plan.

Civic society organisations initiate forums to facilitate citizen dialogues and reflections on policy issues for transmitting policy ideas to the empowered space. The deliberative practice initiative by the Philosophy and Social Democracy Studio, which comprises the youth and university students, highlights social innovations and youth agency. The Philosophy and Social Democracy Studio regularly holds forums and youth workshops to invite students for discussion on social and policy problems from plural perspectives, cultivates students' ability of reasoned argumentation and justification through deliberative practice, and invites legislators and politicians to interact with young participants. The deliberative experiment includes the Citizen Parliament, in which student participants play the role of legislators to propose and deliberate on specific bills. The aforementioned practices help participants understand legislative processes and practise questioning and deliberation. To connect public discourses with the empowered space, organisers invite legislators from the Third Force parties for face-to-face communications with student participants regarding policy proposals. Such communication helps legislators understand the ideas and discourse of the youth.

Four legislators from the Third Force parties take turns having individual discussions with student participants regarding the differences in opinion between the legislators (viewpoints based on the ideology of their political party) and the students on the bills proposed by the students. The legislators also discuss which student policy proposals their party might support and the reasons for the support. Student participants can ask questions and have face-to-face discussions with legislators. The students can then talk to each other to share their views and ideas or criticisms of the legislators. The organiser sends the workshop report to the Third Force parties so that the youth participants' ideas and thoughts can be heard in the empowered space. Civic forums initiated by civic society organisations increase participants' abilities of critical thinking and democratic deliberation and exert a diffusion effect. Ongoing innovative deliberative practices facilitate contemplation on transmission and on how a democratic government might institutionalise youth participation.

Co-governance and new youth institutions

Representatives from the public space can involve themselves in the process of co-governance through certain mechanisms and institutions.

Governmental committees provide opportunities for policy stakeholders and citizen representatives to voice policy ideas and proposals, participate in decision-making processes and deliberate on policy programmes to achieve policy outcomes. One mechanism through which NGOs are incorporated into governance is the National Council for Sustainable Development (NCSD). The premier serves as the chairperson of the Council, which has 24 to 30 members. Council members are selected from among administrators of government agencies, experts and scholars, as well as representatives of civil society groups, with these three categories of participants having equal representation. NCSD connects leading members of civil society and other stakeholders with government representatives for joint consultation on sustainable development strategies and policies, thus providing space for continuous dialogue with stakeholders to facilitate timely policy responses and the bottom-up identification of emerging issues. Another example is the Taipei Citizen Participation Committee of the Taipei City Government, which includes experts, NGO representatives and members selected from the public, and aims to enhance transparent and collaborative governance. The committee has incorporated policy proposals from the public space through the mechanisms of open government and participatory budgeting (Chapter 7).

Institutionalised mechanisms and informal transmissions are interrelated. In particular, integrated watershed governance is unique in its involvement of multiple actors and multiple levels of institutions and in the complexity of the requisite expertise and set of interests. The public and private sectors have reached a consensus to adopt a collaborative governance model through the participatory platforms of intermediary organisations. The Flood Control Alliance has negotiated and coordinated with the government to set up institutionalised mechanisms for information disclosure and public participation. According to the regulations for public participation in the integration of the Shimen Reservoir and its catchment area, public partici-pation is required in the entirety of planning, designing and conducting site surveys by government agencies and in public hearings and meetings (such as conference and review meetings). Furthermore, informal mechanisms have been established, such as the National River NGOs Meeting, hosted by community colleges. In addition to the functions of education, dialogue and consensus-making among NGOs and community colleges, the National River NGOs Meeting serves as a communication platform that connects the public space and empowered space. It invites government agencies to par-ticipate and communicate with ENGOs, which shapes the development of stakeholder relationships and integrated watershed governance. The focus of NGO participation in integrated watershed governance has transformed from broadening participation to ensuring effective cooperation (Chou, 2015). Furthermore, the government has established a common natural resource management mechanism for areas, such as national parks and conservation areas that fall within traditional territories, per the Indigenous People Basic

Act. The co-governance mechanism empowers tribespeople to have a voice in the policy-making process and facilitates greater dialogue.

Cross-boundary cooperation among local governments is another mechanism in which industry representatives, experts and NGO representatives can serve as external committee members to participate in cross-boundary policy issue discussions. However, currently, limited cooperation occurs among local governments in Taiwan because of different party ideals and the lack of institutionalisation. Most of the limited cooperative efforts are confined to the common manifesto or symposiums, with agendas being restricted to issues such as traffic and garbage disposal. Informal cooperation mainly includes the meetings conducted by county governors and city mayors as well as the efforts of regional cooperation organisations that have not yet been legalised. An example of formal cooperation is two cities or multilateral parties signing government agreements and collaborating to set up a private legal corporation for providing public services (Liu & Hsu, 2011).

The force of the better argument as well as the epistemic quality of deliberation and decision should be given the highest priority in institutions of committees. It matters whether consensus is an approach to decision-making or the product of decision-making – that is, as an unforced convergence among independent committee members (Moore, 2018). In a study on the operation of the National Health Insurance Committee (NHIC), Luo (2017) found that insurants can exercise influence through election mobilisation as well as agenda obstruction and veto power in the NHIC. The government dominates the administrative mechanism and plays the roles of facilitator, mediator and arbitrator. Although medical service providers can access financial and professional resources, they are less influential due to the internal heterogeneity and mutual competition among them. The decisions made by committees are affected by the majority under the traditional representative system as well as by the manipulation of the administrative authority. Thus, stakeholders have influence over decision-making in the committee mechanism, and this influence is affected by access to resources. The democratic functions of committees are still under debate.

Since 2016, the cabinet-level Youth Advisory Committee has provided an important transmission mechanism for the youth to participate in policy proposal and formation processes. The tasks of the committee include collecting the opinions of young people, actively providing policy recommendations that concern the youth, and addressing other matters related to promoting youth participation in public affairs. The term of the committee members is 2 years. The Youth Advisory Committee convenes meetings once every 4 months, and government agencies related to the issues under discussion may be invited to attend these meetings. The premier serves as the convener of the meeting. Moreover, the committee comprises two deputy conveners: one is a minister without a portfolio appointed by the premier and the other is elected by the young representatives. The number of committee members ranges between 25 and 30, and 20–25 youth representatives are selected. These representatives must be Taiwanese students between 18 and 35 years of age. The youth representatives are recommended by the ministries related to youth issues and appointed by the premier.

The Youth Advisory Committee uses forums and online platforms to incorporate youth narratives, stories and debates into policy-making processes. Committee members regularly hold youth forum tours on different issues that concern young people to collect their ideas and communicate with them. These communications include discussions on the regeneration of old houses; the employment of local youth in Yilan; the relationship between art, drama and education in Tamsui, New Taipei City; and how to run fisheries and sustain them in Tainan City. Such face-to-face meetings can compensate for the inadequacy of online participation and broaden youth participation. In meetings initiated by the Youth Advisory Committee, young citizens are invited to propose policy ideas for problem solving, and these meetings enable government agencies to respond to citizen proposals. A verbatim record of the meeting is posted on the website of the Youth Advisory Committee, and the relevant agencies may respond to participants' ideas, questions and recommendations. The committee members translate the contents of the meeting so that the presented ideas and terms can be understood by the participants and government officials. Moreover, the translation enables good ideas and opinions to be incorporated into the proposals of the committee. The official website lists the specific proposals made by the committee members and explains how the government will address the recommendations. The following statuses are used to represent government action: sent to the agencies for research and discussion, in progress, citizen proposal to be fully adopted, citizen model to be partly adopted, and citizen model temporarily not adopted. The aforementioned transmission mechanism can effectively connect the discourses in the public space with those in the empowered space.

Election and performance evaluation

Electoral campaigns create deliberative spaces where candidates, the public, the media and social groups can engage in meaningful conversation and articulate policy ideals and preferences. These deliberative spaces include televised debates, online discussions of campaign issues and talk shows with presidential candidates. Electoral campaigns enhance social deliberation as a whole. Recent experiments in political innovation include the 'Instant Fact-Check' project by Watchout and the Taiwan FactCheck Centre. The Instant Fact-Check covers claims made by politicians, and it did so in real time during the televised 2018 mayoral election debates. Before the 2020 presidential election debate, Watchout and several public and mainstream media outlets collaborated to initiate the 2020 READr Presidential Candidate Fact-Check Project, which invites ordinary people, volunteers and the media to collaborate. Considering that candidates tend to self-promote and attack opponents with false statements, and that the media can only present the debate situation in real time, the aforementioned project aims to record the candidates' speech completely, check the facts and justify them, and undertake in-depth coverage and long-term follow-up on issues for increasing the authenticity of information obtained by readers, presenting the detailed political opinions of candidates, reducing false information and allowing citizens to practise democracy with sufficient and correct information. The project participants provide a verbatim transcript of the candidates' conversation, verify the transcript and mark different categories. The content issue has the following classifications: 'conversation contains verifiable content', 'general narratives', 'personal experience and opinions', and 'content outside the scope of verification'. Moreover, the policy categories include labour, environmental protection, and domestic and foreign affairs.

The fact-check project builds a database of candidate conversations. It then verifies conversations marked as 'conversation contains verifiable content' according to the Verification Guidelines of the Taiwan FactCheck Centre and publishes the obtained results on its website. The media organisations involved in the project work together to revise the verification guidelines according to the verified information and based on the principles of openness, transparency, cautiousness and responsibility (READr, 2020). The citizen collaboration project creates a deliberative space and linkages among the media, the public and civic society so that they can work together to fact-check politicians' claims. It also urges politicians to take responsibility for their remarks and claims. Environmental groups particularly focus on fact-checking candidates' environmental policy content. Until 9 January 2020, 2 days before the election, 11 media organisations had completed 230 fact-checks on speech content. A total of 47 of these checks were on content related to environmental issues. In addition to the public speeches of the candidates, inspections were also performed on the three presidential candidates' political briefings, a presidential candidate debate held on 29 December 2019 and candidate speeches posted on social media.

The Taiwan Environmental Information Centre, an independent media organisation, aims to provide readers with sufficient and truthful information as the basis for environmental action and voting choices. The fact-check reports of the information centre are not only used to check whether candidates' speeches are based on facts but also as a reference text for readers to make political decisions, including voting choices. An examination of three presidential candidates' 'Energy and Climate' speeches indicates that nuclear energy and green energy have become the focus of discussion in this area. For the two aforementioned topics, the results of the fact-checks indicated one-sided facts, and the frequency of error messages was the highest. Thus, people may easily receive inaccurate messages or be misled on these issues. Moreover, for the reference of people voting for legislators, the Changhua County Environmental Protection Alliance announced a list of recommended legislators proposed by several NGOs in Changhua County. This list contains candidates' opinions regarding environmental protection issues and their concerns regarding local development projects, candidates' environmental attitudes, and intention surveys conducted by the Taiwan Environmental Protection Alliance. In the evaluation results, the alliance praises candidates who have clear opinions or proposals regarding environmental issues (Taiwan Environment Information Centre, 2019).

Candidates' justification of policy proposals and their willingness to converse with the young generation are crucial factors for winning support. During the 2020 presidential election process, people were highly concerned about the ongoing demonstrations in Hong Kong that were triggered by the introduction of the Fugitive Offenders Mutual Legal Assistance in Criminal Matters Legislation (Amendment) Bill by the Hong Kong government, the cross-strait relationship, and China's impact on Taiwan's sovereignty. Politicians from the DPP and KMT accused each other of creating a feeling of impending doom for the country. This rhetoric is referred to as Wang Guo Gan, which is the Mandarin name of a popular snack made from dried mango strips. DPP supporters alleged that the election of KMT candidate Han Kuo-yu would cause the end of Taiwan's autonomy because Han favours better relations with China. KMT supporters alleged that Tsai's re-election would be harmful for the Republic of China because of the DPP's historically limited support for the 'Republic of China' name and constitution as well as their preference for renaming the country under a new constitution (The Storm Media, 2019). The Wang Guo Gan rhetoric was influential in the campaign. The KMT tended to emphasise economic growth through the improvement of the cross-strait relationship; however, they did not propose a clear and complete cross-strait policy or strategy and did not justify their policy position. President Tsai strongly expressed her determination to guard Taiwanese sovereignty and democracy and expressed her concerns regarding the rights of citizens residing in Hong Kong. Thus, Tsai addressed the main discourses in the public space (i.e. Taiwanese autonomy, subjectivity and freedoms) and the young generation's concerns about the China factor in Taiwan.

Another citizen action involves asking politicians and candidates to promise support for policy ideals and programmes advocated by civic society organisations before the election and then overseeing whether politicians fulfil campaign promises to engage in reform or consider the voices of their constituents in policy-making. For example, the Awakening Foundation, a civic society organisation that practices advocacy for women's rights, women's political participation, and at least one-third representation for each sex in the cabinet, reviews each political party's gender policy and asks candidates to support civic society's gender policy programmes, comments on election culture and oversees whether the gender policy can be fulfilled. The Awakening Foundation states that although each political party has selected some gender experts or outstanding female social movement activists in the list of legislator-at-large candidates, the parties and presidential candidates have only offered slogans and have not submitted complete and concrete policy arguments for promoting gender equality. The foundation asks each party to propose clear and complete gender policy proposals (e.g. gender-friendly workplace policies and policies promoting work–family balance, childcare and public long-term care planning, and female labour participation) and argues that they should offer suitable policy proposals to attract voters who are concerned about gender and human rights issues. The Awakening Foundation asks nominated legislative candidates who have a women's league background or who are gender experts to make political commitments to voters who are concerned about gender issues. If elected in the future, these candidates are requested to work hard to improve the gender blindness and gender discrimination culture of various political parties and to actively combine the power of political parties for promoting various gender-related policies.

An increasing number of civic society organisations have begun to oversee the performance, conduct and speeches of politicians and candidates. These organisations publish performance evaluation results before elections. The common initiative of civic society organisations is to evaluate the preformation of governments. The evaluation process can strengthen the interaction between civic society organisations and local governments, and the government may be urged to better respond to public concerns and social expectations. On the eve of the 2014 local election, the Taiwan Environmental Protection Union and 27 civic society organisations together proposed 20 claims, such as non-nuclear homeland, saving energy and carbon reduction, waste management, environmental audit, strengthening food safety, forest conservation, green industry transition and promoting public transportation. The Taiwan Environmental Protection Union evaluated the environmental performance of 22 counties and cities on four major dimensions and criteria: energy transition, pollution prevention, public participation and environmental governance. The union reviewed the performance of local governments and published the evaluation results for 2018 to urge local governments to make efforts on environmental protection. They criticised that, among 22 cities and counties, only the Hualien County Government refused to provide relevant documents for civic evaluation, and that government did not make sufficient efforts for environmental protection. The obtained results indicated that resources affected governance performance, and that metropolises generally had suitable environmental performance. The Taiwan Environmental Protection Union divided the evaluation results into three levels and announced which cities' performance had improved or deteriorated. They also provided transparent information and environmental governance performance evaluations from the civil society perspective, which could be an important basis for citizens to judge whether to support and vote for a certain politician.

Moreover, the energy transition alliance called 'Citizen is Energy', formed by 20 national and local civic society groups in 2015, periodically evaluates the energy policy of each city and county and urges local governments to improve their performance and engage in energy transition reform. Civic evaluation teams mainly review energy savings and green energy policy programmes as well as the design of citizen participation mechanisms. Citizen is Energy first visits local governments and explains the evaluation criteria and then conducts interviews with local government officials regarding policy implementation output and future planning. The evaluation criteria include 'whether a platform is established to incorporate civic society' and 'whether programmes that facilitate the use of different types of electricity and green energy production are implemented'. The civic evaluation could urge local governments to increase interaction with stakeholders and civic society and to enhance dialogues and citizen participation.

Conclusion

This chapter analysed the main transmission mechanisms acting in different sites. Greater citizen campaigning, engagement in deliberative workshops, oversight of the government and experimentation with democratic innovation mechanisms (combined with new communication technologies) by civil society organisations have connected public spaces to the empowered space to influence policy-making. Emergent public participation experiments create deliberative spaces for marginalised groups involved in the transmission mechanisms to make policies fit their needs and expectations. For example, in the case of PB, the Bureau of Social Welfare of the Taoyuan City Government has promoted a participatory budget for welfare services for people with disabilities since 2016. It invites family caregivers, non-profit organisations and people with disabilities who are concerned about disability issues to participate in deliberations and make proposals based on the needs of people with disabilities. Proposals obtain support and legitimacy through deliberations, and field and online voting is conducted by persons with disabilities for these proposals. These proposals are executed by the selected proposal unit. The Taoyuan City Government also conducts participatory budgeting for migrant workers. The aforementioned innovative experiments have the potential to enhance inclusiveness and political equality.

Elections are effective accountability mechanisms, and politicians are concerned about winning elections. Public opinion affects the outcome of elections. Therefore, public opinion trends are crucial for politicians. People's political participation is no longer just a moment of voting but a continuous, dynamic process of oversight. Reform and innovations, such as open government, open data, information disclosure and public participation platforms, accelerate the flow of information and ideas and strengthen the transmission of policy discourses and debates. Through the use of information and communication technology, NGOs, which oversee the performance of politicians and facilitate legislative transparency, have effective influence on the empowered space. The functions of NGOs include promoting transparency in policy deliberation and decision-making processes, evaluating legislators' performance and local governance, fact-checking politicians' claims, promoting political consumerism and reminding voters to examine the performance of all current legislators and to call for removing unqualified legislators from the candidate list. These civic actions have caused politicians to pay increasing attention to public opinion trends during their term of office, and they cannot ignore the supervisory power of the people. The threat of recall also has a significant effect on politicians. The trend of public opinion or the spread of online information affects the image of political figures and political parties. The petition dubbed Recall Han Kuo-yu is a typical example of this phenomenon.[3] We Care Kaohsiung, an NGO, launched a campaign and petition to have the itinerant Mayor of Kaohsiung and full-time presidential candidate Han Kuo-yu recalled as the mayor in 2019. Kaohsiung voters ousted Mayor Han in a recall election in June 2020. Han is the first Taiwanese politician to be recalled. Citizens take actions that connect public discourse and deliberative moments in the street and virtual community.

Notes

1 Such as the bill declassifying all government documents relating to the 228 Incident and White Terror as well as the period of mobilisation aimed at suppressing Communist rebellion.
2 Respectively, the energy governance group, the energy conservation group, the power group, the new and renewable energy group and the green energy technology industry group.
3 As required under the Civil Servants Election and Recall Act, the first phase must include the submission of signatures from 1% of the Kaohsiung electorate, or 22,814 residents. The next phase must include a petition with signatures from 10% of the Kaohsiung electorate, or 228,134 residents, within 60 days. For a recall to be enacted, 25% of Kaohsiung's electorate must vote in favour of recalling Han, with 'yes' votes exceeding 'no' votes.

References

Boswell, J., Hendriks, C., & Ercan, S. (2016). Message received? Examining transmission in deliberative systems. *Critical Policy Studies, 10*(3), 263–283.

Burall, S. (2015). *Room for a view: Democracy as a deliberative system.* London: Involve.

Chen, D.-Y., Liao, P.-Z., & Huang, H.-I. (2017). *Government public communication: New types of online participation and communication strategy.* Taipei City: Taiwan E-Governance Research Centre.

Chen, Y.-C. (2016). *Taiwan's e-participation in public policy: A comparison study between vTaiwan and Join Platform* (Unpublished master's thesis). National Taiwan University, Taipei City, Taiwan.

Chou, S.-C. (2015). Intermediary organizations and integrated watershed management. *Taiwan: A Radical Quarterly in Social Studies, 100,* 283–289.

Citizen of the Earth. (2019, July 31). White paper on energy transition. *Citizen of the Earth.* www.cet-taiwan.org/node/3524

Curato, N. (2015). Deliberative capacity as indicator of democratic quality: The case of the Philippines. *International Political Science Review, 36*(1), 99–116.

Fan, F.-T., Chen, S.-L., Kao, C.-L., Murphy, M., Price, M., & Barry, L. (2019). Citizens, politics, and civic technology: A conversation with g0v and EDGI. *East Asian Science, Technology and Society: An International Journal*, *13*, 279–297.

Hsiao, Y.-T., Lin, S.-Y., Tang, A., Narayanan, D., & Sarahe, C. (2018). *vTaiwan: An empirical study of open consultation process in Taiwan* [Manuscript in preparation]. osf.io/jnq8u

Huang, D.-Y. (2017). *Report of the 'eID Card?' open policy-making* [research project commissioned by Ministry of the Interior. Taipei, Taiwan].

Huang, T.-Y., & Chen, D.-Y. (2004). E-Government and the realization of deliberative democracy. *Taiwan Journal of Democracy*, *1*(4), 1–34.

Huang, T.-Y., & Hsieh, C.-A. (2013). Practicing deliberative democracy in Taiwan: Processes, impacts and challenges. *Taiwan Journal of Democracy*, *9*(2), 79–104.

Lin, H.-Z. (2019). The implications of recent models of the National Conference of Participatory Democracy for the design of plural participation of the national technology conference. *Research Portal*, *9*, 1–12.

Liu, M.-T., & Hsu, Y.-C. (2011). Analysis on the model and case of cross-boundary cooperation among local governments between Taiwan and Germany. *Public Administration*, *41*, 37–72.

Liu, T.-I. (2018, February 22). 12 years of Taiwan air pollution policy. *The News Lens*. www.thenewslens.com/article/89348

Luo, K. L. (2017). Who calls the shots? A case study of stakeholders' participation in the Taiwanese National Health Insurance Committee. *Taiwan Democracy Quarterly*, *14*(3), 103–145.

Ministry of Economic Affairs. (2020). *Energy Bureau 2017–2018*. http://energy whitepaper.tw/

Moore, A. (2018). Deliberative democracy and science. In A. Bächtiger, J. Dryzek, J. Mansbridge, & M. Warren (Eds.), *Handbook of deliberative democracy* (pp. 640–653). Oxford: Oxford University Press.

Public Policy Participation Network Platform (Join Platform). (2020). *Home page*. https://join.gov.tw/

READr. (2020). *2020 READr President Election Fact-Check Project*. www.readr.tw/project/fact-check-2020

Stevenson, H., & Dryzek, J. S. (2014). *Democratizing global climate governance*. Cambridge: Cambridge University Press.

Taiwan Environment Information Centre. (2019, October 3). The Energy Transformation White Paper is still in the Executive Yuan after one year of citizen deliberation. *Taiwan Environment Information Centre*. https://e-info.org.tw/node/220486

The Storm Media. (2019, November 18). Taiwan Hashtag: Wang Guo Gan 亡國感 vs. Mang Guo Gan芒果乾 [Video]. *YouTube*. www.youtube.com/watch?v=Z8VPuUEpvj0

Tsao, C.-H. (2018). *A study on content analysis of e-participation: A case study of the public policy participation platform* (Unpublished master's thesis). National Central University, Taoyuan City, Taiwan.

Tu, W.-L. (2019). Combating air pollution through data generation and reinterpretation: Community air monitoring in Taiwan. *East Asian Science, Technology and Society*, *13*, 235–255.

vTaiwan. (2020). *Home page*. https://vtaiwan.tw/

Part II

Deliberative policy-making and democratic innovations

5 The democratisation of science in deliberative systems

The controversy over nuclear waste repository siting

Introduction: science and policy in deliberative systems

Research on deliberative systems with detailed discussions on the relationship between science and policy and the role of science in deliberative systems is limited. Berg and Lidskog (2018) argue that dynamic interactions between the spheres of policy and science is the crucial part in a democratisation of global environmental governance. The democratisation of science can affect the establishment and functioning of deliberative arrangements in the policy sphere, which might stimulate the democratisation of science to varying degrees. Knowledge supports and justifies policy, whereas policy influences the production and stabilisation of knowledge. As Jasanoff (2012) argues, science and policy are mutually shaped and co-produced. Berg and Lidskog (2018) posit that science should be considered a distinct sphere with deliberative qualities, but also that the policy and science spheres are interrelated. Different degrees of democratisation within the science sphere may have various impacts on the democratic potential of arrangements with the policy sphere. The authors propose two forms of democratisation, one moderate and one radical. The moderate democratisation of science allows public input to evaluate and complement scientific practice. Solving environmental problems requires not only abstract and universal scientific knowledge but also practical and contextual knowledge. The moderate form entails the inclusion of complementary knowledge that could help extend scientific understanding, which contributes to improving and expanding the consistency of the scientific frame (Berg & Lidskog, 2018, pp. 9–10).

The radical democratisation of science involves public contestation of existing scientific framings of environmental problems. If the process of inclusion within the science space can shape scientific approaches and stimulate new research directions, it could lead to the identification of new environmental risks and alter the understanding of what constitutes an environmental risk. It also includes a broader set of problem framings, which would enhance the deliberative capacity of environmental governance. Therefore, the deliberative space would be enlarged, and the reason-giving process would be more equal. The deliberative capacity of environmental governance depends on the abilities of each of these spheres as well as their interaction effects (Berg & Lidskog, 2018, pp. 10–17).

According to McCormick (2007, 2009), democratising science movements contests, reframes and engages in the production of official scientific research and seeks to legitimise lay perspectives. It often allows creating new research, changing related government regulation and shaping public opinion. These developments challenge how expert knowledge is produced, reframe existing knowledge and democratise knowledge production. In the process, activists attempt to gain new credibility through their access to technical information, scientific language, technical advances and expertise. One of the primary methods used for democratising science movements is the lay–expert collaboration, which allows activists to form partnerships with researchers working on problems identified by laypeople and transform the insular nature of expert systems into those that consider local experiences. Activists use their own experience as a factor in scientific study and to serve as a bridge between laypeople and scientists. This chapter analyses the science-policy interactions.

Nuclear waste disposal disputes

The removal of the Orchid Island repository and the uncertainty surrounding the final low-level radioactive waste disposal site have been long-standing problems. Nuclear-related conflicts, public distrust and opposition from anti-nuclear groups challenge the governing capacity of administrative agencies. Most Taiwanese low-level nuclear waste has been temporarily stored on Orchid Island (Lanyu), the homeland of the Tao aborigines. Orchid Island, a 45.7 km² island, is 76 km off the coast of southeast Taitung County. The Tao's anti-nuclear waste movement, supported by the Christian church, environmental groups and broader social groups, forced state-owned Taipower to halt further shipments in 1996.[1] In 1997, the Tao tribe was verbally promised by Taipower and the government that the nuclear waste would be removed by the end of 2002. However, Taipower delayed the removal of the Orchid Island repository because of the failures in final low-level radioactive waste disposal siting (see Fan, 2006, 2009).

Taipower established the Candidate Site Selection Committee in 1993, which proposed incentives and compensative voluntary programs. However, the committee remains unable to complete the site selection process because of the political complexities and intense protests by residents. The Legislative Yuan passed legislation called the 'Act on Sites for the Establishment of Low-Level Radioactive Waste Final Disposal Facility' (hereafter referred to as 'Act on Sites'), which introduced a local referendum and compensation mechanism of up to NT$5 billion to enhance the legitimacy and public acceptance of Act on Sites in 2006. The site selection group of the Ministry of Economic Affairs selected Daren Township of Taitung County, Mudan Township of Pintung County, and Wangan Township of Penghu County as the three potential sites on 19 August 2008, which immediately prompted diverse forms of citizen mobilisation to express their views. The majority of residents in Daren Township and Mudan Township are indigenous peoples. The aboriginal anti-nuclear alliance organised the 'Anti-Nuclear Alliance Swearing Ceremony', where people took an oath to ensure a 'nuclear-free homeland' as their goal. The alliance also sought support by disseminating information to tribal members and the community through blogs and social media. Subsequently, members of the Penghu People in Taiwan Association also joined the movement to oppose the use of Penghu as a disposal site. In September of the same year, the Penghu County Government declared the Dongji Island of Wangan Township a basalt nature reserve, thereby removing Wangan from the 'recommended candidate site' list.

The referendum mechanism is a manifestation of direct democracy, which provides a channel for public participation and enhances the legitimacy of decision-making. However, because of the allocation of risks and benefits, as well as the conflicts of multiple perspectives and values related to site selection, if opposing citizens are not afforded adequate information and rational communication, the outcry at the grassroots level can be difficult to appease. Under these conditions, opportunistic political elites can easily manipulate information and inflame public emotions to achieve their political objectives (Tang et al., 2009). Anti-nuclear groups expressed their concerns about whether the referendum questions were designed to induce specific answers by leading people to believe that they had no other option. They also raised the issue of weighting the public's vote, and stated that local referendum ballots from citizens residing near the nuclear waste disposal site should be given greater weight than votes cast by others.

Research methods

This chapter is based on the qualitative data collected in the author's previous research projects (see Fan, 2017a; Huang et al., 2011). The documentary research mainly involved examining materials, such as official documents and reports, regarding the nuclear waste controversy as well as reports and leaflets from environmental group campaigns. Interviews and conversations were conducted on Orchid Island during the summers of 2013 and 2015. The research team spent time building local relationships at the beginning of the field study. Because we were outsiders to the community, we generally assumed a listening role during our conversations with the Tao people. We used a purposive sample of stakeholders and actors in nuclear waste controversy, followed by snowball sampling to obtain other available information and differing perspectives from the interviewees. We selected 15 interviewees, including homemakers, farmers, fishermen, young members of non-profit organisations on Orchid Island, and anti-nuclear waste activists of different generations. In addition, the nuclear engineering, radiation protection and health experts who had participated in anti-nuclear citizen actions, as well as North Coast Anti-nuclear Action Alliance members, were interviewed. In

July 2014, the author hosted the Nuclear Waste Regulation and Monitoring Mechanisms Workshop; scholars from various academic disciplines and former officials of the Atomic Energy Council (AEC) were invited to participate in the meeting to promote expert discussion and share arguments from different points of view. Local and stakeholder perceptions, experiences and discourses regarding the nuclear waste accident, and views on official risk assessment and regulation, were compared and analysed. To understand how citizen participants and stakeholders evaluate the consensus conference, in-depth interviews with residents and key stakeholders were conducted in 2010. The interviews were conducted as part of a formal evaluation of the process.

Democratising science in deliberative systems

Consensus conference

A citizen consensus conference was held by the academic deliberative democracy research team commissioned by the Fuel Cycle and Materials Administration (FCMA) of the AEC in 2010.[2] The main goals were to provide a platform for dialogue, allow informed citizens to conduct rational dialogues on nuclear waste disposal issues and raise varying levels of concern and points for consideration to provide a reference for future site-selection processes. The consensus conference mainly followed the model of its Danish counterpart, with some key modifications. For example, the consensus conference was broadcast on television to make information more transparent, the process more deliberative and the public more aware, thereby expanding the effects of social education. Audiences who were concerned about the issues could visit a venue beside the consensus conference meeting room for further discussion.

The organisers promoted activities through diverse channels, including posters, media campaigns, telephone survey invitations and the Internet, receiving 173 valid applicants. The organisers employed the stratified random sampling method and selected participants according to the standards established by the executive committee. These standards were as follows: for every 20 participants, at least one must have an aboriginal status; five participants should be selected from each of the registered eastern districts and islands; at least one person must have an education level of below junior high school; at least one person must be over 60 years of age; and the gender ratio of the participants should correspond to the national gender ratio. The steering committee as impartial arbiter recommended experts from fields related to nuclear energy, social and environmental studies and public deliberation.

The deliberation activities spanned four days and were held on 27–28 February 2010 and 13–14 March 2010. The discussion topics in the consensus conference included the following: 'How should low-level radioactive nuclear waste be managed?' and 'What do citizens care about the most regarding low-level radioactive nuclear waste?' The issues were also distinguished by 'environmental and health risks' and 'social-cultural and economic development' orientations. The first day of the consensus conference mainly focused on the participants' initial understanding of the problems by introducing the idea of deliberative democracy and the purpose of the conference, as well as the background of the low-level radioactive disposal and site selection controversy. The second day focused on the environmental and health issues related to low-level radioactive site selection. The third day involved a question-and-answer session between the citizens and experts. During the fourth day, the citizens discussed and formulated a consensus report, which included the following nine items:

1. What is the relationship between nuclear waste disposal and energy policies?
2. What are the selection parameters of the nuclear waste disposal site?
3. Is low-level nuclear waste disposal an urgent issue? Can the existing nuclear power plant sites become candidates for disposal sites? What are the positives and negatives of the site-selection considerations?
4. The final low-level radioactive waste disposal site's ordinance framework and specification principles.
5. How can we expand citizen participation?
6. Disclosure of information related to nuclear waste disposal site selection.
7. Compensation for nuclear waste disposal sites.
8. How can we handle matters regarding time limitations for facility construction design and the influences and concerns of health and safety?
9. Real-time monitoring of the social, environmental and health issues should be provided during the nuclear waste disposal site selection, construction, operation, closure and supervision periods.

Citizens' perceptions regarding the potential health and environmental effects of the final disposal facility influenced the focus of the site-selection operation. In the summary report of the consensus conference, the citizen panel presented their views on the site-selection parameters and stated that the current site selection ordinance specifications should not only include 'the standard site selection principles and consideration choices' but also 'citizen representatives' to 'eliminate any possible expert blind spots' (Citizen Panel Report, 2010). The citizen panel emphasised that the 'known potential sites are home to pristine forest ecology and biodiverse land', highlighting their concern for the sites' influence on the ecology and species. The citizens also questioned whether 'existing nuclear power plant sites could become candidate disposal sites' and suggested that the 'government should seriously consider storing low-level radioactive waste in the originating nuclear power plants' (Citizen Panel Report, 2010). The rationales for the proposals presented by the citizen panel included the point that 'Taiwan's land is limited and land resources should be cherished', 'the nuclear power plant siting requirements should be more stringent', 'the lands of the existing nuclear power plants that are not fully loaded should be used as experimental disposal sites', and 'converting existing nuclear power plants into nuclear waste disposal sites is more convenient because no new ports need to be built, nuclear waste transportation is not an issue and social unrest and communication costs can be reduced' (Citizen Panel Report, 2010).

The consensus conference report provided a wide range of recommendations as a reference for the government, and it received official responses from the AEC. The director of the FCMA personally responded to the concluding report produced by the 20 participating citizens on the last day of deliberation. Most of the citizens perceived the director's responses favourably, which indicated that citizen discussion activities can enhance public trust and deepen interactions between the government and the people. However, according to the in-depth interviews conducted after the deliberation activities, the public generally felt that insufficient time was allocated for the conversations, and they expressed concern regarding the effects of the consensus conference and future policy decisions.

Anti-nuclear waste movement and civic forums

A series of protests organised by the anti-nuclear organisations have taken place since the 1980s. The nuclear disaster in Fukushima initiated diverse responses of social activists, which have called attention to nuclear hazards and are regarded as the revival of antinuclear campaigns in Taiwan (Ho, 2014). The anti-nuclear waste activists formed a new heterogeneous anti-nuclear alliance with other civic society organisations, interdisciplinary scientists and academia, and the nuclear engineering experts who joined anti-nuclear campaigns after the Fukushima disaster in 2011. By joining such civil anti-nuclear campaigns, researchers who used to work in nuclear-energy-related projects have become a new type of expert, or expert-activists. Tens of thousands took to the streets of Taipei in 2014 in an anti-nuclear protest. Protesters wore yellow ribbons that read: 'Stop the Fourth Nuclear Power Plant. Give Power Back to the People'. Issues of nuclear risks and nuclear waste disposal have become main concerns of these opponents of nuclear energy. The anti-nuclear movement attracts media coverage and gains public and government attention to influence public opinion and pressure the government to address controversial issues of nuclear waste disposal site selection more effectively. Citizen activism facilitates dialogue and deliberation in public spaces and forces the government to respond to civic discourses and concerns and stop the construction of the fourth nuclear power plant.

Civic groups built alliances with counter-experts to create knowledge and were able to use science to heighten the political nature of the nuclear waste disposal problem and risk assessment, which opened narrow scientific approaches that tended to ignore lay perceptions, daily life experiences and embodied knowledge. In December 2011, the media reported that scholars from the Academic Sinica detected cesium-137 and cobalt-60 (radiocaesium, the by-products of nuclear fission processes in nuclear reactors) in sediments of the intertidal zone and tidal pool near the nuclear waste depository on Orchid Island from 2008 to 2010. The AEC maintained that the cobalt-60 pertained to the ashes generated during a nuclear waste container examination in the repository. They recognised the problem of drum rust and decay caused by the highly humid environment in the late 1990s and ordered Taipower to initiate a program of repackaging the waste into fresh drums. This repackaging program started in 2007 and was completed in November 2011. Taipower asserted that the dose of these synthetic radionuclides was less than the standard level and therefore harmless to human bodies. Furthermore, Taipower claimed that because the amount of detected cobalt-60 was considerably lower than the standard level, the incident should not be referred to as a 'leakage' but only as 'a trace release'; when the covers of the trenches were removed to collect and transport nuclear waste samples to the examination centre, a small proportion of radioactive dust from inspections and repackaging operations were blown outside the depository (Fan, 2017b).

The radiation exposure instigated a severe public grievance on Orchid Island. On 20 February 2012, the anti-nuclear campaign '220 Expel the Demons from Orchid Island' was initiated. During the campaign, the Tao people expressed their anger by throwing mouldeds (tribal staple food) at the depository, signifying that Taipower must take back all its nuclear waste. They demanded that all nuclear waste on the island be removed, and that the island should never be leased to authorities for use as a nuclear waste depository site. Finally, the Tao people threw barrels, representative of nuclear waste, into the sea, signifying their determination to permanently reject nuclear waste (The Lanyu Youth Action Alliance et al., 2012).

The radiation leakage accident and Tao activism led to AEC's promoting parallel environmental monitoring on Orchid Island with an emphasis on information transparency and public participation, as well as on verification, sampling and analysis by a third party. The Orchid Island residents, NGOs and local government representatives were invited to participate in the environmental sampling and radiation detection work in the villages on Orchid Island. The AEC claimed that, before the detection and sampling work in each village began, the participants were informed about the radiation detectors and sampling approach to be employed in the work, and the locations for detection and sampling were determined by the chiefs of villages and participating civilians. The AEC also stressed that authorised radiation detectors must be employed. The various sampling analyses were commissioned to the laboratory of the Nuclear Science and Technology Development Centre in National Tsing Hua University, certified by the Taiwan Accreditation Foundation. The laboratory announced that no abnormal environmental radiation was detected in the villages (Atomic Energy Council, Executive Yuan, 2013).

However, the reliability of the results of the governmental environmental parallel detection operation was doubted by the local anti-nuclear waste organisations of Orchid Island. The environmental detection was conducted at fixed points. The parallel detection method was employed, through which residents or representatives gathered some agricultural crops or soil from Orchid Island and sent them to laboratories. However, the interviewed Tao people questioned the independence and impartiality of the third-party certification institutions which are seen as having a close relationship with Taipower; this caused the Tao people's distrust of the monitoring results (Fan, 2017b). Civic groups' distrust of the AEC led to the establishment of the AEC's Citizen Participation Platform to increase dialogue and mutual understanding; this is discussed in more detail later in this chapter.

In addition to marches, campaigns and petitions, environmental groups held forums and workshops to facilitate the inclusive union of civic groups, citizens and experts to engage with one another and clarify the nuclear energy and nuclear waste problems and to promote collective consideration of the relevant policy issues. The Green Citizens' Action Alliance allied with a Gongliao self-help organisation, singers and musicians to hold 'No Nuke' and 'Love Music, Save Beach' activities at the Ho-hai-yan Rock Festival and to promote a 'low-carbon community'. The Green Citizens' Action Alliance engages in research on global energy issues and nuclear risks. It supervises energy policy, holds symposia on energy issues and argues for 'decreasing electricity usage growth to zero' as the fundamental solution to the energy problem. Civil society organisations also produce documentaries on nuclear energy and nuclear waste and broadcast the films at civic forums and workshops to encourage discussion and reflection.

Continuing the street activities of the Sunflower Movement, the National Nuclear Abolition Action Platform (NNAAP) initiated 'Deliberation on the Street: Questions on the Fourth Nuclear Power Plant' to let the on-site people conduct group discussions, reflect on and clarify nuclear energy disputes and ask the authorities to respond to 'citizens' anti-nuclear opinions'. The NNAAP was established by more than 200 civic groups after the national 309 march on 9 March 2013, which attracted 220,000 people who joined the activities to ask to 'terminate the no. 4 nuclear power plant' and achieve 'Zero Nuclear Energy'. The alliance includes a variety of civic society organisations, such as environmental protection groups, labour rights and human rights groups, gender equality groups and education groups, and aims to facilitate social dialogue and further build solidarity and consensus.

Considering the limits of the participatory mechanisms and public distrust of technocratic authority, the NNAAP promoted nationwide deliberative public forums on nuclear waste disposal and site selection criteria to facilitate discussions on nuclear waste, especially in places where nuclear power plants are located or places that might become potential sites to host nuclear waste storage facilities. The NNAAP hosted eight citizen forums based on the concept of deliberative democracy from March to October in 2016. Eight civic forums for local NGOs and citizens were held; the locations included the northern and southern coastal areas, where three nuclear power plants are located; Orchid Island; Taitung, which is a potential site for permanent low-level radioactive waste storage; Tainan; Kaohsiung; and Taipei. Forums have discussed whether to send nuclear waste abroad for storage, the criteria and processes that should be used for the selection of a permanent national nuclear waste disposal site, which government agency should be responsible, and how affected residents should participate in the process. The NNAAP invited local civic groups, politicians, village representatives and educators to join the civic forum to deliberate nuclear waste issues to build solidarity and produce policy suggestions.

The NNAAP held a press conference on 15 October 2016 to present their consensus, urging the government to conduct citizen deliberations on nuclear waste issues and allow the public to oversee and participate in issues related to nuclear waste disposal and management. They also suggested that the government should respect local knowledge and emphasise the principles of environmental justice. The consensus document called for local residents directly affected by waste disposal facilities to be granted a veto or additional 'weighted' votes in a local referendum that would determine participants through proximity to facilities rather than along county lines (Gerber, 2016). Deliberative forums help to tighten the connection between civic society groups. From the individual local forum to the joint national forum, participants from different regions and townships with historical context have focused on different aspects of nuclear waste issues and formed slightly different points of view. But participants all emphasised the importance of environmental justice and called for informed consent and veto rights (Hsien, 2016).

Participants expressed their opinions on public policies constructively and communicated rationally with others to reach consensus in the spirit of deliberative democracy. Such practices will foster a culture in which laypeople are willing to participate in politics and engage in deliberation. Deliberation has occurred within the anti-nuclear movement and the NNAAP. Deliberative forums enable the participation of affected communities to shape public discourse, and help to strengthen public communication, improve public consciousness of nuclear waste issues and seek common ground on site selection (M. F. Fan, 2019, pp. 12–13).

Public forums hosted by civic groups and online platforms provide opportunities for people to communicate with others who have contrasting perspectives. These forums contribute to knowledge production and shape public discourse. For example, the Green Citizens' Action Alliance cooperated with other anti-nuclear civic groups to hold symposia to facilitate discussion and make information transparent. Mom Loves Taiwan, an organisation that aims to supervise the safety of nuclear energy and nuclear waste disposal, strives to make information transparent, clarify current problems and raise public awareness of issues regarding energy transition and climate change. Since 2018, the group has initiated 'live classrooms' to broadcast films, and has invited foreign and domestic experts and civic groups to attend the forums to discuss issues of nuclear safety, nuclear waste and energy policy. Furthermore,

Taiwan's Public Television Service produces a programme called *Our Island*, which broadcasts special reports on issues related to nuclear energy and nuclear waste on Orchid Island. This programme plays an important role in attracting public attention and facilitating ongoing dialogue on nuclear energy and nuclear waste.

AEC's integrating mechanisms of public engagement

The anti-nuclear movement creates a political opportunity to structure governance processes by integrating mechanisms of public engagement. The doubts of civic groups regarding the role of the AEC's regulations in nuclear waste supervision as well as the operation of expert committees have led to meta-deliberation and broadened public participation in related discussions.

a) Expert committees

Expert committees tasked with central and local governance – such as those concerned with nuclear safety and health risks and New Taipei City's Nuclear Safety Supervision Committee – engage in scientific deliberation. The doubt expressed by environmental activists and residents regarding the dry storage facility reflects their considerable distrust in Taipower, the AEC and the culture underlying nuclear energy regulation. This is a result of previous incidents calling Taipower's competence into question, and it involves a perception of delay or the failures in final low-level radioactive waste disposal siting. The project to construct an intermediate dry storage facility for spent fuel near the no. 1 nuclear power plant passed the Environmental Impact Assessment in 2008 under the condition that two expert consultation committees, composed of local government representatives, civic groups and stakeholders, would be established to consider the issues of nuclear safety and health risks. In addition, nuclear waste could be stored for 40 years and then must be removed.

Two expert committees were formed and comprised experts and scholars recommended by the New Taipei City government, Taipower and the AEC. The goal of the committee was to seek professional consensus, and the AEC consulted local-government representatives, government agencies, civil society groups and stakeholders to arrive at a policy decision. The discussions of the two expert commissions were oriented towards technical details and risk assessment. Although some representatives recommended by members of the public expressed divergent views, the experts reached consensus on some topics, including the content of emergency measures, greater research into health and radioactivity and more stringent health monitoring. The commission asked Taipower to provide a comprehensive response to the questions and doubts raised in the meeting. After several committee meetings, residents and environmental groups still doubted the project, and the New Taipei City government held the opposition position. For example, one participant from the Wild at Heart Legal Defence Association made allegations of conflicts of interest in the safety analysis review made by members of the AEC, and the participant doubted whether the AEC would declare who the commission members were. The ENGOs also noted that the contractor, the Nuclear Research Institute, was a subordinate unit of the AEC. They doubted the integrity of the AEC's role in supervising and reviewing the safety of the storage of nuclear waste (M. F. Fan, 2019).

Faced with strong opposition from local environmental groups in the site selection process for a permanent nuclear waste facility, the Executive Yuan passed a draft of the Administrative Institution Radioactive Waste Regulation Centre Establishment Act in November 2016. According to the legislation, the Administrative Institution Radioactive Waste Regulation Centre would comprise 11–15 directors. The board of directors would include disinterested social members, members of civil society groups and residents, who must constitute at least one-third of the board. The Centre would be responsible for selecting the site of a permanent nuclear waste facility and would supervise nuclear waste management. The draft was sent to the Legislative Yuan for review. The establishment of institutions responsible for nuclear waste governance can foster a dialogue and exchange of knowledge among different disciplines (e.g. engineering, public health, environmental studies, social studies of science and law) and across agencies.

(b) AEC's Citizen Participation Platform

The AEC set up the Citizen Participation Platform according to the 'Citizen Participation Platform Operation Regulation' on 6 October 2016. The AEC invites civic groups and residents to participate in meetings and forums to provide opinions and recommendations regarding issues of nuclear power plant safety supervision, radiation protection safety control, nuclear accident emergency response, radioactive waste management and environmental radiation monitoring to make information transparent and enhance public communication. The discussion topics of meetings are designated by the AEC or raised by citizen groups and the public. The AEC invites civil society organisations and relevant agencies to participate in discussions and allows the public to sign up for these discussions. The official AEC website provides meeting records and broadcasts of the meetings.

The first public participation platform meeting was held in August 2016 to discuss the operation of the platform and the plan to hold a meeting every 2 months. The Vice Director of the AEC serves as the chairman. The founding president of the Taiwan Environmental Protection Union – Professor Xin-Min Shih from National Taiwan University – was invited to be the co-chairman, which could help to increase the credibility of and trust in the meeting. Professor Shih has expressed the importance of public participation in the policy-making process, and indicated that the active participation of civic groups is required for the suitable operation of the platform and so that public voices can be heard. The present generation is responsible for enabling the future generation to find solutions to problems and to help the AEC perform supervision to the best of its ability.

The theme of the second platform meeting, held on 21 October 2016, was reviewing the decommissioning plan for the no.1 nuclear power plant. Opinions and suggestions were expressed concerning the two main topics discussed during the meeting: (1) Taipower's decommissioning plan for the nuclear power plant, especially regarding the planning of the nuclear waste storage facility in the plant area, and (2) the procedure for reviewing the decommissioning plan for the no. 1 nuclear power plant, especially regarding information disclosure and public participation. The Ministry of Economic Affairs and environmental groups (e.g. the Yilan Humanities Foundation, Green Citizen Action Coalition, Mother Supervision Nuclear Power Plant Alliance, Housewives Alliance, Environmental Protection Foundation and North Coast Anti-Nuclear Action Alliance) were invited to participate in the meeting. One participant asked a question regarding future plans for land reuse after decommissioning. The participant received a positive response from the director of the FCMA that the bureau would ask Taipower to consult local residents regarding land reuse planning.

The meeting conducted in March 2017 involved discussions on the topic of 'Environmental radioactivity monitoring and regulations of nuclear power plants and public supervision'. One environmental group participant suggested that local government officials, civic groups and residents should have opportunities to participate in inspections, which should not be restricted to committee members of the Nuclear Plant Safety Monitoring Council. The Vice Director of the AEC responded to the opinions in a manner that reflected the principles of deliberative democracy – listening, understanding and open-mindedness:

> Thank you for your opinions. Your suggestion is very concrete. Indeed, that rule was only recently drafted. We have fully understood your opinions. After the meeting, I will discuss your opinions with my colleagues from the FCMA. Unless they give sufficient reasons to convince me, I will adopt your opinion.
>
> (Atomic Energy Council, Executive Yuan, 2017)

Thus, the chairman recognised the opinions provided by civic groups and local residents and indicated that the AEC would attempt to implement the suggestions. However, the meeting stipulated that each person only had 3 minutes to speak. The AEC chairman indicated that further suggestions provided by mail and telephone would also be welcome and that residents who were not invited to participate in the platform meeting could express their opinions or leave a message on the AEC's website. Civic groups suggested that people should have not only consultation rights but also an effect on decisions. The AEC responded positively that they would incorporate public opinions when making decisions and make an effort to broaden public participation.

The AEC's discussion platform facilitates dialogue and positive interaction between the government and civil society organisations. Further examination is required regarding the AEC's response and how to practically implement citizens' views or suggestions.

Institutional evolution: Orchid Island Committee on Nuclear Waste Removal, a negotiation platform and fact-seeking committee

Different participatory mechanisms have different functions in deliberative systems. Due to Taipower's failure to find an alternative to Orchid Island for nuclear waste storage, the economics minister visited Orchid Island and apologised to the Tao tribe, seeking the tribe's understanding that Taipower had done its best in regards to site evaluation. The minister also explained the government's plan for handling the nuclear waste and forming a monitoring panel. The cabinet-level Orchid Island Repository Removal Promotion Committee and the Non-Nuclear Homeland Promotion Committee were organised in 2002. The Orchid Island Repository Removal Promotion Committee comprises 26 members, one-third of whom are representatives of Tao tribespeople from Orchid Island. In addition to government and Tao tribal representatives, the other committee members include experts and scholars, indigenous legislative representatives and representatives from the Taitung government. The Committee established an official website as a communication channel to make information transparent and declared the following core principle: 'We acknowledge that the past closed procedure for establishing the nuclear waste repository on Orchid Island was a serious mistake'. The committee reached a consensus that respect should be shown to the Tao tribe, as indicated by the following declaration: 'Orchid Island should be excluded from the list of alternative sites for final nuclear waste disposal'. The committee declared that the most important principle is the removal of the nuclear waste repository from Orchid Island, which should not become the final disposal site.

A few committee members had doubts regarding the timetable of repository removal; however, site selection is not the mission of the committee. In the face of strong protests from the Tao tribespeople concerning the delay in the removal of the waste repository, the government and Taipower went to Taitung to negotiate with Tao representatives and promised to pass the act on site selection and exclude Orchid Island from the list of potential sites. The Orchid Island Repository Removal Promotion Committee held several meetings during 2002–2008 to discuss the issues of removal of the nuclear waste repository, radioactivity prevention and compensation restoration. However, the administration of former president Ma Ying-jeou suspended the meetings upon gaining power in 2008.

During the anti-nuclear movement and marches in March 2013, anti-nuclear groups and residents from North Coast, Taitung and Orchid Island formed the 'Nuclear Waste Victims Alliance' and forced the government to have face-to-face talks with representatives of the activists. Due to the efforts of the residents, the former premier, Jiang Yi-huah, agreed to set up a participatory mechanism. Then, the government organised the cabinet-level negotiation platform on nuclear waste in 2013. This platform was the first cabinet-level platform consisting of representatives from Orchid Island, North Coast and Taitung. The platform allowed anti-nuclear groups to unite to propose their views and demands to the premier. The representative from the Orchid Island Tribal Culture Foundation appealed for the immediate removal of nuclear waste from Orchid Island and argued that the issue of waste removal should be decoupled from the selection of the final site for the nuclear waste repository. The Taitung Anti-Nuclear Waste Alliance, which opposes the selection of rural townships as potential final nuclear waste repository sites, also stated that it was strange to continue to make Orchid Island responsible for the nuclear waste until the final site had been decided, despite it being someone else's responsibility to relocate the waste. Representatives of the North Coast expressed their opposition to Taipower's dry storage facility project, a mid-term storage site, at the first nuclear power plant in Shimen and noted that local residents had no opportunity to participate in the decision. After a face-to-face meeting, the premier indicated that the government would consider decoupling the issues of nuclear waste removal and low-level radioactive repository site selection. However, residents and groups from the three nuclear power plants and Orchid Island as well as anti-nuclear groups believed that the government failed to propose concrete plans, offer definite promises and restart meetings of the Orchid Island Removal committee. Thus, the anti-nuclear waste alliance withdrew from the negotiation platform in April 2014 to express their dissatisfaction with the government.

After the third power transfer in 2016, President Tsai apologised to the indigenous peoples on Indigenous Day, 1 August 2016, by declaring,

> In that year, the government deposited nuclear waste on Orchid Island without informing the Tao people. The Tao people on Orchid Island suffered from the harm of nuclear waste. For this, I would like to apologise to the Tao people on behalf of the government . . . I will also ask the relevant departments to submit a true investigative report on the relevant decision-making process of nuclear waste storage on Orchid Island.
>
> (Office of the President, 2016)

President Tsai visited Orchid Island and held a forum in August 2016. The president indicated that the DPP government regards nuclear waste removal from Orchid Island as a priority and that the Executive Yuan will convene the Tao people, relevant ministries, Taipower and scholars to set up an investigation team. With the participation and supervision of the tribe, the investigation report was to be submitted within 6 months and serve as a basis for subsequent negotiations with the Tao people regarding reconciliation and compensation methods before the final site decision. The cabinet-level

Fact-Seeking Committee on the Set Up of the Orchid Island Nuclear Waste Repository, which included three representatives of the Tao tribe and two scholars, held its first meeting in October 2018.

The investigation team collected official documents from relevant agencies to perform its investigation. It also interviewed workers from the repository and held forums on Orchid Island to explore the elder Tao residents' views on the process of repository construction as well as the Tao residents' opinions on removing the nuclear waste repository as soon as possible. The investigation report was published in September 2018 and indicated that, according to existing official documents, the government prohibited residents from approaching the repository on account of it being a 'defence facility' or 'military land'. The letter from the International Science Committee in 1971 also recommended 'strict confidentiality'. No evidence indicated that the informed consent of the Tao tribe was obtained to set up the repository. Until 1982, when the repository was completed and open to visitors, the Tao people did not know that a nuclear waste repository had been constructed during the martial law period (Hsieh, 2017).

In response to the instructions of President Tsai and the premier, the AEC agreed to separate the issues of repository removal from Orchid Island and the search for a new location in 2017. Taipower proposed two plans for repository removal, namely 'returning to the origin' and 'sending to centralised storage facilities'. Under the plan of 'returning to the origin', the barrels from the island would first be transported to three nuclear power plants and the Longtan Institute of Nuclear Energy Research in Taoyuan City. The AEC asked Taipower not to limit the selection of potential permanent sites to remote uninhabited islands, isolated areas or relatively socially vulnerable areas, but to take all of Taiwan into consideration. The cabinet emphasised that the selection process should include close cooperation and consultation with the local authorities and population (Strong, 2017).

At the meeting of the Presidential Office Indigenous Historical Justice and Transitional Justice Committee in March 2018, the convener of the cabinet-level Fact-Seeking Committee and other committee members urged the government to formulate compensation regulations as soon as possible to compensate the Tao tribe. President Tsai agreed to the proposal and asked the Executive Yuan to enforce it. The AEC asked Taipower to actively handle the removal as soon as possible to realise the goal of indigenous transitional justice and indicated that compensation is one means by which to resolve disputes and help right past wrongs (Z.-X. Fan, 2019).

Based on the report of the inquiry, the government planned to offer NT\$2.55 billion (US\$83.6 million) to indigenous Tao residents on Orchid Island. In addition, the government would provide NT\$220 million in compensation every 3 years for land use until the nuclear waste is completely removed. According to the spokeswoman for the Executive Yuan, the compensation would be used for long-term social welfare, health care, education and environmental protection under the consensus of tribes and government representatives. Guidelines for the compensation were approved by the Executive Yuan, and a fund management board that includes local residents was to be established (Huang, 2019). However, at a protest in front of the Executive Yuan on 29 November 2019, anti-nuclear activists comprising Tao elders announced that the Tao tribespeople will not accept the compensation. The Tao activists called attention to their four demands: establishing a communication platform, legalising nuclear waste disposal and paying compensation, continued investigation, and redirecting the funds to the relocation of the waste disposal site (Lin, 2019). Currently, greater deliberation on nuclear waste removal is required to formulate a solution that better respects tribal subjectivity and pursues transitional justice.

Debates on nuclear energy and national referendums

The NNAAP submitted a referendum petition, representing 126 anti-nuclear groups around Taiwan, and 2,800 signatures to the Central Election Commission for initial screening in April 2019. The proposed referendum would ask voters the following question: 'Do you agree that until a repository for high-level radioactive waste is built and operational, Taiwan should not build, expand or continue construction of nuclear plants and should not extend the lifespans of existing ones?' Anti-nuclear groups believe that no additional nuclear waste should be created before a solution for the final disposal of radioactive waste is found. Under the recently revised Referendum Act, the required number of signatures on a referendum petition is 0.01% of the electorate in the first stage and 1.5% of the electorate in the second stage. The electorate in the 2016 presidential election was 18,782,991. Therefore, 1,879 signatures were required in the first stage of the current referendum drive and 281,745 were required in the second stage. A referendum vote is declared valid if 25% of the electorate casts ballots and a majority votes in favour of the petition.

Pro-nuclear groups call for 'nuclear energy as clean energy and the use of nuclear energy to develop green energy'. Such groups initiated a referendum on nuclear energy alongside the nine-in-one local elections held in November 2018. Ultimately, 59.41% of Taiwanese voters (5,895,560) voted for repealing the planned end of nuclear power stations in a referendum that asked voters if they agreed to abolish paragraph 1 of Article 95 of the Electricity Act, which stipulates that 'all nuclear energy-based power-generating facilities shall completely cease operations by 2025'. However, considering strong opposition from local governments and the difficulties of solving nuclear waste disposal, the Minister of Economic Affairs said in January 2019 that Taiwan will not extend the lives of existing nuclear power plants, nor will it resume construction of the mothballed fourth nuclear power plant. Nuclear advocates are pushing for another referendum on nuclear energy because they feel that the DPP government intends to disregard the results of the first referendum.

The leader of the Nuclear Energy Rumour Terminator,[3] Huang Shih-hsiu, who drafted the referendum on whether Taiwan should remove legal provisions that mandate it to become nuclear-free by 2025, is a former assistant to former KMT chair Hung Hsiu-chu. It appears that the KMT currently intends to use advocacy for nuclear energy as a wedge issue against the DPP. Yet, pushing for a referendum against the storage of nuclear waste materials on Orchid Island – originally the result of KMT policy – is likely to allay criticism of Huang and the Nuclear Energy Rumour Terminator for downplaying the issue in the past, including public incidents in which Huang attempted to defend nuclear waste storage on Orchid Island, which led to demands by indigenous groups for Huang to apologise for what they perceived as discriminatory comments against Tao tribespeople and Taiwanese indigenous people. Huang suggests that the social responsibility of nuclear waste disposal should be shared among all members of society by every household literally sharing a bottle of nuclear waste. In a closing statement in a televised debate, Huang made the claim that, because the parents of the current generation of Taiwanese people were raised through the use of nuclear energy, the current generation has a moral obligation to remain committed to nuclear energy. Some people regard Huang's claims as outlandish (Hioe, 2019).

People who support nuclear energy development joined the Nuclear Energy Rumour Terminator and used Facebook and social media to express their opinions publicly. They have also participated in televised debates on the referendum for nuclear energy, emphasising that they were participating to promote communication among the public. Furthermore, they emphasised their responsibility to spread scientific information and clarify the disputes regarding nuclear energy. Some members and supporters of the Nuclear Energy Rumour Terminator have pan-blue political interests, atomic energy engineering backgrounds or relevant working experience in nuclear energy; as a result, they might be unrepresentative and partisan. The Nuclear Energy Rumour Terminator advocates nuclear energy development and seems to be closely linked to a desire to restrict debate and discussion to 'factual', 'objective' and 'rational' elements.

Referendums give citizens the opportunity to vote directly on legislation; however, voters often lack the information required to make informed choices. Public deliberation initiatives can be the catalyst that brings deliberative democracy into partnership with existing democratic institutions (Carson et al., 2018, p. 700). During the televised debates on the nuclear energy referendum, the existing and emergent proponents and opposition alliances attempted to convey their understanding of nuclear information to others within their private and public spaces of action to clarify the controversy and influence voters. Although the Nuclear Energy Rumour Terminator has conflicting and competing opinions on nuclear energy and challenges the credibility of environmental activists or counter-experts' claims, their actions facilitate additional reflection on the nuclear dilemma. The nuclear controversy has become one of the most critical issues of the 2020 election campaign. Anti-nuclear

Table 5.1 Modes of transmission and hybrid forms of governance

Modes of transmission	Policy ideas and discourses
Consensus conference	• Site selection principles must consider public opinion and include citizen representatives, in addition to considering the ecological impact. • Whether existing nuclear power plant sites can become candidate disposal sites must be evaluated.
Anti-nuclear waste movement and citizen forums	• The slogans included 'Nuclear go zero', 'saying goodbye to nuclear energy, welcome the era of wind and solar renewable energy', 'phase out nuclear power, usher in green energy and safeguard Taiwan's future', and 'no more nuclear energy till the nuclear waste problem is resolved'. • Local knowledge to be respected, principles of environmental justice to be upheld and residents directly affected by waste disposal facilities to be granted a veto or additional 'weighted' votes in a local referendum.
AEC's Citizen Participation Platform	• Civic groups and residents should be able to participate in the inspection of environmental radioactivity; citizen opinions should be incorporated into decision-making.
Institutional evolution: Orchid Island Committee on Nuclear Waste Removal, the negotiation platform and fact-seeking committee	• The relocation of nuclear waste stored on Orchid Island. • Orchid Island will not be the candidate for the permanent site; a compensation plan was formulated.
Debates on nuclear energy and national referendum	• Until a repository for high-level radioactive waste is operational, Taiwan should not build, expand or continue the construction of nuclear plants and should not extend the lifespans of existing ones (The NNAAP). • Nuclear energy should be used as clear energy and to develop green and renewable energy (Nuclear Energy Rumour Terminator).

groups have challenged the KMT candidate, who supports nuclear energy, which has caused further debate and dialogue on energy policy. Debates and online forums for deliberation can produce increased awareness of the reasons underlying opposing views, and could also result in the fostering of a more deliberative culture (Ankeny, 2016, p. 14). Table 5.1 highlights multiple modes of transmission and hybrid forms of governance.

The functions of civic activism and mini-publics

Mansbridge et al. (2012) identified epistemic, ethical and democratic functions as the three functions of a deliberative system. This section analyses the contributions of civil society organisations and alliances of citizens and experts in achieving the aforementioned functions in the deliberative system. It helps to address the problem of epistemic injustice, which involves fairness in the entire process of framing a problem as well as the possible outcomes (Mabon et al., 2015) and different ways of knowing to be included in a series of communicative activities.

Epistemic function: clarify problems and tensions of uncertainty

Research on the nuclear waste storage citizens jury in South Australia shows that deliberations featured discussions about complexity, uncertainty and whether the distant planning horizons of contemplating nuclear waste storage would reduce the capacity of the citizen panel to reach a common view (Calyx & Jessup, 2019, p. 9). However, this case is slightly different. Although citizen panels faced the challenge of reckoning with tensions of uncertainty between competing expert testimony, citizen participants had reached consensus on the core problem, important criteria and principle for site selection. The consensus conference on siting nuclear waste allowed citizens with varying views to communicate and discuss core problems rationally after obtaining adequate information and to highlight relevant issues and principles for site location proposals in the future.

The most crucial concern regarding the final nuclear waste disposal site for participants of the consensus conference is how radiation may affect residents' health. According to the public propaganda information provided by Taipower and the AEC, Taiwan's natural background radiation is approximately 2 mSv annually, and each chest X-ray delivers approximately 0.1 mSv. The low-level radioactive waste disposal site will adopt a multi-barrier safety design and security control standards for the facility's operation, closure and supervision protocols. The facility is expected to emit approximately 0.25 mSv of radiation annually (Taipower, n.d.). During the consensus conference, the director of FCMA explained the background radiation values and emphasised the safety of the low-level radioactive waste disposal facility. One expert with a nuclear engineering background then raised their concerns regarding the potential impacts on groundwater and the construction quality. Furthermore, the anti-nuclear groups expressed doubts regarding the safety of the final nuclear waste disposal facility and the related information provided by Taipower. One interviewee from a local environmental group believed that the nuclear waste disposal site had risks and asked, 'If they [Taipower] believe that the site is safe and will not pollute the environment, why have they come all the way to aboriginal lands?' (Interview with a member of an ENGO,

2010). During the citizen discussion forum, representatives from the environmental groups and a number of citizens also raised similar questions.

In the section of the consensus conference on expert testimony, the representative from the environmental groups highlighted the problem of information asymmetry. They stated that Taipower has substantial promotional resources, whereas anti-nuclear activists and nuclear opponents have extremely limited resources. For example, the Taitung civic groups questioned the ethics of Taipower when it sponsored 'good neighbour' activities in local celebrations, concerts, community gatherings and school occasions to advertise the safety and benefits of the nuclear waste disposal facility, and when it conducted placement marketing in local media outlets and variety shows. During the consensus conference, the environmental group experts questioned the credibility of Taipower's continual inferences regarding the final disposal site in Rokkasho Village, Japan, and provided information indicating that the Rokkasho residents perceived that the 'economic effects of nuclear fuel in the Aomori Prefecture were not as significant as expected' and the 'average income for the actual native residents of Rokkasho Village remains low' (Citizen Panel Report, 2010).

The citizen panel also presented people's doubts on the capabilities of existing institutions and government agencies responsible for the low-level radioactive repository siting. The citizen panel stressed the importance of 'information disclosure' in the nuclear waste disposal site selection process. They stated that 'although information should be fully transparent, a gap between the government and citizens' perception of information disclosure remains, resulting in doubts and distrust' (Citizen Panel Report, 2010). Additionally, 'the information required by the public or relevant groups is beyond scientific data; the government should provide sufficient information on the entire program, research, or investigation process' (Citizen Panel Report, 2010). The citizen panel stated that civic organisations and experts should be allowed joint supervision of the construction and operations of the disposal site.

Unprecedented public deliberations and Public Television's live broadcasts of the consensus conference can increase community awareness and information disclosure. Participating citizens and experts develop positive perceptions of the public deliberation process, but identify the problem of inadequate information. Because of time constraints, interactions between citizens and experts, and opportunities for further exchanges, were limited. Additionally, the form and design of citizen questions and expert responses did not provide experts with the opportunity to further clarify the issues among themselves. The consensus conference enhanced the government's understanding of citizens' views on the nuclear waste disposal issues. Overall, the officials of AEC tended to recognise the outcome of citizen deliberation positively, which influenced how they view the core of the problems and motivated government officials to place greater emphasis on citizen participation in nuclear waste discourses.

Environmental groups have the potential to act as trusted information proxies to guide the political judgments of citizens in situations characterised by limited information (MacKenzie & Warren, 2012). The main anti-nuclear groups, such as the Taiwan Environment Protection Organisation and the Homemakers United Foundation, established in 1987, and the Green Citizens' Action Alliance, established in 2000, demonstrated their deep knowledge of the science and the social problems surrounding nuclear energy and nuclear waste disposal. The Green Citizens' Action Alliance seeks to clarify the controversy and convey their understanding of impacts to others within their private and public spheres of action. Members of the Alliance have administered surveys and exchanged ideas with civic groups in Japan after the nuclear accident in Fukushima, which have contributed to scientific literacy and the public's right to information. In addition, public forums held by civic groups have provided opportunities for people to communicate with others with competing opinions; such interaction has the potential to facilitate knowledge production and shape public discourse.

Because the risks of the nuclear waste depository are not easily perceivable or verified, the antinuclear waste campaigns have shifted their focus to searching for scientific evidence. Antinuclear waste groups have tested the radiation and suspected that the values disclosed by the officials were substantially lower than those measured by the NGOs. The controversy over the monitored data involves measurement location selection, measurement approaches and sampling methods. Selecting a location for measurement is considerably controversial. The nuclear engineering experts working as the consultants of the NGOs suspected that the radiation values as announced by the government at the locations of the nuclear facilities were excessively low; particularly, the lowest background radiation value announced by the government was that of Orchid Island, followed by Shihmen and Jinshan (the locations of the no.1 and no. 2 nuclear power stations). The experts asserted that the government officials set their testing devices overly far from the depository, thus affecting the results (Fan, 2017b). Furthermore, the Homemakers United Foundation created the 'Map of Citizen Radioactivity Measurement' (Crowd Source Gigermap) and holds courses and workshops on using the radioactivity map to obtain detailed information and knowledge.

Counter-expertise acts as part of advocacy groups or as allies to advance the goals of progressive social movements fighting environmental health injustice (Arancibia & Motta, 2019), which involves scientific knowledge production that foregrounds new evidence, different interpretations of data or new methods. After the Fukushima disaster in 2011, a few nuclear experts who used to work for nuclear-energy-related industry have become experts-activists. Counter-experts have concerns regarding nuclear safety and have changed their position from support to opposition of nuclear energy. They have published articles and books to transmit nuclear energy knowledge and communicate with those who have competing points of view. Moreover, they serve as ENGO consultants and discussants in public forums to communicate with the public and provide expertise in civic activism. Expert activists and civil society groups form alliances with counter-experts to play a more crucial role in democratising science in the deliberative systems.

Ethical function

The ethical function of a deliberative system is less about individual ethical motivation for citizen action and more about promoting equality and mutual respect among citizens (Mansbridge et al., 2012; Rosenberg, 2007). The citizen panel of the consensus conference tends to argue that citizens' perceptions regarding the potential health and environmental effects of the final disposal facility, local concerns and values need to be considered in the site selection and assessment processes rather than only the technical perspective or scientific positivism. As the report of the consensus conference stated: the site selection ordinance specifications should include not only 'the existing [scientific] standard site selection principles and consideration choices' but also 'citizen representatives' to 'eliminate any possible expert blind spots' (Citizen Panel Report, 2010). It highlights reflection on lay knowledge and respect for lay citizens' opinions. As previously mentioned, the citizen panel argues for the alternatives of site selection, and suggestions reflect their reasoning.

Public forums conducted by the NNAAP show ENGOs challenging the notion of 'social–technical divide', in which technical aspects are generally brought into the public domain only after technical experts have defined the 'problems' and decided on a 'solution'. The deliberative forums provided an opportunity for young people and local residents to learn to deliberate and communicate with others who might have competing points of view. A high level of reflection on the controversial nuclear waste disposal and site selection issues was exhibited at the citizen forums, which contributes to the shaping of political discourse (M. F. Fan, 2019).

Anti-nuclear waste activists and civil society organisations not only make efforts to promote equality and mutual respect among citizens but also challenge technocracy and expert domination to promote mutual respect among local residents, the Taipower company and technocrats. ENGOs and anti-nuclear groups seek to promote equality and mutual respect and fight for the environmental rights of the Tao tribe, indigenous peoples and residents in rural townships to be informed of the nuclear waste siting controversy and to be equal participants in the decisions on site selection. The Green Citizens' Action Alliance speaks for vulnerable groups and the environment and argues that policy must obey three principles: information transparency, public participation and social justice. It advocates the 'nuclear go zero' principle and organises civic anti-nuclear waste forums with other civic groups of the NNAAP.

The Tao representatives participated in the meeting of the Indigenous Historical Justice and Transitional Justice Committee, chaired by President

Tsai, and participants in the cabinet-level Fact-Seeking Committee on the Set Up of Orchid Island Nuclear Waste Repository demonstrated a respect for and listened to Tao local voices and opinions. The government adopted the tribal people's preference of removing the repository first and then solving the problem of permanent site selection. The cabinet-level Orchid Island Repository Removal Promotion Committee's acknowledgement of the serious mistake of the past closed procedure for establishing the nuclear waste repository on Orchid Island indicated acceptance of the Tao tribe's demand for removing the nuclear waste repository. The actions undertaken by the aforementioned committees indicate that the government is reflecting on substantive issues and policy procedures and seeking reconciliation by communicating with the Tao people regarding the compensation programme. The government is also strengthening cross-agency dialogue to resolve disputes and appease the Tao people's dissatisfaction with the delay in removing the nuclear repository.

Democratic function

The democratic function of a deliberative system is to incorporate multiple and diverse voices, interests, concerns and claims into the political process (Mansbridge et al., 2012, p. 12). The consensus conference facilitates dialogues and speaks for those who cannot directly participate in public debate. The citizen panel expressed concerns regarding the potential ecological impact. The term 'sustainable development' was mentioned numerous times in the consensus conference's discussion process and the final citizen report. Some participants of the consensus conference emphasised that potential site locations often have rich biodiversity, and they oppose storing nuclear waste on uninhabited islands, indicating stronger sustainability discourse and ecological priorities. Their concluding report stressed that nuclear energy and waste policies are relevant to the idea of 'ecological sustainability', where emphasis is placed on biodiversity and 'citizen welfare'.

The concept of 'intergenerational equity' has also become a critical discourse during the discussion of links between nuclear energy and nuclear waste disposal issues. The development of nuclear energy and nuclear waste treatment involve the responsibility of this generation to future generations. If this generation continues to develop nuclear energy, future generations will inevitably bear the responsibilities and risks of nuclear waste disposal. The citizen panel believed nuclear waste disposal and energy policies must consider 'the needs of various generations' and 'fully integrate public concerns'.

Site selection debates involve differing views on local visions and the quality of life. According to the tribal chairmen and community leaders, most residents in the potential site of Nantian Village of Daren Township, Taitung County support the site. The primary consideration for residents of this area is economic development, and they hope to obtain the compensation funds and welfare measures (such as jobs, electricity, local construction and medical benefits). Numerous villagers believe that the final disposal site would provide positive benefits in local construction and welfare for the local residents. However, residents of neighbouring villages greatly value the environment and the sustainable development of the tribespeople, and refuse to expose the local ecology and health of their tribe to possible negative influences.

'Environmental justice' has become the core of the discourse of anti-nuclear groups. The environmental group highlighted that the current potential sites have all been mentioned in the past, and now they are reselected again; however, no one is aware of what comprises the selection criteria. They believe the reselection is caused by the 'minimum resistance principle', stating 'maybe the aborigines cannot effectively fight for their own rights. If this development provides such significant benefits, why is the government always attempting to locate it in areas with vulnerable populations?' (Interview with a member of ENGOs, 2010). Some tribespeople consider the selection of traditional aboriginal lands as potential sites to be disrespectful to their history and culture. The citizen panel also stressed 'environmental fairness' in their conclusion reports. They argued that the risks of nuclear waste disposal should be borne by the metropolitan and industrial areas that use the most energy. The potential sites are all teeming with biodiversity and 'use minimal electricity, and should not bear the risks of nuclear waste disposal' (Citizen Panel Report, 2010).

The AEC recognises the report provided by the citizen deliberation activities. An official interviewee from the AEC indicated some doubt regarding the effects of the deliberation activities before the citizen panel was held:

> I wonder whether people would just try to argue their points without understanding the subject first or fail to find a solution to the problems? However, as the activity progressed, I started to believe that consensus conference can produce a rational dialogue platform.
>
> (Interview with AEC official, 2010)

The consensus conference provided an opportunity for dialogue between the experts and the citizens, and allowed the citizens to set the agenda based on their framework of the issues as well as gain more information and social learning experiences through their participation. The government agencies and Taipower obtained the citizens' views on the nuclear waste issues through the citizen deliberation activities. This activity also affected the government's views on deliberative democracy and civil literacy. The government's attitude has transformed from hesitance to emphasising the importance of public participation in nuclear waste disposal discourses.

Similar to other environmental groups that aim to represent the voices of those who cannot directly participate in public debate, such as people affected by climate change in other parts of the world as well as future generations and species (Riedy & Kent, 2015), the Green Citizens' Action Alliance attempts to ensure that the voices of the minority – workers, indigenous people, the environment and species – are included in the public space. The anti-nuclear movement has generated a lively space of inclusive discourses and ideas. Civic activism calls for the ideas of environmental justice, environmental rights, the good life and transitional justice (Fan, 2014). In the activism against nuclear waste that occurred after the Fukushima accident in 2011, Tao tribespeople called for 'pursuing our happiness of tomorrow' (Tao Foundation, 2011). Emergent civic organisations have been formed to represent specific identities and roles and express particular concerns and discourses. For example, Mom Loves Taiwan emphasises mothers' worries regarding the negative effects of nuclear energy, problems in dealing with nuclear waste, their children's well-being and their land. The Papa Promise No Nukes Alliance, which was established on Fathers' Day in 2013, advocates for fathers to make promises to their children and take actions to firmly oppose the no. 4 nuclear power plant and nuclear energy for the next generation. Civic groups have continued to evolve and create their specific discourses. Referendums and public debates enable increased dialogue among people who have different views and reflections on a particular issue in a democratic manner. Proponents and opponents of nuclear energy have contested sociotechnical imaginaries. They engage in efforts to shape policy and practise citizenship through engagement.

Conclusion

This chapter identified the important roles of the anti-nuclear movement and civil society organisations in democratising science in deliberative systems. Citizen activism and ongoing dialogues on the nuclear waste controversy highlight the dynamic interactions and connections between the spheres of policy and science in deliberative systems. Environmental groups and civil society organisations built an alliance and collaborated with interdisciplinary and nuclear engineering experts who joined anti-nuclear campaigns after the Fukushima disaster. The anti-nuclear alliance created shared discourses to mobilise people from different social positions to exert pressure on the government to change the previous expert-dominated model and respond to citizen concerns as well as the demand for concerned citizen engagement in decision-making. Anti-nuclear waste activism and citizen forums have facilitated dialogue and interaction among the Tao tribe, civic groups, the public, Taipower and the government, as well as reflection on the nuclear waste siting controversy. Moreover, people involved in the anti-nuclear waste movement and counter-experts have questioned official claims, challenged official measurements and their validation, and engaged directly in monitoring radioactivity and sharing scientific information.

Local activists and civic society organisations have played versatile roles in transmitting and connecting the intertwined spheres of deliberative systems. Civic society organisations engage in democratising science and simultaneously facilitating participatory initiatives, which has accelerated the evolution of participatory institutions. The dynamic interactions and connections between the spheres of policy and science in deliberative systems have been shaped by interconnected communication practices and the interplay of multiple factors, including specific accidents (e.g. the Fukushima accident and radioactivity leakage on Orchid Island), political power changes and politicians' responses to protest and anti-nuclear movements. Civil society organisations have challenged the official framing of the issue of nuclear waste siting, shaped policy towards prioritising the removal of nuclear waste from Orchid Island and influenced the evolution of governance institutions.

Institutions and participatory mechanisms of nuclear waste governance have developed and evolved over the past decades. The idea of environmental justice has become crucial in the discourse of the nuclear waste controversy. President Tsai's promotion of the goal of transitional justice has resulted in public policy shifting from treating the Tao tribe as a passive nonentity or Orchid Island as a site for dumping nuclear waste to working respectfully with Tao tribespeople as equal participants in the creation of policy programmes (e.g. working with the Tao tribe on truth-seeking, compensation, community research and parallel environmental monitoring). Tsai's policy emphasises the concept of indigenous self-determination and the right to participation. The older Tao tribespeople tend to wear traditional attire in anti-nuclear marches, public meetings and forums to represent the uniqueness of their tribe. Tao activism and the ongoing dialogue among the tribespeople can contribute to reconstructing subjectivity and countering exclusion and injustice.

This chapter traced multisided deliberative practices and communicative activities as well as their interplay in a democratic system. Multiple modes of transmission have different functions, limitations, actual effects and failures, which work together to contribute to building deliberative capability and social learning. Ongoing communication and deliberations have led to the decisions to remove the nuclear waste repository from Orchid Island, separate the removal issue from the final repository siting decision and exclude Orchid Island from the list of potential final repository sites. These decisions indicate a reflection on the past decisions to ship nuclear waste to Orchid Island and delay the removal of the waste repository, and to respect the Tao tribe's narratives and discourses and emphasise collective decision-making. However, the government has failed to solve the nuclear waste facility siting problem. The decision to ship the nuclear waste back to its origin does not include a broad range of discourses and views, especially those of residents near the three nuclear power plants.

As an accountability mechanism, the Control Yuan exercises the power of corrective measures and has asked the AEC, Ministry of Economics, Ministry of Labour and Taipower to improve the management of inspections and repackaging operations, which rendered Tao workers vulnerable to radiation exposure during 2007–2011. The state has recognised policy drawbacks and has adopted a standard that involves making systemic changes and adjusting governance towards participation and reciprocity. In light of the continuing controversy over the final siting of the nuclear waste repository, the AEC plans

to amend the act of nuclear waste site selection to raise compensation in an effort to increase public acceptance. The active participation of civil society organisations, the Tao people and local residents in the ongoing dialogues contributes to improving the democratisation of deliberative systems. Representatives of the Non-nuclear Country Promotion Task Force of the National Council of Sustainable Development asked Taipower and AEC to enhance social dialogues on nuclear waste siting and management. Recently, Taipower has commissioned the Centre for Democratic Innovation and Governance at National Chengchi University to promote public deliberations on nuclear waste and invite members of the young generation to participate in dialogues. Further examination is required regarding how Taipower and the AEC respond to citizens' views and suggestions. Opening decision-making criteria to democratic deliberation, facilitating stakeholder deliberation and obtaining consensus on the rule-making for selection is necessary. Different forms of knowledge must be included and deliberated in the process of reaching a legitimate outcome.

Notes

1 Most low-level nuclear waste has been stored on Orchid Island since 1982. Spent fuel is temporarily stored in the pools of the three nuclear power plants: no. 1 nuclear power plant in Shihmen (1978~), no. 2 in Jinshan (1981~) and no. 3 in Maanshan (1984~).
2 The Principal Investigator is Professor Tong-Yi Huang at the Department of Public Administration, National Chengchi University. The author is the Co-Principal Investigator.
3 The Nuclear Energy Rumour Terminator advocates nuclear energy development and seems to be closely linked to a desire to restrict debate and discussion to 'factual', 'objective' and 'rational' elements.

References

Ankeny, R. (2016). Inviting everyone to the table: Strategies for more effective and legitimate food policy via deliberative approaches. *Journal of Sociology Philosophy*, *47*(1), 10–24.

Arancibia, F., & Motta, R. (2019). Undone science and counter-expertise: Fighting for justice in an Argentine community contaminated by pesticides. *Science as Culture*, *28*(3), 277–302.

Atomic Energy Council, Executive Yuan. (2013, October 2). Orchid Island residents participating in the parallel monitoring operation in 2013. *Atomic Energy Council.* www.aec.gov.tw/newsdetail/headline/2999.html

Atomic Energy Council, Executive Yuan. (2017). The meeting record of AEC public participation platform held on 2 March 2017. *Atomic Energy Council.* www.aec. gov.tw/share/file/focus/YNxny6xM7Y~37EOqEj2uQA__.pdf

Berg, M., & Lidskog, R. (2018). Deliberative democracy meets democratised science: A deliberative systems approach to global environmental governance. *Environmental Politics, 27*(1), 1–20.

Calyx, C., & Jessup, B. (2019). Nuclear citizens jury: From local deliberations to transboundary and transgenerational legal dilemmas. *Environmental Communication, 13*(4), 491–504.

Carson, L., Hartz-Harp, J., & Briand, M. (2018). Deliberative democracy as a reform movement. In A. Bächtiger, J. Dryzek, J. Mansbridge, & M. Warren (Eds.), *Handbook of deliberative democracy* (pp. 697–709). Oxford: Oxford University Press.

Citizen Panel Report. (2010). Citizen panel report. A report on the Citizen Consensus Conference held by the Academic Deliberative Democracy Research Team and commissioned by the Fuel Cycle and Materials Administration of the Atomic Energy Council, Taipei, Taiwan.

Fan, M. F. (2006). Nuclear waste facilities on tribal land: The Yami's struggles for environmental justice. *Local Environment: The International Journal of Justice and Sustainability, 11*(4), 433–444.

Fan, M. F. (2009). Public perceptions and the nuclear waste repository on Orchid Island, Taiwan. *Public Understanding of Science, 18*(2), 167–176.

Fan, M. F. (2014). Nuclear technology risks and value conflicts: The STS and justice perspective. In W. J. Wang, D. Fu, & M. F. Fan (Eds.), *Taiwan: An island swamped in technological controversies* (pp. 48–66). Hsinchu: National Chiao-Tung University Press.

Fan, M. F. (2017a) Technological risk, impact assessment and democratization of science (MOST 103- 2410- H- 010- 013- MY3). Taipei, Taiwan: Ministry of Science and Technology.

Fan, M. F. (2017b). Whose risk? Whose regulatory and testing standards? The case of the radioactive waste controversy on Orchid Island. *Journal of Communication Research and Practice, 7*(1), 107–139.

Fan, M. F. (2019). Risk discourses and governance of high-level radioactive waste storage in Taiwan. *Journal of Environmental Planning and Management, 62*(2), 327–341.

Fan, Z.-X. (2019, February 25). The draft of Orchid Island Compensation Operation Guidelines will be finalized and submitted to the Executive Yuan by March. *CNA.* www.cna.com.tw/news/aipl/201902250101.aspx

Gerber, A. (2016, October 16). Nuclear waste forums' results revealed. *Taipei Times.* www.taipeitimes.com/News/taiwan/archives/2016/10/16/2003657277

Hioe, B. (2019, February 25). Taiwan will debate its nuclear future once again ahead of 2020 elections. *The News Lens.* https://international.thenewslens.com/article/114389

Ho, M.-S. (2014). The Fukushima effect: Explaining the recent resurgence of the anti-nuclear movement in Taiwan. *Environmental Politics, 23*(6), 965–983.

Hsieh, L.-H. (2017, June 30). Truth exposure: Two premiers approved the construction of Orchid Island Nuclear Waste Repository. *Newtalk.* https://newtalk.tw/news/view/2017-06-30/90876

Hsien, B. Y. (2016). *The nuclear waste policy discourse in a diverse society: A case study of a citizen forum for nuclear waste* (Unpublished master's thesis). National Chengchi University, Taipei, Taiwan.

Huang, T.-T. (2019, November 29). Residents of outlying Taiwan island call nuclear waste compensation 'vote-buying'. *Taiwan News.* www.taiwannews.com.tw/en/news/3827158

Huang, T. Y., Tu, W. L., Fan, M. F., & Lin, T. L. (2011). *Citizen participation in siting of the final low-level radioactive waste repository* (NSC 98-3114-E-004-001). Taipei, Taiwan: Ministry of Science and Technology.

Jasanoff, S. (2012). The politics of public reason. In F. Dominguez Rubio & P. Baert (Eds.), *The politics of knowledge* (pp. 11–32). New York, NY: Routledge.

Lin, C.-N. (2019, November 30). Tao protest, reject compensation for waste. *Taipei Times*. www.taipeitimes.com/News/taiwan/archives/2019/11/30/2003726721

Mabon, L., Shackley, S., Vercelli, S., Anderlucci, J., & Boot, K. (2015). Deliberative decarbonisation? Exploring a framework of ethical governance for low-carbon energy. *Environment and Planning C: Government and Policy, 33*(2), 256–271.

MacKenzie, M. K., & Warren, M. E. (2012). Two trust-based uses minipublics in democratic systems. A systemic approach to deliberative democracy. In J. Parkinson & J. Mansbridge (Eds.), *Deliberative systems: Deliberative democracy at the large scale* (pp. 95–124). Cambridge: Cambridge University Press.

Mansbridge, J., Bohman, J., Chambers, S., Christiano, T., Fung, A., Parkinson, J., Thompson, D. F., & Warren, M. E. (2012). A systemic approach to deliberative democracy. In J. Parkinson & J. Mansbridge (Eds.), *Deliberative systems: Deliberative democracy at the large scale* (pp. 1–26). Cambridge: Cambridge University Press.

McCormick, S. (2007). Democratizing science movements: A new framework for contestation. *Social Studies of Science, 37*, 609–623.

McCormick, S. (2009). From 'politico-scientists' to democratizing science movements: The changing climate of citizens and science. *Organization and Environment, 22*(1), 34–51.

Office of the President. (2016). The president apologises to the Indigenous Peoples on behalf of the government. www.president.gov.tw/NEWS/20603

Riedy, C., & Kent, J. (2015). Australian climate action groups in the deliberative system. *Environmental Politics, 24*(3), 363–381.

Rosenberg, S. (2007). An introduction: Theoretical perspectives and empirical research on deliberative democracy. In S. W. Rosenberg (Ed.), *Deliberation, participation and democracy: Can the people govern?* (pp. 1–22). London: Palgrave Macmillan.

Strong, M. (2017, February 15). Taiwan utility told to remove nuclear waste from island within 9 years. *Taiwan News*. www.taiwannews.com.tw/en/news/3095581

Taipower. (n.d.). Low-level radioactive site selection – starting from 'voting': Final low-level radioactive waste disposal site selection and referendum. Taipei: Taipower.

Tang, C. P., Tsai, H. T., & Fan, M. F. (2009). The study of referendum on the low-level radioactive waste facility siting (Research project commissioned by the Fuel Cycle and Materials Administration). Taipei: Atomic Energy Council.

Tao Foundation. (2011, December 30). The Tao tribe 'pursuing our happiness of tomorrow' – 1230 anti-nuclear waste action. *Coolloud*. www.coolloud.org.tw/node/65707

The Lanyu Youth Action Alliance (Producer), Chien, Y.-C. & Lin, S.-L. (Directors). (2012, February 20). *Cry: 220 anti-nuclear waste protest on Orchid Island* [Video]. *YouTube*. www.youtube.com/watch?v=B804p0faqfo

6 Indigenous political participation and deliberative governance

The controversy over mining on traditional territories

Environmental governance as deliberative systems

Indigenous movement and environmental protests against the dominance of the state are traditionally regarded as nondeliberative. The systemic approach of deliberative democracy argues that protests constitute an integral part of public deliberation in terms of public conversation that occurs in multiple sites of communication, and that the adversarial nature of the protests has the potential to facilitate dialogues among stakeholders (Mendonça & Ercan, 2015). A systemic approach of deliberative democracy recognises the potential contribution of indigenous knowledge and democratic practices to policy-making and wider deliberative systems.

Hébert (2018) argues that 'dispossession of land, incorporation and subalternity with the institutional structure of a state, and cultural assimilationist pressures' are the three major dimensions of the colonial indigenous situation that reveal the denial of self-determination. Most state administrations have been top-down, with few channels of substantial deliberation and decision-making going up the governance chain, but indigenous people have demonstrated resilience in maintaining their deliberative practices. As he argues, the dual processes of deliberation are simultaneously at play, including those official modes within colonial or state institutions and those that continue to play themselves out in the interstices of colonial institutions and autonomous spheres of activity, such as the aspects of conflict resolution, governance of traditional territories and the forging and maintenance of alliances. In the analysis of Me'Phaa deliberation, Hébert (2018, p. 100) argues that indigenous political agency transcends the community level and is active at all scales. They are involved in regional organisations, themselves linked within broader national, continental and global networks of indigeneity. As he argues:

> The various scales at which Indigenous people express their political agency can have a mutually reinforcing effect on each other and contribute to countering these dynamics of exclusion. The maintenance and revitalization of collective decision-making processes, the elaboration of

formal structures of autonomous government, and the participation in global networks of solidarity all nourish one another. They can be seen as both products of deliberation and as spaces facilitating it.

(Hébert, 2018, p. 100)

Tamura (2014) further argues that social movements and the intimate sphere can be examined as sites or parts of a deliberative system as a whole in terms of the macro-deliberative effect of micro-deliberative actions, even if their modes of communication and actions are non-deliberative. Simultaneously, each social movement and the intimate sphere can be regarded as a deliberative system by itself because they can create opinions and would also be sites of decision-making. Tamura (2014) argues that we can 'consider decision-making over everyday life as one site of decision-making and, therefore, acknowledge it as a separate deliberative system' (p. 81). There is no need to attribute 'empowered space' exclusive to governments. He argues for reconceptualising deliberative systems as 'entities with a nested structure', and urges us to rethink grassroots movements in deliberative democracy (Tamura, 2014, p. 81).

Following Stevenson and Dryzek (2014), Davis (2018) outlines some characteristics of indigenous deliberative systems as follows: less distinction exists among the private, public and empowered spaces; empowered space involves authority vested collectively in Elders chosen for intelligence, diligence and talent; public space involves consultative and deliberative mechanisms in group decision-making; closeness between elders and society creates frequent and direct transmission between public and empowered spaces; and closeness creates accountability between elders (empowered space) and society (public space). The Annual Sovereign Union Forums are an example intended to examine the ways that Aboriginal sovereignty can be recognised by government. As to decisiveness, examples include treaties with other aboriginal nations, agreements and petitions to the state, the Uluru Declaration and the use of the Voice to Parliament to create a deliberative forum linked to the state. In his study of the sustainable management of Australia's Murray-Darling Basin, Davis (2018) argues that deliberative democracy can add to our understanding of indigenous environmental governance because indigenous deliberative forums act as transmitters of indigenous claims and values to the state through the deliberative system. Indigenous deliberative forums can improve indigenous environmental governance; they legitimate and transmit indigenous values, help counter dominant state and scientific perspectives, build trust between state and indigenous actors and develop legitimate shared narratives for water co-management.

This chapter discusses indigenous grassroots participation and the coevolution of deliberative systems and considers indigenous activism and political communication as part of the macro-deliberative system as well as a micro-deliberative system in itself. Drawing on the controversy on mining on Truku indigenous lands, this chapter explores how indigenous political participation and environmental activism contribute to policy ideas transmission and connect with communications, narratives and dialogues in multiple spaces in the wider deliberative systems that could enhance the deliberative capacity of governance. After the introduction of the context of mining on Truku land, it discusses life narratives and discourses on land claims, and connectivity of communication activities and sites for articulation and contestation of discourses and policy ideas transmission mechanisms.

Indigenous participation in a changing political context in Taiwan

Taiwan's indigenous peoples number around 559,000, comprising approximately 2.37% of the population. Recent research suggests their ancestors may have been living in Taiwan for approximately 5,500 years in relative isolation before Han immigration began in the 17th century. There were nine officially recognised indigenous tribes throughout most of the last century. These tribes were classified by Japanese colonial authorities, and the designations were kept by the Taiwanese government. In 2001, the government promulgated the Status Act for Indigenous Peoples to promote the recognition and reconstruction of indigenous identity. Currently, 16 tribes are recognised. The rise in the number of officially recognised ethnic tribes highlights the efforts to protect indigenous diversity and to respect the will of indigenous peoples seeking to promote their unique ethnic identities (Gao, 2015).

The Taiwanese political system transformed from an authoritarian dominant-party system to a democracy in the late 1980s. The heterogeneous and ambivalent complexity of colonial history and geographical contexts has had a considerable effect on indigenous representatives and indigenous forms of deliberation. Each ethnic tribe has its own particular form of democratic practices and deliberation that are connected to their traditional social organisations and culture. Indigenous representatives and township and village officials set up by the state affect traditional elder leadership and functions. Moreover, emergent young indigenous activists and NGOs in the tribal community actively participate in tribal public affairs and challenge the current relationships and interactions with the state and tribal representative institutions. Indigenous groups and activists demand open access to information and participation in the policy-making process to achieve responsive policies that meet tribal needs.

Government policies concerning the nation's indigenous citizens have evolved significantly over the past few decades. On Indigenous Day, 1 August 2018, indigenous rights advocates protested on Taipei's Ketagalan Boulevard, urging President Tsai Ing-wen to deliver on her promise, made 2 years prior, to promote transitional justice for the nation's aboriginal tribes. President Tsai delivered a landmark apology on 1 August 2016 to indigenous people on behalf of current and past governments, promising to reinstate traditional indigenous territories and promote the preservation of their culture and language. She also unveiled the Indigenous Historical Justice and Transitional Justice Commission.

According to The Indigenous Peoples Basic Act and the Council of Indigenous Peoples' current guidelines on traditional territories, any land development, wildlife conservation or anthropological projects in traditional tribal territories must be approved by the indigenous community. However, indigenous rights advocates have reported the government as failing to stop developers from obtaining permission to implement construction projects on traditional indigenous territories, thus jeopardising the preservation of their culture (Maxon, 2018). There are ongoing plural conversations within tribal communities and between tribes, and interactions between indigenous peoples and non-indigenous residents that shape indigenous policies and deliberative systems.

Conflicts of mining on Truku indigenous lands

Taiwan has approximately 173 mining courts, and half of them are situated on indigenous lands. Of these courts, the biggest is located in Hualien on indigenous reserved land and is owned by the Asia Cement Corporation (ACC). The dispute surrounding the Ministry of Economic Affairs' (MOEA's) approval of ACC's extension of its mining permit for another 20 years without the need for environmental impact assessment (EIA) procedures has sparked much tribal grievance and attracted considerable public attention. Indigenous communities and environmental groups have protested against mining activities on indigenous reserved land in Hualien. Thousands of protesters demanded the protection of indigenous land rights and that the government make its environmental assessment reports public.

Dialogues among tribespeople have been ongoing regarding the impact of mining on tribal land and the well-being of their population. ACC's mining court is located in Bsngan tribe lands, where six smaller tribes reside. There are 510 households, including those from the Dgarung (20 households), Rowcing (100 households), Skadang and Huhus (120 households), Ayug (50 households), and Qrai (220 households; see Figure 6.1). ACC's development in Taroko National Park stems from the long history of indigenous people being forced off their lands by Han Taiwanese. The approval for the mine was originally set to expire in 2017, having originally been approved in 1973. This conflict raised suspicions about the legitimacy of the documentation with which the ACC justifies ownership over the land. Many doubt that the Truku people agreed to give up their lands to the ACC, suspecting coercion from the government or developers. Furthermore, the legal case filed against the ACC has lasted over 15 years without firm resolution, despite the government's past attempts to pass off a false resolution on the issue, the making of meagre settlement pay-outs to affected residents of the area (even in cases of deaths caused by accidents from the mine), and the pollution of the local drinking water (Hioe, 2017).

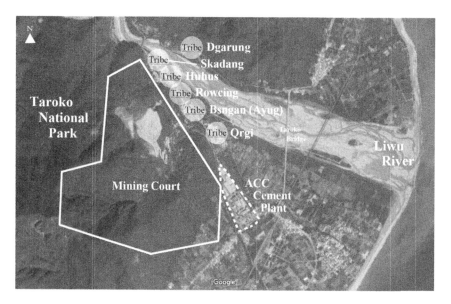

Figure 6.1 Location of the Truku tribe and the ACC

Source: Modified from Google Maps and Citizen of the Earth, Taiwan (see Google Maps, 2020; Citizen of the Earth, Taiwan, 2019).

The Control Yuan censured Hualien County Government, the Xiulin Township Office and the Council of Indigenous Peoples for neglecting tribal livelihood and failure to enforce regulations on the mining industry (The Control Yuan, 2019). The Control Yuan officials criticised Hualien County government for allowing mining activities on indigenous reserved land that ignored sensitive geology and landslide problems in the areas. Control Yuan officials stated that the distance between the mine and the residences of the indigenous tribe is a mere 370 m, and that if mining activities continue for another 20 years, the distance could be reduced to 179 m from the Truku people who live in and around the area. The Hualien County government charged miners unreasonably low rents for forest land without considering the environmental cost of the mining. However, the ACC claims that it has duly compensated the indigenous people for the right to use their land and cited that half of its workers are indigenous. In addition, the ACC has sought to defend itself with the claim that its mine predates modern regulations as well as contemporary administrative divisions (Chen, 2017).

In addition to concerns of indigenous land rights, environmental damage and distribution inequality, land development conflict involves the deficit of the participatory and procedural dimension of environmental justice. Wild at Heart Legal Defense Association indicated that consultation sessions necessary under Taiwan's Indigenous Peoples Basic Law were neglected prior to the approval of new mining permits. Indigenous activists argued that although the Indigenous Peoples Basic Law stipulates that any development project near an indigenous community must be approved by the community, the ACC never obtained the Truku people's consent or passed an EIA (Chen, 2017).

Research methods

The research methods used are documentary analysis and in-depth interviews. The documentary research mainly involves examining relevant official reports and government publications regarding issues of traditional territory and land use; records of legislatures, news media, propaganda materials and leaflets; and websites of indigenous groups and environmental group campaigns. These materials help to support, supplement and cross-check the correctness of my interpretations of situations and related arguments. They strengthen the reliability of the data collected by other methods. Interviews using open-ended questions and snowball sampling were employed. Open-ended questions usually encourage unpredictable discourses to cast new light on the research, and snowball sampling promotes the emergence of some relevant interviewees introduced by the others. Activists from self-help organisations and members of environmental groups were interviewed in 2019 to understand how activists and residents perceive the mining controversy and how they initiate discursive practice and mobilise, and how environmental groups participate in the process of knowledge production, provide professional assistance to local residents and activities, and participate in negotiation processes and policy-making in the deliberative systems.

Life narratives and discourses on land claims and living safety

Discourses as a distinct analytical category perform a coordinating function in that citizens do not need to directly communicate with each other to inform their actions. Discourses organise people's views and consequently affect their decisions and actions (Curato, 2015; Stevenson & Dryzek, 2014). There are three discourses on the mining controversy: indigenous land and informed consent rights; living safety and environmental uncertainty; and economic sustainability and job opportunity. These discourses emerged from my interpretative analysis, and these categories are key to understanding the controversies in the indigenous context. This section identifies the content of these discourses and key actors and advocates of each discourse, while the discourses remain at the centre as a guiding thread.

The first discourse relates to indigenous land rights and environmental justice. A self-help organisation interviewee described an unreasonable situation: large tracts of indigenous reserved land were rented to the ACC in 1974 during the authoritarian era, and counterfeit abandoned land documents appeared when the self-help organisation was established in 1996. Although tribespeople have competing perspectives on the ACC's effect, most tribespeople expressed their dissatisfaction with the government's approval of the ACC's application to extend mining without consulting the tribe or obtaining their consent. For the tribespeople, 'reserved land' means traditional territory rather than state-owned land, and asking the older tribespeople to sign to abandon their land for mining in exchange for an inadequate amount of money is unjust and unacceptable. As one Truku woman who has lived in the mine area for 30 years expressed, 'ACC is stepping on the shoulders of our people and distributing dividends to shareholders. This is our land. This is our home. How can you do this? Do you have peace of mind?' (Lin & Hsieh, 2019). An Ayug resident complained that the government does not consider indigenous historical context, territories of Truku life or particular lifeways and culture; it only considers whether it obeys laws since the ACC commenced mining activities in the area in 1974. State policy and mining activities conflict with indigenous livelihood and lifeways, which are regarded as land deprivation and the ruin of traditional land use (Interview with a member of an ENGO).

The second discourse is living safety and environmental uncertainty. Tribespeople and environmental groups have raised serious concerns regarding irreversible negative effects on the environment and health. Residents from an Ayug village near the mining pit called themselves 'victims' and expressed life narratives of extensive suffering due to the mining effects of air pollution and noise. Tribespeople doubt that ACC emphasises scientific data and standard compliance, but no one can guarantee living safety. The self-help organisation member asked in the ACC shareholders' meeting: 'Can you solve the problems of flooding, explosion shock, dust and conveyor belt noise? It has been 44 years. You [ACC] are lying all the time'. Tribespeople and environmental activists expressed their anger outside the meeting (Lin & Hsieh, 2019).

Local residents express their anxiety about the fragile geology and call attention to the landslide near the mine quarry that collapsed in 2016. According to Water and Soil Conservation Bureau data, three streams have landslide potential among the ACC courts, and two streams pass through the mine court. The Ayug tribal village is affected by the streams, and the nearby wild creek is covered with grey mud due to mudslides from the mining court. One resident indicated that, since the ACC started mining, heavy rain has caused streams to rise and flood houses, so residents have no choice but to raise the door to prevent mud coming in. According to residents who oppose the activities of the ACC, the mine court is old, and not requiring the ACC to pass an EIA is unreasonable, which makes them worry about how more than 20 years of ACC mining activities will affect the geology and cause negative environmental effects. The self-help organisation is concerned about environmental uncertainty and how the ACC could guarantee safety in 2021. Ayug residents believe that the mine is too close to the tribe and expressed anxiety regarding unstable sludge caused by explosive work during mining in extreme weather, which has threatened rights to life and property (Interview with an Ayug villager).

The third discourse is economic development, job opportunities and livelihood. Local perceptions of the ACC are heterogeneous among tribespeople. A strong sense of ambivalence regarding dependency on the mining industry is present in the community. Some tribespeople have worked for the ACC for a long period and tend to believe that the company has done its best to reduce the effect of mining on the environment. These employees and the tribespeople whose village is above the mine pit tend not to oppose the ACC because the effect of mining on the village above the pit is not as substantial as that on the village under the mine pit. The ACC chairman said in the shareholders' meeting, 'the indigenous people welcomed us at that time because there were no jobs, then two or three generations later you said that we are not welcome and have to leave; that is a very unreasonable thing'. The ACC has made efforts to create relationships with local residents. In addition to offering job opportunities, the ACC provides funds for tribal activities and scholarships and created the ACC Ecological Park to demonstrate its emphasis on environmental protection. The small-scale mining fried mountain experiment demonstration is used to demonstrate that the effect on the environment is limited. The ACC's engagement in local communities has influenced how tribespeople perceive mining effects. The discourse is associated with the ACC and its indigenous workers, who call for coexistence of the company and tribal economic sustainability. As one tribal resident who works in the ACC said, 'I live just under the mining pit and can prove and feel that the ACC offers many goodwill reward programmes to care for local tribes. I hope the ACC can extend its mining permit' (Hsu, 2019).

Discourses from the perspective of the self-help organisation and tribespeople who work for the ACC have been articulated in private and public spaces. Various avenues and sites are available for the articulation and contestation of discourses and transmission mechanisms for public space to affect empowered space.

Policy ideas transmission and shaping policy-making

Indigenous activists and environmental groups mobilised to facilitate new dialogues and discourses and created networks and coalitions in response to the state's dominant policy; they also engaged in deliberation on controversies over indigenous lands and regulations of mining through various means in multiple spaces. Civic activism contributes to transmission and forces the government to set up a negotiation mechanism to facilitate dialogue between the tribespeople, the ACC and the government. Deliberative activities are dynamic and interconnected with deliberation of other institutions in the deliberative systems. The Control Yuan's censuring the MOEA and Hualien County government serves as an accountability mechanism, which pushes the MOEA to respond to public and local discourses and demands.

Deliberation in the environmental movement and online petitions

Self-help organisations and activists mobilised and utilised resources and networking to obtain wider support, public attention and concerns from outsiders; the resources employed included workshops, campaigning, petitions, lobbying and litigation. Indigenous activists and environmental groups asked the government to amend the Mining Act to better protect the rights of the Truku people. A march against the ACC's mine on Truku indigenous lands in and surrounding Taroko National Park was held in front of the Executive Yuan on 25 June 2017, with over 2,500 in attendance. In addition to the demand for an end to the ACC mine and passage of mining industry reform, activists also call for social justice for indigenous people in Taiwan.

Indigenous activism against the ACC has integrated modern music and traditional cultural rituals. Apart from speeches and musical performances, Truku activists incorporated a smoking ceremony to communicate with ancestral spirits to demonstrate their determination to guard traditional territory and to spread awareness on indigenous issues and appeals. Protesters set off smoke bombs and played mining sounds to represent the loud noises that are constantly produced by the ACC's mine, which has caused considerable negative effects on the environment and the daily lives of Truku residents.

A renewed wave of outrage followed director Chi Bo-Lin's death in a helicopter. In his documentary 'Beyond Beauty: Taiwan From Above', Chi honed in on environmental damage to Taiwan's natural landscape, including Asia Cement's mining in Hualien County's Sincheng Township. The film prompted public outrage against Asia Cement's development project. A petition calling for ACC's permit to be revoked had received over 200,000 signatures at the time of the protest, initiated on March 23 by the Citizen of the Earth Foundation via Facebook. The self-help organisation said that if government did not start to amend the Mining Act by 22 November 2016, which is when the ACC's original permit was set to expire, then the group would block the entry to the mountains 'to defend indigenous land' (Maxon, 2018; Hioe, 2017). An online petition that calls for accelerating the legislative process of the amendment has received over 242,000 signatures as of October 2019.

Members of the self-help organisation express their concerns about living safety and the struggle for traditional territories to the public. They display photos of mining effects and news on their website and Facebook page with a song by a popular indigenous singer opposed to the ACC. Furthermore, they broadcast films of tribespeople's narratives of the negative effects of the ACC to transmit information, raise awareness of the controversy and communicate their perceptions of mining effects on the environment. The self-help organisation also discloses information and posts the local Environmental Protection Administration's environmental monitoring data to illustrate the ACC's pollution. On the self-help organisation website, a member mentioned that, 'according to the immediate manufacturer chimney monitoring data in Hualien in the past month, ACC's emissions exceed the standard. The data are telling, and pollution is not invisible'. Truku tribes' voices, perceptions of the negative effects of mining and citizen activism have attracted media attention and public concern.

The Citizen of the Earth Foundation has been engaged in activism in favour of indigenous rights in relation to the mining controversy for more than 30 years. The tribal activists established links with prominent environmental and indigenous groups. Citizen of the Earth has many discussions with tribal activists and suggests the self-help organisation adopts the rhetoric 'return my traditional territory' to gain legitimacy because the call 'return my land' might lead people to misunderstand that protesters only want money. Facebook content and posts and the blogs by the self-help organisation and the Citizen of the Earth Foundation have attracted public and media attention and concern from outsiders. Some citizens left messages and expressed their opinions and support for the Truku tribe on Facebook. The Facebook page, articles and comments on blogs about the controversy have attracted the attention of the virtual community and citizen media, who echo their message by posting and writing related commentary to accelerate transmission. For example, Indigenous Youth Front posted articles from the self-help organisation, shared similar situations of the Bunan tribe in Nantou County that suffered from negative mining effects, and appealed for support for the Mining Act amendment petition.

Indigenous TV broadcasting produced a special report to highlight the controversy and depict the Truku tribe's viewpoints. In July 2019, the indigenous TV programme 'Indigenous Views' broadcast a special forum titled 'ACC's extension cancelled and Mining Act amendment stuck. Procrastination?', which invited tribespeople and civic groups to participate in discussing the problems and provided audience members with the opportunity to call in and ask questions of the panel directly. The five panel members were drawn from the self-help organisation, the Truku tribal assembly, a tribal man whose father used to work for the ACC, Citizen of the Earth, and a lawyer from the Legal Centre of Indigenous Peoples. The self-help organisation emphasised that God and ancestor spirits want the tribespeople to guard our land, and unscrupulous development will cause nature's counterattack. The tribal participant indicated that the ACC must engage in tribal community development rather than using it for short-term benefits and subsidies. The lawyer appealed to legislators to review and pass the Mining Act amendment as soon as possible to guard indigenous land and informed consent rights. Citizen of the Earth called for improved mining management and strategic EIA. One audience member called in and questioned whether the ACC might notify workers that they will lose their jobs if the ACC cannot obtain the mining permit. The caller argued that the ACC's union should work with the self-help organisation to ask the ACC to propose a long-term plan for industry transformation which includes employee placement. The programme attracted public attention, facilitated ongoing conversations and reflected on the concept of justice and sustainable development and long-term relationships between land and people.

Tribal assembly as a platform for dialogue

The Bsngan tribal assembly was established in 2000 according to the rule of indigenous consultation to obtain the consent of indigenous people. The first meeting was held in November 2017. A tribal assembly member indicated that the Truku people and cadres initially did not completely understand what the tribal assembly could do. They learned the potential functions of tribal assembly, including helping to make tribal affairs visible, attracting the attention of President Tsai and the media, expressing opinions in public, and inviting geology experts to participate in fact-finding investigations on behalf of the tribespeople. The tribal assembly functions as a platform for dialogue and as a channel to speak to outsiders. The platform aims to meet the needs of tribespeople in different positions and link various opinions, including those of tribespeople who work for the ACC and the self-help associations, to express their concerns. The tribal assembly integrates traditional culture and modern administrative concepts, including tribal group migration, local administration and election systems, traditional territories and the concept of neighbouring tribes, in the consultation and consent regulation. It consists of a general assembly, presidium and cadre joint meeting, and operates using continual negotiation, communication and discussion. According to the organisation charter, the tribal assembly emphasises open and inclusive principles and communication (Presidential Office Indigenous Historical Justice and Transitional Justice Committee, 2018).

The operation of the tribal assembly and traditional ways of negotiation and decision-making mechanisms have conflicts. First, the concept of the tribe and the establishment of the tribal assembly within the current regulations conflict with traditional concepts of territories for each tribal village, tribal relationships and alliances; this causes the division of space. The Truku tribal assembly integrates both the traditional autonomy concepts of 'tribal alliance' and 'associated tribe' in the consultation and consent regulation. Second, tension is involved in making a final decision and selecting which tribal village is entitled to exercise the consent right. Truku tradition emphasises tribal norms and the communication process of seeking consensus (Program of Indigenous Views, Taiwan Indigenous Television, 2019). However, according to the regulations for consultation on consent of indigenous people, the tribal assembly makes the decision based on a household majority vote. For a resolution to pass, half of the tribal household representatives must attend the assembly and more than half of the household attendees must vote to support passing it. In contrast to a general voting system, the voting units are each household.

The government's institutional rules might produce division among tribespeople and disadvantage the small tribes. Members of the self-help organisation are concerned that six tribes can exercise consent rights, but the majority of the households do not appear to oppose ACC activities. The Ayug village under the mining court has suffered most from the negative effects of mining but has only approximately 20 households. Ayug villagers argue that each small tribe should establish its own tribe assembly and return to its own land, culture and traditional territory rather than grouping the large tribal assembly and small tribes together, saying 'it involves the living safety of our tribespeople who live under the mine court; why let the other five tribes determine our life and death?' (Interview with an Ayug villager).

The interviewee from the self-help organisation believes that the Ayug village should establish its own tribal assembly and should not be subject to the decisions of five other tribes. Tribespeople must obey Gaya, the natural law of Truku. Gaya is the norms that the elders pass down. This law is regarded as the highest guiding principle. The tribe must obey Gaya for traditional territory division. In the past, if a tribesman had to enter another tribe's territory for hunting, he had to obtain a hunting permit. Similarly, the ACC's mining court is located in Ayug territory; therefore, the Ayug village has the right to decide, rather than the other tribal villages. Forming the tribal assembly composed of six tribes disobeys Gaya. However, members of the tribal assembly have a slightly different opinion.

In addition to the Ayug, the nearby Orgi and Rowcing tribes are regarded as related because the Rowcing tribe is located behind the mountain and faces the threat of landslides. However, the presidium is required to define the related tribes. For some tribespeople, the Ayug village's independence from the tribal assembly might ruin the symbiotic relationship (Program of Indigenous Views, Taiwan Indigenous Television, 2019). However, the self-help organisation interviewee said, 'institutional rules oppress and limit Ayug [autonomy]', and seek tribespeople's support for Ayug's separation from the Bsngan tribal assembly. Ayug activists held the meeting on the establishment of the Ayug tribal assembly on 23 November 2019 and aimed to guard living safety and social justice and show their determination to seek Ayug self-awareness and autonomy.

Members of the tribal assembly have reflected on potential mechanisms to increase the legitimacy of Truku democracy. Because the ACC controversy is complex and involves competing views, the director-general of the tribal assembly indicated that tribespeople expect to have a platform to discuss whether and how the current laws of indigenous consent could be applicable to the current divided situation of the tribe. Tribespeople continue to patiently discuss and deliberate on the mining controversy in traditional and modern socio-political processes. They do their utmost to attend meetings in accordance with the rules made by the government, such as three-party negotiation meetings, working groups' meeting, tribal assembly and cadre meetings of the tribal assembly. In addition, traditional socio-political processes of everyday conversation and gatherings play a crucial role. Tribal social relations involve the intertwining of kinship, neighbourhoods, partnership and friendship. Because tribespeople face a great controversy and threat to their livelihood, they are willing to continue discussions on complex issues, even though some might be emotional. Environmental activists engage in communications with tribespeople who do not oppose the ACC to increase mutual understanding and seek common ground, and stimulate more conversations among members of the self-help organisation to build solidarity and seek consensus (Interview with a member of an ENGO).

Negotiation meeting of three sides

In response to the instructions of President Tsai, the Indigenous History and Transitional Justice Committee invited the tribespeople, the ACC, and the MOEA and Bureau of Mines to a three-sided negotiation meeting to discuss and resolve conflicts. The first three-sided negotiation meeting comprising the tribe, the ACC and the government was held on 25 March 2018. The chairperson was from the Truku tribe and a member of the Indigenous History and Transitional Justice Committee. The chairman indicated that the negotiation meeting was the first step for the government to manage the indigenous peoples' call for transitional justice. Before the meeting started, an elder Truku leader dressed in a traditional costume performed a traditional blessing ceremony. At the beginning of the meeting, the chairman made a speech in the Truku language and in Mandarin. The chairman said that the venue is called Bsngan, which is the convergence place where ancestors gather to cooperate, barter and create collective memories. He emphasised that this negotiation meeting was a platform on which each side could express opinions and seek a means of collaborating to guard life safety and the land for future generations. The meetings were broadcast online and held every three months to continue negotiations.

The agenda for the first meeting included three parts: presentations by the Bureau of Mines, the ACC and the tribal assembly regarding the current situation; discussion of the fact-finding investigation and living safety concerns; and resolution confirmation. The MOEA minister indicated that he visited ACC's mining court to evaluate the situation and asked the ACC and the Bureau of Mines to empathise with the tribespeople. He discovered that some houses still had leaking problems, and he asked the ACC to improve and invite local residents to examine the sediment and flooding during typhoon season to assuage the fears of residents.

The negotiation meetings facilitated more dialogue and deliberation among tribespeople. A representative of the Bsngan tribe assembly indicated that tribespeople have engaged in discussion for long periods and have incorporated opinions from the self-help organisation, scholars and experts, Citizens of the Earth and ENGOs, and lawyers into the presentation of their statement. The tribe assembly proposed 'three principles', eight appeals and one mechanism. The 'three principles' entail the government signing and enacting a legally binding document, acknowledging indigenous land and natural resource rights in accordance with the Indigenous Peoples Basic Law and two international conventions on civil rights, and respecting the tribal consent processes and providing sufficient time for tribal discussions. The first mechanism is a call for establishing a commission under the Indigenous Historical and Transitional Committee to assist in a fact-finding investigation. The eight appeals are as follows: (1) the government should cancel ACC's mining licence extension; (2) tribal consent rights should be practised; (3) the state should undertake a survey on how the ACC obtained mining licences and land in the past to clarify whether the township was involved in negligence or fraud; (4) a third party should conduct environmental safety monitoring and reports; (5) the state and the ACC should apologise to and compensate the tribe after performing a complete investigation and obtain the tribe's forgiveness; (6) the ACC should propose a mining, closing and industry transition plan; (7) the ACC must return the deprived land and rights to the tribe; and (8) tribal consent must be obtained for previous and new mining development projects using the Mining Act amendment.

The tribal responses were positive. The MOEA minister promised that the MOEA will negotiate with the ACC to manage concerns of shallow collapse and landslide safety that worry the tribespeople most and asked the tribe to suggest trustworthy and professional institutions to oversee the process. The ACC manager indicated that the ACC will invite tribespeople to participate in safety monitoring work, scholarships will be offered for tribal youth to learn about such work, and the reports will be made public.

The first meeting focused on two issues: living safety and the fact-finding investigation. The three parties reached a consensus on six points, four of which regarded living safety: (1) the government and the ACC agreed that tribal people and a third party or expert that the tribespeople trust must fully participate in mining court and tribal safety data collection, assessment and follow-up supervision; (2) the MOEA and the ACC should provide funding for safety monitoring; (3) the ACC should invite tribal representatives to participate in the ACC's current safety measurements and respond to tribal opinions; and (4) the ACC and the government agencies should consult tribespeople regarding several safety concerns and improvement requirements proposed by the tribe and evaluate the proposed programmes within 1 month. The two points regarding the fact-finding investigation were: (1) involve tribal representatives, the government, and the ACC in forming a working task group to negotiate the establishment of an investigation committee and timeline within 1 month, and (2) undertake the investigation in a fair and just manner in compliance with the laws, Truku Gaya (Truku social norms, moral standards and ancestors' legacy) and transitional justice.

The meeting made tribal voices heard and improved mutual understanding. Representatives of the trial assembly recognised the meeting as an opportunity for the tribe to express opinions and hoped the negotiation process could help gradually increase mutual understanding and empathy for each other, although strong distrust of the ACC remains. The self-help organisation issued a statement on Facebook recognising that the chairman and members of the Indigenous Historical and Transitional Justice Committee did their best to listen to tribespeople's voices and let tribespeople express opinions sufficiently (SuyangAyugBalay, 2018). However, the self-help organisation was not satisfied because this meeting did not discuss the legitimacy of the ACC's extension and the plan for closing the mining court. The MOEA and ACC did not respond to the following tribal concerns: (1) The MOEA did not promise to offer the documents for the ACC's extension to provide the tribespeople with full information to examine its legitimacy; (2) the ACC did not promise to undertake an EIA or obey the new rules of the Mining Act; and (3) the MOEA did not answer the question of the legal effect of tribal denial of consent or conditional consent regarding the mining licence extension (Wei, 2018).

The second negotiation was held in July 2018. The Council of Indigenous Peoples, the MOEA and the Bureau of Mines presented the progress on the fact-finding investigation and living safety. Tensions were high regarding safety issues between the ACC and the self-help organisation. One geology expert representing the tribe doubted whether the ACC's application proposal for mining extension mentioned the fault line in the ACC's court and argued that the company must prove that the court has no fault line; otherwise the mine is deemed to threaten public safety and interests. The ACC responded that discussing hypothetical questions is time intensive. However, a self-help organisation representative argued that, in the Central Geological Survey, the MOEA identified the mining zone as an environmentally sensitive area, and geology affects the drainage problem. The chairperson decided to allow the tribal safety working commission and expert discussion mechanism to discuss the fault line concern. The self-help organisation expressed their dissatisfaction with the slow progress of the investigation and lack of response to industry transformation, and they hoped the government would commission a geology survey soon. Those at the meeting reached some points of consensus, including on improving the neighbouring drainage system plan and creating a linkage of the ACC's emergency response and evacuation programme with the township's emergency response plan; it was also agreed that the proposal of tribal transition to sustainable development would be discussed in the task commission (Lin & Sun, 2018). The self-help organisation issued a statement on Facebook to express disappointment that the ACC continues to say it complies with regulations as a shield to avoid answering questions and alleviating doubts. The third meeting held in December 2018 highlighted the completion of the drainage project discussed in the previous meeting and concerns of mining transformation.

The dialogues of the first meeting appeared to indicate mutual respect and listening. However, the second meeting lacked listening and justification and caused tribal distress. As the self-help organisation stated on Facebook, 'the government and the ACC are only willing to reiterate uncontroversial items and avoid reasonable doubts as if asking everyone to perform a harmonious drama. Three-party negotiation seems to self-destruct as it functions' (SuyangAyugBalay, 2018). They also criticised the ACC's failure to humbly respond to tribal doubt. This demonstrates that considering conflicts seriously and attempting to deliberate over conflicts is better than avoiding talking.

The self-help organisation has doubted the form of the three-sided negotiation. They indicated that they hope to hold a two-sided negotiation between the government and the tribe because they believe the tribespeople are 'victims' and ask why the perpetrator, the ACC, must join the negotiation. They believe that the government and the ACC had common interests during the negotiation meeting, and the self-help organisation was in a disadvantaged situation because the tribal assembly tends to support the ACC, and only representatives of the self-help organisation oppose the ACC's mining extension. The negotiation platform reached an impasse in 2019. The self-help organisation interviewee indicated that, because the ACC decided to appeal and had no intention to participate in the three-sided negotiation meeting, the self-help organisation was not willing to participate in the meeting. They asked that the discussion on geology and fact-finding investigations and mining court transition have a concrete outcome, and they will decide on further action after the government publishes the fact-finding investigation.

Litigation declares indigenous informed consent rights

Self-help organisations and residents near the mine filed a petition against extending mining rights. However, the Executive Yuan said that it was lawful for the MOEA to grant the mining extension, and the Indigenous Peoples Basic Law was not pertinent to the topic. The self-help organisation filed a lawsuit against the MOEA and the ACC. On 11 July 2019, the Taipei High Administrative Court repealed the ACC's right to operate a cement mine because the extension violated the Indigenous Peoples Basic Law, and the indigenous people living nearby should have been consulted (Liao, 2019).

The ACC argued that their rights had been severely affected, saying that the extension of mining rights was a decision made at an inter-ministerial meeting at the Executive Yuan. According to the current Mining Act, mining extension is not applicable in the Indigenous Peoples Basic Law. The ACC expressed regret for the verdict and has demanded that lawyers appeal the case to guard employee and stakeholder benefits and amend social perceptions. The union members support the company's decision to appeal the ruling.

The Bureau of Mines indicated that they would further evaluate the legal, industrial development, social and environmental dimensions and indigenous rights to determine whether to appeal the case or not. Then, they decided not to appeal to demonstrate their respect for indigenous will. They announced that the MOEA would participate in a negotiation meeting to discuss the current situation collectively and attempt to settle the controversy.

Although the Truko residents won the lawsuit against the ACC's mining extension, those who work in the ACC hold competing positions. The ACC's corporate union at its Hualien plant held a news conference, saying that from 20 to 22 July 2019, they received signatures from 380 households, 832 residents, or 70% of all indigenous households in the Bsngan community, supporting the extension of the company's mining rights (Xu, 2019).

The self-help organisation and activists responded favourably to the verdict and thanked the Legal Aid Foundation, Wild at Heart Legal Defense Association, and Citizen of the Earth for their assistance. They argued that the Bureau of Mines should cancel the ACC's mining extension and not appeal, and called for the ACC to cease mining operations on their land. The self-help organisation claims that the tribespeople should have sufficient time to exercise the right of consultation and consent freely, in advance and in informed conditions.

Citizen of the Earth argued that the MOEA and the Bureau of Mines violated the Geology Act and Cultural Heritage Preservation Act when reviewing the ACC's mining extension proposal by not asking the ACC to conduct an investigation on environmentally vulnerable zones. This not only neglected residents' safety but also ignored mining's effects on the environment and cultural assets. According to NGOs, the result of the verdict demonstrates the problem of mining institutions and regulations, and the developers maintaining mining rights during the extension application in accordance with Article 13 of the Mining Act is unreasonable. NGOs asked the Bureau of Mines to ask the ACC to conduct an EIA and propose a complete plan for closing the mine court and conducting an economic benefits assessment. Unless the MOEA turns down the ACC's extension application, the ACC's mining cannot be stopped if the Mining Act is not amended.

The Legal Aid Foundation lawyer mentioned that this was the first national verdict that the tribespeople won because of the judge's consideration of Article 21 of the Indigenous Peoples Basic Law to rule that the developer failed to put indigenous consultation and consent into practice. The lawyer argued that the current Mining Act favours the industry because the ACC can continue mining even when the mining extension has been cancelled. The Mining Act exhibits hegemony of developmentalism and must be amended urgently.

Deliberation on the Mining Act amendment

On Indigenous Day 2016, the leader of the anti-ACC Return Truku Traditional Territories Movement represented the tribe to accept President Tsai's apology and petition the government to ask the ACC to put indigenous consultation consent rights into practice. President Tsai assigned this task to the Council of Indigenous Peoples, who indicated that the mining permit extension should follow the consultation and consent principle. On 7 December 2017, the Executive Yuan announced its draft of the Mining Act amendment. The amendment included enhanced environmental protection and established an EIA process and environmental rehabilitation plans, realised indigenous rights of consultation, enhanced safety management, legalised a compensation mechanism, opened data (e.g. monitoring) and promoted transparency and participation in the policy-making process, and removed unreasonable rules. If the draft passes, the ACC must make up the EIA within three years. However, ENGOs have argued that the draft still favours the mining industry because new rules of indigenous consultation rights only apply to new application cases.

In 2017, the anti-mining movement forced President Tsai to promise to reform mining, and the draft has been submitted to the Legislative Yuan as a priority. The review process is slower than expected. Since April 2018, the Economics Committee has held more than 10 review meetings, and the draft has been negotiated three times among the parties, reaching consensus in May 2019, when it was submitted to a Legislative Yuan meeting. The most controversial and key items of the amendment are whether to incorporate Article 21 of the Indigenous Peoples Basic Law into the Mining Act and whether asking firms to consult the tribe and obtain tribal consent is necessary. However, the Bureau of Mines and the MOEA interpret indigenous consultation rights as the right to participation; as such, obtaining indigenous consent is unnecessary. ENGOs indicated that this ignores indigenous land rights.

During the Legislative Yuan Economic Committee review meeting, quarrels occurred among legislators, and DPP legislator Shu-Fen Lin expressed her anger towards the MOEA for favouring the industry and towards a few DPP legislators for their support for the MOEA's position. Although the Council of Indigenous Peoples and a few legislators supported incorporating indigenous consent rights, some legislators had a different position. This made environmental activists express doubt related to the involvement of industry interests and political donations. Citizens of the Earth disclosed the details of political donations from the mining industry and called for public supervision (Interview with the member of an ENGO).

Finally, the Economic Committee reached a consensus on the requirement of making up the EIA for old mining fields, and the draft states that mining courts with an area of over 1 hectare must make up the EIA; large mining courts must make up the EIA within 3 years; and small mining courts must make up the EIA within 5 years. If a mining court does not pass the EIA, then the mining court will be closed. If the Legislative Yuan passes the amendment, then approximately 120 mining courts, including the ACC's mining court, must make up the EIA.

Local activists and civic organisations have appealed to legislators and pressured the government to tighten regulations on mining permit licencing, accelerate the legislative draft review process, and call for the public to require legislators to pass the amendment. Moreover, Watchout continues to inspect legislators' performance and broadcast the meetings in a timely manner on their website. On the 'Issue lab' of the Watchout website, Watchout asks the question, 'What mountain and forestry do you want?' to raise public awareness and stimulate reflection and thinking on the mining controversy. Watchout provides relevant information on the current situation of the amendment process and informs the public of which legislators are concerned about the amendment, the differences among versions of the amendment proposed by different political parties and legislators, and which legislators support or oppose indigenous consultation and consent rights. In addition, Citizen of the Earth broadcasts the deliberative progress of the Economic Committee online to allow the public to understand and supervise the progress. Watchout's functions are meaningful in connecting the public space and the empowered space; it allows the public to evaluate whether the empowered space responds to public discourse.

Functions in the deliberative system and consequentiality

As mentioned, I use the epistemic, ethical and democratic functions of a deliberative system developed by Mansbridge et al. (2012) to structure the discussions on the case study. This section analyses the contributions of civic groups and indigenous activism in achieving these functions in the deliberative system.

First, alliances of the self-help organisation and NGOs have epistemic functions, and civic activism and indigenous movements help make tribal narratives of mining effects visible. Citizen of the Earth published a special report that revealed the negative effects of the mining industry since the 1970s and demonstrated a high level of knowledge and understanding of the mining industry's effect on the environment and the tribe, highlighting current environmental regulatory and governance problems. Citizen of the Earth seeks to clarify the controversy and convey this understanding to others within both private and public spheres of action. Citizen of the Earth has the potential to act as 'trusted information proxies to guide citizens' political judgments in situations characterized by limited information' (MacKenzie & Warren, 2012). ENGOs and self-help organisations challenge the ACC's claims on scientific data and safety standards, arguing that the ACC's mining court is in a disaster-prone zone and identifying risks of landslides and flooding during typhoon seasons and environmental uncertainties in extreme weather. Citizen of the Earth provides relevant information and knowledge about the mining industry and a chart of differences before and after the amendment to help the public understand the controversy and contribute to public environmental education. Lawyers also disseminate knowledge to other indigenous tribes and local residents to help them understand the mining controversy and raise their awareness of informed consent rights. During the process, civic groups attempt to gain knowledge on indigenous groups and traditional methods of land use and appeal to legislators to respect the environment, which affects the welfare of all Taiwanese people, and engage in mining reform.

Civic activism draws attention to and enables actors to address 'undone science', which refers to a situation of unequal power that involves a conflict between a social movement and industrial and political elites and that is associated with absent knowledge (Hess, 2015). Local residents doubt and distrust the ACC's scientific claims of safety and illuminate the epistemic claims they wish to evaluate; the scientific data are simply not available. Citizen of the Earth argued that the ACC has not conducted long-term environmental or geological research and has attempted to collect more monitoring data since the anti-ACC movement in 2017; data collection is not yet complete (Interview with a member of Citizen of the Earth, 2019). Tribal activists' and residents' calls for more information and participation in living area safety assessment during the three-party meeting resulted in the MOEA funding further research. Indigenous activism also led to the incorporation of EIA procedure requirements in the draft of the Mining Act amendment. The living safety investigation committee comprising tribal representatives, experts and officials contributes to knowledge production and coproduction of flood control, drainage and evacuation plans.

Second, the ethical function of a deliberative system is to promote equality and mutual respect among citizens (Mansbridge et al., 2012; Rosenberg, 2007; Riedy & Kent, 2015). Citizen of the Earth seeks to promote equality and mutual respect in the deliberative system by fighting for indigenous peoples' rights to know, consent to, and participate in decisions on mining. The three-party negotiation meeting promotes equality among tribes, the ACC and the MOEA, and shows respect for tribal concerns and opinions. The government changed their methods of interaction with the Truku people from neglect and lack of recognition to willingly undertaking face-to-face communication and negotiation. The interaction and dialogue of the MOEA and the Bureau of Mines with the Truku participants in the negotiation forum demonstrated respect for Truku differences, but only partial responsiveness. Multiple discourses have equal opportunities for deliberation in the negotiation process, which indicates high degrees of inclusiveness. This interaction highlights the dynamic process and continuing political and social shaping of deliberation practices.

Third, the democratic function of a deliberative system is to incorporate a diversity of voices, interests, concerns and claims into the political process (Mansbridge et al., 2012). Representatives of the tribal assembly emphasise 'social justice', arguing that the government and the ACC should not simply state that the extension of mining complies with the law to justify mining development. Members of the self-help organisation in the Ayug tribal village express a distinctive identity of place, which reveals a 'place-based value' that involves a commitment to one's past and a commitment to the future of human and ecological community (Norton, 1997; Fan, 2008). Environmental damage caused by mining is regarded as the ruin of tribal life narratives.

Tribespeople call for the right to know regarding the living safety assessment and the truth; transitional justice must be obtained through fact-finding investigations and reconciliation. Face-to-face negotiation could facilitate the government's reflection on mining policy and issues of historical injustice and respect for tribal land rights.

Citizen of the Earth seeks to ensure that the voices of the tribespeople and victims are injected into the public space for consideration in influencing the empowered space, including the tribespeople, the environment and species that are affected by mining. Citizen of the Earth also expresses concern about workers' welfare and calls for social responsibility of corporations, arguing that the ACC must transform towards stopping mining, increasing benefit sharing and providing local residents with job opportunities. Rather than asking the tribespeople who support the ACC whether they agree with the company's continued mining, Citizen of the Earth believes that the question must be reframed to ask whether they agree with the ACC's continuing mining on the condition of assuring safety, benefit sharing and a time limit. Government and the ACC have to take responsibility for the negative impacts caused by mining (Interview with a member of an ENGO, 2019).

Consequentiality could also be regarded as the capability of a deliberative process to oppose structural oppression and inequality (Felicetti, 2017, p. 20). The tribal struggle for justice and civic activism has forced the government to coordinate and initiate new dialogues among the Truku tribe, the ACC and the MOEA, and establish the fact-finding investigation committee to address historical injustice.[1] Civic activism creates and enlarges deliberative space, enhances the deliberative capacity of environmental governance and shapes rule-making for mining. However, legalisation of indigenous communities' consent on mining permits still faces the challenge of industry interest and requires more deliberation and negotiation.

Conclusion

This case presents the external and internal political changes to the indigenous deliberative system through indigenous participation. The self-help organisation of the Ayug village allied with environmental groups and indigenous activists and mobilised to facilitate deliberation regarding indigenous lands and mining regulations by using various means, including campaigning, petitioning, lobbying, and litigation. Activists have mobilised and utilised resources to seek wider support, public attention, and concern from outsiders. This chapter offers insights into the contributions of indigenous political participation in deliberative systems and expands understanding regarding the dynamic interactions between indigenous activism and the state during ongoing tribal grassroots participation and social negotiation.

This case presents the inadequacy of tribal consultation processes at the beginning of mining decisions on indigenous land. The Truku people's political participation demonstrates the ability of indigenous peoples to respond to contemporary political and environmental challenges. Ayug villagers established the self-help organisations and transcended their original tribal village boundaries to communicate with neighbouring tribal villagers who had competing viewpoints and participated in negotiation with government officials and the ACC. Tribal arguments and activism for guarding indigenous traditional territories pressured the government to incorporate tribal concerns and adopt tribal requests to participate in safety investigations and invite technicians they trust to participate in environmental monitoring; these actions help to democratise the knowledge system.

Residents near ACC mining are not homogeneous. Even people who share characteristics of one identity usually have multiple identities (O'Neill, 2000, p. 176). Identity is produced through the dialectics between self and society in the ongoing process of social reconstruction (Mead, 1934). Tribespeople continue to redefine complex problems of dependency on mining and environmental impacts of development projects, and reflect on social relationships, tribal subjectivity and traditional boundaries and difference during the process of ongoing dialogues. The colonial history and process of modernisation have shaped the fluid and evolutionary relationships that exist among the Truku people, nature and land. Truku grassroots participation and ongoing dialogue facilitate social learning and reconstruct tribal subjectivity. It is necessary to facilitate tribal deliberations about what sustainability of different dimensions mean for the tribe, and it might help to build solidarity.

This case demonstrates the coevolution of micro- and macro-deliberative systems. Participatory governance in traditional territories and the Tsai government's pursuit of dialogue for historical and transitional justice are mutually reinforcing. Indigenous democratic practices and the relationship and interaction between indigenous peoples and the Taiwanese government have been shaped through and by social processes. Deliberation practices could help create a sense of agency and reconstruct tribal subjectivities. During the process of this engagement, people are transformed through interactions with others and with nature and are also able to transform the societies and environments we inhabit (Evanoff, 2002). Colonial history and the state's power and policies have challenged the traditional norms and rules of indigenous tribes, various events and tensions connect conversations among tribespeople in different tribal villages and sites, providing spaces to reconstruct Truku tribe subjectivities. The Truku tribe still faces the challenge of operating the tribal assembly, interacting with state officials and participating in public policy changes. It reveals the coevolution of tribal deliberative systems and their interaction with the state. Indigenous political participation and civic activism spark ongoing dialogues as well as reflection on social justice, sustainable development and the relationship between people and land.

Note

1 The working group commissioned the College of Indigenous Studies of National Dong-Hwa University to undertake a one-year fact-finding investigation.

References

Chen, R. (2017, October 17). ISSUE: Undermining Taiwan's indigenous environments. *The News Lens.* https://international.thenewslens.com/article/81206

Citizen of the Earth, Taiwan. (2019). The Yani Xinchengshan Mine has lost more than 20 years of digging and the Taroko tribe won! *Citizen of the Earth, Taiwan.* www.cet-taiwan.org/node/3514

Curato, N. (2015). Deliberative capacity as indicator of democratic quality: The case of the Philippines. *International Political Science Review, 36*(1), 99–116.

Davis, R. (2018, July). Indigenous deliberative forums as transmitters in indigenous environmental governance: Enablers and barriers. Paper presented at the International Political Science Association Conference, Brisbane, Australia.

Evanoff, R. (2002). *A constructivist approach to intercultural dialogue on environmental ethics* (Unpublished Ph.D. dissertation). Lancaster University, Lancashire, UK.

Fan, M.-F. (2008). Environmental citizenship and sustainable development: The case of waste facility siting in Taiwan. *Sustainable Development, 16*(6), 381–389.

Felicetti, A. (2017). *Deliberative democracy and social movements: Transition initiatives in the public sphere.* London: Rowman & Littlefield.

Gao, P. (2015, February 1). Taiwan review: Promoting indigenous rights. *Taiwan Today.* https://taiwantoday.tw/news.php?unit=12,29,33&post=23754

Google Maps. (2020). User-created map. www.google.com.tw/maps/@24.1446895,121.6375273,5452m/data=!3m1!1e3?hl=zh-TW

Hébert, M. (2018). Indigenous sphere of deliberation. In A. Bächtiger, J. Dryzek, J. Mansbridge, & M. Warren (Eds.), *Handbook of deliberative democracy* (pp. 100–109). Oxford: Oxford University Press.

Hess, D. (2015). Undone science, industrial innovation, and social movements. In M. Gross & L. McGoey (Eds.), *The Routledge international handbook of ignorance studies* (pp. 141–154). Abingdon: Routledge.

Hioe, B. (2017, June 25). Demonstration against Asia Cement's mine on indigenous lands draws 2,500. *New Bloom.* https://newbloommag.net/2017/06/25/asia-cement-taroko-gorge/

Hsu, C.-N. (2019, July 17). Past opponent now supports coexistence and prosperity. *China Times.* www.chinatimes.com/newspapers/20190717000544-260118?chdtv

Liao, G. (2019, July 11). Taroko residents win lawsuit against Asia Cement's mining extension. *Taiwan News.* www.taiwannews.com.tw/en/news/3743219

Lin, J.-M., & Hsieh C.-W. (2019, June 24). Against mining development, the Taroko tribespeople attend Asian Cement's shareholders' meeting to protest. *PTS News Network.* https://news.pts.org.tw/article/435351

Lin, S. W.-Q., & Sun, T. Z.-X. (2018, July 22). The second three party negotiation meeting on ACC focuses on the fault line and caused tensions. *Taiwan Indigenous Television.* http://titv.ipcf.org.tw/news-40779

MacKenzie, M., & Warren, M. E. (2012). Two trust-based uses minipublics in democratic systems. A systemic approach to deliberative democracy. In J. Parkinson & J.

Mansbridge (Eds.), *Deliberative systems: Deliberative democracy at the large scale* (pp. 95–124). Cambridge: Cambridge University Press.

Mansbridge, J., Bohman, J., Chambers, S., Christiano, T., Fung, A., Parkinson, J., Thompson, D. F., & Warren, M. E. (2012). A systemic approach to deliberative democracy. In J. Parkinson & J. Mansbridge (Eds.), *Deliberative systems: Deliberative democracy at the large scale* (pp. 1–26). Cambridge: Cambridge University Press.

Maxon, A. (2018, August 1). Aborigines urge Tsai to deliver on vow. *Taipei Times*. www.taipeitimes.com/News/taiwan/archives/2018/08/01/2003697771

Mead, H. (1934). *Mind, self and society*. Chicago, IL: University of Chicago.

Mendonça, R. F., & Ercan, S. A. (2015). Deliberation and protest: Strange bedfellows? Revealing the deliberative potential of 2013 protests in Turkey and Brazil. *Policy Studies*, *36*(3), 267–282.

Norton, B. (1997). Environmental values: A place-based theory. *Environmental Ethics*, *19*, 227–245.

O'Neill, O. (2000). *Bounds of justice*. Cambridge: Cambridge University Press.

Presidential Office Indigenous Historical Justice and Transitional Justice Committee. (2018, March 25). Piling Humi, presentation of tribal assembly on the first three party's negotiation meeting [Video]. *YouTube*. www.youtube.com/watch?time_continue=5503&v=Jy_8OVoh9L8

Program of Indigenous Views, Taiwan Indigenous Television. (2019, August 17). Piling Humi: Tribal assembly is the process of tribal subjectivity: It needs to find way and consensus [Video]. *YouTube*. www.youtube.com/watch?v=LZTgT6wzjlg

Riedy, C., & Kent, J. (2015). Australian climate action groups in the deliberative system. *Environmental Politics*, *24*(3), 363–381.

Rosenberg, S. (2007). An introduction: Theoretical perspectives and empirical research on deliberative democracy. In S. W. Rosenberg (Ed.), *Deliberation, participation and democracy: Can the people govern?* (pp. 1–22). London: Palgrave Macmillan.

Stevenson, H., & Dryzek, J. S. (2014). *Democratizing global climate governance*. Cambridge: Cambridge University Press.

SuyangAyugBalay. (2018, March 27). *Facebook self-help organization* [Facebook page]. *Facebook*. Retrieved 25 April 2019 from https://zh-tw.facebook.com/SuyangAyuBalay

Tamura, T. (2014). Rethinking grassroots participation in nested deliberative systems. *Japanese Political Science Review*, *2*, 63–87.

The Control Yuan (2019). The rectification case. www.cy.gov.tw/CyBsBoxContent.aspx?n=133&s=6605

Wei, S. (2018, March 25). The first three party negotiation meeting of ACC controversy reach consensus on six items: Tribal full participation. *CNA*. www.cna.com.tw/news/firstnews/201803250190.aspx

Xu, Z.-Y. (2019, July 29). ACC's corporate union announces 70% residents support ACC and oppose stigmatization. *ETToday*. www.ettoday.net/news/20190729/1500881.htm

7 Democratic innovations and participatory budgeting in deliberative systems

Introduction

PB has been widely discussed and has been institutionalised in numerous cities worldwide. PB is a form of collaborative governance in which citizens participate in decision-making processes that dictate how part or all of the available government funds will be spent (Hartz-Karp, 2012). For PB to be effective, an ongoing participatory process is required, which involves building civic capacity and infrastructure. A considerable body of PB research has been conducted from the perspective of the government and has been analysed with a focus on the exercise itself; therefore, related research has overlooked crucial activities of civil society actors, the relationships between multiple deliberations and the dynamics in a deliberative system. Little research has focused on the intermediation role and the value of third-party groups in civil society in PB, which assists in achieving meaningful citizen participation in resource allocation and democratic development (Justice & Dulger, 2009).

Since 2014, the concept of PB has been incorporated in election slogans and advocated by several county mayoral candidates. PB has been implemented in all Taiwan's major cities. Initiators of PB include departments and agencies in both central and local governments and several local councillors. The 'outsourced' model of PB – in which promoting PB, designing participation procedures and organising and mobilising the public have been outsourced to NGOs or teams led by scholars – has mostly been adopted outside Taipei City. Taipei is the only municipality that has attempted to institutionalise PB on a city-wide basis (Wan, 2018).

The current mayor of Taipei City, Ko Wen-je, the founding chairman of TPP; previously a renowned doctor who organised a medical fan club for the previous DPP president, Chen Shui-bian (2000–2008), he ran for mayor of Taipei in 2014. Ko reported in his election white paper that the democratisation of Taiwan had reached a bottleneck. He further indicated that the political system could not effectively respond to public opinions, which incurred protests and citizen movements, and that he believed that PB could compensate for the inadequacy of indirect democracy in the current situation by delegating some of the power to the people to formulate budgets, thereby empowering people to influence policy-making and achieving the dual purposes of eliminating disadvantages and increasing profits (Ko, 2014).

The Department of Civil Affairs was responsible for implementing PB by order of the mayor; the deputy commissioner proposed the idea of government–academia alliances by inviting local universities and community colleges to become partner organisations with the District Administration and provide the support of knowledge and resources for the implementation of PB. In this model, the administrative system plays a central role, and it is complemented by professional support from academics and community colleges. This government–academia alliance developed various mechanisms, such as government execution, academic consultation and civil support, aimed at increasing local cooperation, active support and sustainable development. The mechanisms were then integrated into a one-stop contact window for the promotion of PB (Taipei City Government, 2017b). During the Citizen Participation Committee's second assembly on 8 July 2015, the Taipei City Government passed the Procedures for the Proposal and Review of the Participatory Budgeting System in Taipei City at the city and district levels (amended on 29 December 2016). The procedures are divided into five phases: promotion, proposal review, budgeting evaluation, budgeting review and council supervision. These procedures were implemented to modularise and institutionalise PB in Taipei City.

By exploring the case of PB in Taipei City, this chapter examines how PB operates and connects the sphere of micro-deliberative forums, empowered space and civic society in deliberative systems. Furthermore, the unique government–academia alliance approach and the particular roles of academic institutions and civic organisations as intermediary actors in activating deliberative practices and accelerating the transmission of ideas and adjustments in PB procedures are explored. This chapter begins with a brief discussion of the key concepts of deliberative systems and then introduces the design of PB in Taipei City. Furthermore, the dynamic connections between residents' assemblies and other components of PB, the functions and divisions of labour of participatory processes and activities of PB, and the ongoing communications between government officials, local elites, partnership schools and civic organisations are analysed.

Democratic innovations and democratic imagination

In the analysis of linking mini-publics to the deliberative system, Curato and Böker (2016) argued that a systemic interpretation of deliberative democracy was neither optimistic nor critical, but *ambivalent*. They argued that the interpretation was dependent on whether mini-publics could meaningfully connect to other components of deliberative systems and serve to promote or hinder deliberative democratisation at the wider systemic level. For instance, the Australian Citizens' Parliament (ACP) has a reasonable level of internal quality but has not achieved much consequentiality. Researchers on the ACP has described this event as a successful mini-public, with high internal quality and 'inclusivity' because they mirrored the demographic composition of Australian society. However, these mini-publics sparked little further deliberation outside the scope of this event and have indirect legitimacy-enhancing and capacity-building effects (Curato & Böker, 2016).

In contrast to a mini-public, which is one component of a system, PB has decision-making authority and thus could achieve more consequentiality. Democratic innovations adopt various forms. According to Newton (2012), democratic innovation is 'the implementation of a new idea that is intended to change the structures or processes of democratic government and politics by improving them' (p. 4). Newton further reported that democratic innovation should connect citizens to policy-making processes. Smith (2009, p. 2) argued that two general aspects of democratic innovation are crucial: (1) institutions directly engage citizens; (2) innovations include institutionalised forms of participation in which citizens have a formal role in policy, legislative or constitutional decision-making. According to the experiences of other countries, governments seldom set clear goals before promoting PB. Participants have diverse backgrounds and various expectations (Ebdon & Franklin, 2006). Governments promote public participation in budget management for several reasons, which mainly comprise informing and educating the public, improving government decision-making, creating opportunities for the public to shape policies, legitimising government decision-making and enhancing public trust in the government. However, numerous obstacles hinder meaningful citizen participation in PB, including lack of knowledge, people's belief that their investment is not valued or needed, lack of trust and legitimacy, lack of civic sensibilities, time constraints and self-interest. These factors may hinder community interest (Cabannes, 2004, p. 1).

Hasegawa et al. (2007) expanded on Anderson's (1991) work on 'imagined communities' by proposing the concept of 'social expectation' as 'an internalised social norm for individuals and organisations, thus for society as a whole, about what people should do' (p. 179). Hasegawa et al. (2007) believed that the concept of 'social expectation' relates to Habermas's (1989) concept of the 'public sphere', the space for the formation of public opinion and social agreement through collective discussion. Social expectations are 'a set of new hopes developed through the practice of public conversation and joint action', which are 'a motivation for socially meaningful activities' (Hasegawa et al., 2007, pp. 180–181). Hasegawa et al. (2007) further argued that social expectation operates on two levels, first on particular elite groups and then on the general public. This creates a social climate in which an individual's imagined reference groups or community affects their behaviours. The concept of 'social expectation' offers a valuable perspective to analyse dynamic collaboration among policy actors, as well as civic organisations' and residents' participation in the promotion and evolution of PB.

PB in Taipei City

PB was initiated in Taiwan in 2015 and has since flourished. Proponents of PB claim that PB is consistent with transparent and open government. However, during the trial run of the Taipei City Government in 2015, some city councillors questioned the institutional and political feasibility of PB and deemed PB to be a mechanism that might deprive them of their power and resources. For example, one councillor doubted that PB allowed sufficient room for people's imagination in terms of the budget proposal. Other concerns were raised regarding whether proposals should be considered if they were not feasible, whether councillors could oppose proposals supported by the majority of participants, and whether PB might be used solely to benefit specific people proposing various programmes (Lu & Cai, 2015). The main concern among councillors was the potential conflicts between representative democracy and PB, which involves different ideas regarding PB and the conceptualisation of democracy.

The Department of Civil Affairs of the Taipei City Government is the main governmental agency responsible for promoting PB, and each district's office is responsible for the implementation of PB activities in their district through the civil affairs system. One unique aspect of Taipei City Government's promotion of PB is that the government invited the academic community to form a 'participatory budgeting government–academia alliance' and promoted it with the model of 'local partnership'. Each administrative district was matched to local academic institutions, and the accompanying schools' advice and support were sought for design and implementation. Members of the government–academia alliance include the Department of Civil Affairs, district offices, partner schools (i.e. nine universities in Taipei City, and three community colleges), professional counsellor teams and grassroots organisations. The Department of Civil Affairs developed the 6-in-1 strategy, which combines PB training and deliberative activities related to six themes: preliminary PB courses, advanced PB courses, continued facilitator training courses, proposal presentation, resident assemblies and a deliberative workshop for proposals. The Department of Civil Affairs created the platform and organised meetings to invite the partnership members to discuss PB procedures. Meetings of the PB working team, composed of district office personnel and representatives of partner schools, were held regularly. District offices provided internship opportunities for students, and partner schools assisted in recruiting students to serve as facilitators and recorders for resident assemblies (Taipei City Government, 2017b; see Figure 7.1). The Taipei City Government aims to promote PB and strengthen democracy through professional counselling and the collaboration and participation of universities and educational institutions.

Mayor Ko explained on Facebook why training workshops had been planned across the 12 districts of Taipei City, with a particular emphasis on the

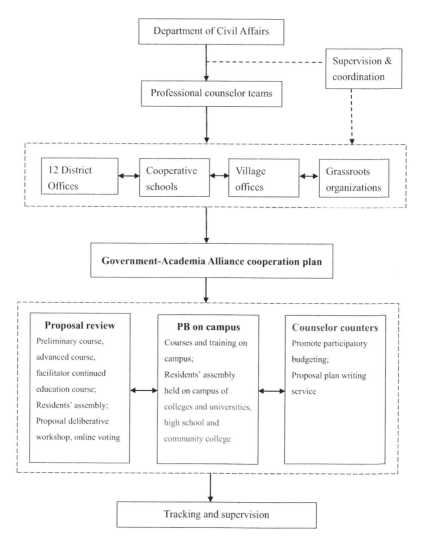

Figure 7.1 Organisation of Taipei City Government's PB partnership cooperation plan
Source: Taipei City Government (2017b).

two basic principles of PB: 'budget transparency' and 'training'. The training workshops comprised three stages designed to help residents understand PB and how proposals can be submitted and voted on and to cultivate their ability to moderate. Training courses on PB were divided into preliminary courses, advanced courses and facilitator continued-education courses. These courses lasted for 3, 6 and 9 hours, respectively. The courses were organised to provide citizens with a step-by-step understanding of PB. Participants who completed the 18-hour training course obtained the '369+Buzzing card', which qualified them to moderate discussions in residents' assemblies. In December 2015, each administrative district began to conduct PB training workshops for citizens and public sector personnel. All three courses had recruited numerous participants by September 2017 (preliminary training course, 4,464; advanced training course, 822; and facilitator continued education course, 72; see Taipei City Government, 2017b). The Department of Civil Affairs adjusts the structure and content of these education courses and determines whether to offer them depending on actual needs.

Taipei City Government oversees each bureau's budgeting to increase the transparency and clarity of the general budget and allow residents to supervise government spending. The budget visualising website was launched in September 2015 and empowers users to develop value-added applications by taking advantage of the accessible and comprehendible data provided on the website. Users can offer opinions or ask questions through the feedback mechanism, and relevant bureaus can respond to residents' questions on the website. The budget visualisation website allows residents to obtain a clearer picture of the city's budget breakdown and enables each bureau to understand residents' budgeting concerns (Taipei City Government, 2020).

Research method

Participant observation, documentary analysis and interviews with policy stakeholders and residents were conducted from 2016 to 2018. The Deputy Commissioner of the Department of Civil Affairs approached scholars with expertise and experiences in deliberative democracy or participatory governance and three community universities before PB was launched in late 2015. I was invited to participate in an academic partnership with Beitou District Office PB working teams to provide suggestions and train students to serve as facilitators in residents' assemblies and training courses. Beitou Community College promotes deliberative democracy and has extensive experience in conducting deliberative activities and, thus, was also invited to collaborate with the Beitou District Office to promote PB. The data employed included official reports, working meeting records, reports of all stages of PB, records of legislatures, archival material and media coverage. Participants and project proposers in resident assemblies, members of Beitou Community College, the head of the village, senior officers from the District Office and Department of Civil Affairs in Taipei City Government and the director from the council office were interviewed to determine their views regarding PB. The interactions and connections of deliberative practices in the political context and their dynamics were also investigated.

Connectivity of deliberative practices at multiple sites

PB procedures focus on facilitating public deliberation, which consists of residents' assembly, proposal deliberative workshops, public exhibition, online voting and the Taipei Citizen Participation Committee's Budget

Review Group for final reading. The PB procedure and deliberative activities in each stage are dynamic and interconnected with the deliberation of other institutions, such as the council, city government and the Taipei Citizen Participation Committee.[1] PB creates new discursive and communication spaces and strengthens the connectivity of everyday talk and micro and macro deliberative systems.

Building partnerships and deliberation on PB design

Establishing the professional counsellor team and the government–academia alliance of Taipei City Government differs from the model of service outsourcing used in other cities and is at the core of PB promotion. The professional counsellor team is composed of experts and scholars of politics, social affairs and public administration in universities and community colleges in Taipei City. Approximately 50 experts and professionals serve as PB counsellors, providing professional knowledge and advice on PB design and promoting training courses.

The Department of Civil Affairs proposed the standard operating procedure (SOP) and invited scholars from partner universities and community colleges to participate in a planning meeting to provide suggestions and deliberate on the design of the procedures and the key rules for PB. The Department of Civil Affairs revised the experimental SOP, promoted PB flexibility and allowed each administrative district office to adjust the rules according to different local circumstances and particularities, following dialogue and wide-ranging discussions. The SOP was then approved by the Taipei Citizen Participation Committee. Furthermore, partnership universities and community colleges can provide feedback and suggestions to the Department of Civil Affairs and district administrative offices during the PB process. The Department of Civil Affairs also invited scholars and civic organisation activists with expertise in deliberative democracy or PB to join the Teacher Group as seeded teachers who instructed the training workshop and participated in the partnership meetings to reach consensus regarding the promotion and implementation of PB.

The Department of Civil Affairs emphasises 'rolling ways of learning', which consists of a PB model for Taipei City that continuously evolves and is transformed through acting, problem-solving, learning and refining. The city government invited academics from partner universities and community colleges to review the procedures and operational problems before the second PB cycle began to reach consensus regarding the revision of SOP procedures and general guidelines while allowing each district office and partnership university to maintain the necessary flexibility to modify the arrangement for residents' assemblies and deliberative practices. The district civil administration office invited partner scholars and representatives of community colleges to join working group meetings to discuss the designs (such as when to hold, how to recruit for and how to conduct residents' assemblies) and procedures and to determine whether the general rules required modifications before PB is promoted and implemented in the district.

Residents' assemblies in 12 districts and on campus

PB proposal review procedures are divided into four phases: residents' assembly, deliberative proposal workshop, proposal exhibition and proposal voting. The Department of Civil Affairs held a briefing session on PB public meetings in each administrative district before the residents' assembly to increase residents' understanding of PB, proposal processes and how to make proposals. Each district office organised the residents' general assemblies.

Residents' assemblies emphasise ideas of deliberative democracy. Participants develop proposals through focus group discussions by sharing ideas, listening to other participants' feedback and then developing and revising a proposal. Moderators and recorders must follow the deliberative procedures to ensure equal opportunity for expressing ideas. Each group can put forward one or two proposals. All participants vote to select proposals for the assembly. In general, proposals with 50% or more votes are selected for the deliberative workshop. Taipei City set 5+1 themes (five themes with one optional, additional theme) for the first year in 2016 to prevent divergent thinking. Each district office discussed the principle of 5+1, which comprised the residents' activity centre and the citizens' hall renovation programme, city community garden promotion, neighbourhood park community environmental improvement, road and sidewalk improvement, commercial area reengineering and other proposals. Each district has developed deliberative designs and procedures according to the local characteristics and the overall considerations of deliberative ideals and feasibility. Different designs and styles have resulted in different effects.

One of the primary concerns regarding the design of the operation of PB raised during the government–academia alliance meeting was whether excluding the head of the neighbourhood is necessary for a budget proposal. At first, a few scholars argued for the need to reduce the possibility of established political power taking political advantage to mobilise people in support of their budget proposals. The government–academia alliance reached the consensus that there was no need to limit the heads of neighbourhoods from proposing budget ideas among residents because the heads of neighbourhoods would fail to obtain public support if their proposal was not perceived to have common good. However, each district office must ensure that participants are randomly distributed to each focus group discussion, and the facilitator must treat heads of neighbourhoods in the same manner as the general public to reduce the risk of neighbourhood political elites dominating the PB process.

In 2016 and 2017, 83 rounds of residents' assemblies were held, with 4,296 participants. According to the 2017 statistics of Taipei City Government, the average age of PB participants was 57 years, and 62% of the participants were female. PB attracted numerous young people, who had previously seldom participated in public affairs, to participate in the residents' general assembly and to be concerned with and involved in community affairs. Among the participants, 48.6% were retired men and homemakers, whereas the neighbourhood heads only comprised 3.3% of attendants. Furthermore, 63% of the participants reported being informed of the residents' assembly from the office of the head of the village (Taipei City Government, 2017b).

The majority of participants in residents' assemblies had favourable deliberative characteristics, such as communicating rationally and listening to other participant's opinions. Few participants were present to vote for a certain proposal without interest in deliberation with others. Among the 93 budget proposals that qualified for online voting in 2017, 27 proposals (24.7%) were put forward by heads of villages. People tend to believe that proposals by political elites or heads of neighbourhoods and villages can obtain more support because they can mobilise people to back their proposal. A few councillors have also stated that PB has become a tool for certain persons, such as heads of neighbourhoods, to compete for resources. However, the Deputy Commissioner of the Department of Civil Affairs recognised that residents are capable of rationally judging each proposal's public value when deciding whether to give their support and that the proposals of the heads of villages sometimes fail to obtain public support. Participants tend to think that people are capable of deliberating, distinguishing the difference between proposals that are beneficial to public and private interests, and voting for proposals based on the importance of the topic rather than who put forward the proposal.[2]

PB also gives students the opportunity to voice their needs and receive responses and support. The 'participatory budgeting on campus' initiative was implemented by the Department of Civil Affairs, the Department of Education, district offices, partner schools, public and private universities, community colleges and public and private senior and vocational high schools in Taipei City. The Department of Civil Affairs works with the Department of Education to teach deliberative democracy and PB to students through curriculum education and participation intending to promote citizenship practice. The initiative offers either 'preliminary courses' or 'preliminary courses plus resident general assembly' at the discretion of the hosting school. Furthermore, basic course completion cards, certifications of training hours and certificates of participation are offered based on the type of training programmes to encourage students to participate in the initiative. In 2017, 1 junior high school, 9 senior and vocational senior high schools, 4 public and private universities and 12 community colleges participated in the initiative, with a total of 1,145 participants. In 2017, 4 out of 71 budget proposals were produced from the assemblies on high school campuses (Taipei City Government, 2017b).

Residents' assemblies held on campus can encourage students to rethink the connection between universities and communities, universities' social responsibilities and how students can contribute to community affairs. Residents' assemblies on university campuses offer students the opportunity to learn to discuss and deliberate with residents who live in the neighbourhood. This space allows the younger and older generations to have active discussions, deliberate on local public affairs and consider how they can work together to improve local communities.

The information desk and citizen proposal information platform

Citizens are also offered instant and convenient consultation channels to facilitate the operation of the PB system. The Taipei Department of Civil Affairs opened information desks in all 12 district offices to assist the public in putting forward budget ideas and proposals to improve their neighbourhoods. Mayor Ko visited the Neihu District office to announce the launch of the information desk service. The media broadcast a drama in which the mayor played the part of an old man living in Da'an District who wanted to see Da'an Forest Park beautified but was confused as to what PB was and how it works. The city government employees gave Ko an application and a form for submitting a proposal and guided him through the process of filling out the forms. During the skit, Ko asked 'Will you put my proposal into practice? Is it for real?', to which one of the employees responded, 'Of course it is for real; have you not heard how mean our Mayor is? We have meetings at 7 am and often work until late at night' (Lin, 2017). The drama aimed to demonstrate Mayor Ko's determination to promote PB and provide residents with assistance so they can share their policy ideas and proposals.

PB counsellor counters have been established by Taipei City Government in 12 district offices. Students from partner schools are trained by the Department of Civil Affairs and district offices to serve as counsellors, help citizens understand the PB system and facilitate citizen participation.[3] Students and members of community colleges have the opportunity to serve as interns or take part-time jobs serving on the information desk to assist the public in completing the process of submitting a proposal. By August 2017, nearly 40 students had served 3,870 citizens at counsellor counters (Taipei City Government, 2017b). Students can play multiple roles (e.g. residents in assemblies, facilitators, intern counsellors) and participate in different areas and stages of PB. Student roles in the participatory process include facilitating, taking notes, providing information desk services, accompanying residents to put forward propositions and communicating information and ideas.

Taipei City Government set up the Citizen Budget Proposal and PB Information Platform websites to facilitate information circulation, increase information transparency and increase citizens' understanding of PB through visualisation of each bureau's budget proposal map. On the online platform, residents can access PB information, register for PB courses and submit a budget proposal that will be discussed at residents' assemblies. The Taipei City Government collaborated with open source communities and activists of the information movement for the budget visualisation project, which is crucial for social learning and reshaping civic society discourses.

Deliberative workshop and citizen proposal review committee

The budget proposals favoured by the majority of voters in the residents' assembly are taken to the deliberative workshops to refine proposals. A PB proposal indicates that 'problems to be resolved' and 'possible solutions' are established (Taipei City Government, 2017b). The principal and related governmental agencies and professional urban planners are invited by the district administrative office to participate in the deliberative workshop to discuss the feasibility of the proposal. The general public can also attend the workshop to provide opinions. Participants are divided into small focus groups to deliberate each proposal. Each group then selects the residents' representatives to attend the follow-up citizen proposal review committee.

To facilitate the smooth operation of the workshop, the Department of Civil Affairs requested that each district office should invite representatives from the principal and relevant authority to discuss the nature of the proposal and the division of labour before the deliberative workshop. The complexity of each proposal case differs. The governmental authority and residents reach consensus more rapidly through deliberation on the proposal and how to implement it if the idea of the proposal is relatively simple. However, if the idea of a proposal is very complex, such as multifaceted and cross-departmental affairs, more time discussions of the ideas of the proposal and identifying the duties of the related government agencies would be required, which involves negotiation and justification. The proposals are then presented to a citizen review committee that will provide professional input and suggestions to refined related ideas. The Department of Civil Affairs invites the relevant authorities, experts and scholars, representatives of the residents and residents who presented the selected proposals to discuss and assess the proposals and prioritise their plans.

A criticism of scholars is that the communication and dialogue in the review committee, gathered to improve PB design and operation after the first year, resemble the review of a commissioned project. Furthermore, scholars have reported that the few experts invited to participate in the process did not appear to grasp the essence of PB, and the experts' comments differed from the original idea proposed by residents.[4] In response to the critiques, the Department of Civil Affairs implemented changes to the design of the review process. In 2017, the proposal deliberative workshop was divided into two phases: proposal discussion and proposal review. In the first phase of the proposal discussion, the proposer and the responsible agencies discuss how to refine the proposal and identify alternatives to infeasible aspects; second, experts and scholars provide advice regarding modifications of the proposal. In the second phase of the proposal review, the citizen review team reviews the publicity, legality and budget feasibility of the proposal. The budgeting proposal must satisfy a feasibility assessment before final approval is obtained. The review committee further considers and assesses the proposal's public interests. In 2016 and 2017, 42 proposal deliberative workshops were held with 1,727 participants (Taipei City Government, 2017b). This approach creates a space for face-to-face communication between government agencies and residents and encourages high-level justification.

Public exhibition and i-Voting

Before proposal voting, the Department of Civil Affairs and district offices organise proposal exhibitions, which include online and on-site exhibitions, to help citizens understand the content of the proposals and allow them to express their opinions. The public can express any opinions regarding the proposals to the district administrative offices, either directly or online, during the period of public exhibition of proposals in the district administrative offices. After discussion within the residents' assembly and review in the proposal workshop, proposals with high or medium publicity that are legal and financially feasible are qualified for voting. Citizens, students, workers and residents aged 16 years or over and living in Taipei City are eligible to vote in District offices. Registered citizens of Taipei City are eligible to vote online. Proposals with more votes than the given threshold are implemented. In 2017, 93 candidate proposals were voted on using i-Voting. The online voting, which ran between 30 June and 13 July 2017, attracted 57,486 votes, and 71 proposals secured sufficient votes for implementation. The three districts with the highest voter turnout were Wenshan (8,355), Da'an (6,186) and Neihu (5,879). The proposal that received the most support was 'Optimisation of Wenshan District's Jingmei Sports Park', which garnered 7,262 votes. Each of the 12 districts collected over 2,000 votes (Taipei City Government, 2017b).

The Department of Civil Affairs attempted to increase residents' interest in PB and encourage voting by setting up voting booths in partner schools and transforming a dining car into a movable ballot box on campus to attract students' and youths' attention. In the PB process for the FY 2018 Budget, Taipei City Government organised 46 residents' assemblies and 31 deliberative and review workshops. A total of 3,896 residents participated in the activities, which led to 42 cases for implementation and 49 cases to be submitted to i-Voting for the final decision. A total of 102,948 people participated in i-Voting (Taipei City Government, 2018). PB participation has increased since 2015. The i-voting process broadens citizen participation and complements other components of PB. For example, residents' assemblies are limited to 60 participants to avoid large crowds affecting deliberative quality.

Budgeting evaluation and review and council supervision

The Department of Civil Affairs is responsible for handling preliminary examinations of the budgets with related agencies, conducting case budget reviews to determine the budget for public affairs and sending budget proposals to the Taipei Citizen Participation Committee's Budget Review Group for final reading. Approved proposals are incorporated into the city government's general budget proposal and sent to the Annual Plan and Budget Review Committee of the government for review. The budget is sent to Taipei City Council for approval before the end of August.

The budgeting system is flexible: low-cost policies are implemented with available funds in the year they are proposed, whereas higher-cost policies are held over a year until new budgets are approved by the Taipei City Council. The final steps of PB procedures are proposal implementation and management. The Department of Civil Affairs introduced a proposal management system website that provides the complete 'production history' of a proposal, which covers conception, review, budgeting and the final results of its implementation. The progress and budget of each proposal are based on the adjustments to which the responsible agency and the proposer have agreed.

The Department of Civil Affairs faces challenges regarding the implementation of certain budget proposals and the justification of certain projects to councillors. For example, the Department of Civil Affairs and responsible agencies may not be able to implement certain proposals concerning a garden city and the renovation of parks if the proposal involves private property, the central government's affairs or the limitations of land use for urban planning, because reviewing and changing urban planning laws takes years. A budget proposal that requires a particular engineering method or information technology system, which only a small number of firms can perform, calls into question whether the proposal involves private profits. Negotiations will be conducted if a proposal contains several items, some of which are regarded as infeasible, or if the proposal can be implemented partly or divided into several stages (Interviewee F, Department of Civil Affairs). The officer of the Department of Civil Affairs reported that some representatives attending deliberative workshops do not review proposals seriously during the first year of PB and some proposals involve problems concerning legal feasibility. The agencies must have flexible outlooks and communicate with the proposer to revise the rules of the subsidies. The Taipei City Citizen Participation Committee plays a crucial role in providing suggestions and being involved in negotiations, and a few commissions have volunteered to be mediators between governmental agencies and proposers to allow both sides to reach a compromise on the implementation of the proposal (Interviewee H, Department of Civil Affairs). The Taipei City Citizen Participation Committee is crucial in enhancing mutual understanding.

Evolving of PB and democratic imagination

The Department of Civil Affairs has considered adjusting and diversifying the channels and times of PB assemblies to encourage the participation of vulnerable groups and residents of all ages. Residents aged 25–45 years have the lowest level of participation. Residents who are providers for their families may not have the time to participate in discussions and proposals (Taipei City Government, 2017b). The Department of Civil Affairs organised a New Immigrants Participatory Budgeting Proposal Meeting on 22 July 2016 at the Wanhua New Immigrants' Hall to allow ethnic minorities the opportunity to propose a PB plan, thus more accurately reflecting the demographic composition of Taipei City.[5] During the Proposal Meeting in 2017, new immigrant participants were divided into small groups for discussion and proposed five programmes. All of the proposed programmes passed with over 50% of the vote. During the PB proposal workshop session, these five programmes were discussed between the new immigrant proposers and representatives from the Department of Civil Affairs, the Department of Social Welfare and the Department of Labour. A member of the Taipei City Citizen Participation Committee and a professor were also invited to participate. The Citizen's review panel then reviewed the proposals in the second phase. Deliberative practice increases the 'inclusion' of participants.

In addition to the new migrant PB assemblies, a few scholars from partner schools suggested that the Department of Civil Affairs could learn from the experience of the New Taipei City Government to conduct PB Disability Assemblies. These deliberative practices echo the argument that 'systemic distribution can promote equality' (Bächtiger et al., 2018, p. 15). Karpowitz and Raphael (2014) argued that political equality in the deliberative system as a whole may be optimally implemented by 'asking the least powerful citizens to deliberate among themselves in their forums' and that

> integrating 'enclave' deliberation among the least powerful participants in civic forums can motivate the marginalised to participate, develop their civic capacities, and create productive tensions between identifying their shared interests and considering how their interest relates to a larger common good.
>
> (p. 7)

In the first year of the experimental implementation of PB, most district offices only held one residents' assembly in the district office or residents' activity centre nearby.[6] Most participants were residents who lived close to the district office because participation was less convenient for those living further from the town centre. Several township and village heads located far from the district office argued that it was unfair to hold residents' assemblies far from their villages. Another crucial concern was that most participants who lived close to the district office tended to vote for budget proposals that were beneficial to the development of nearby neighbourhoods rather than those far away from their own houses. Considering these problems and the positive experiences of resident assemblies held in the subdistricts of Da'an District, the Department of Civil Affairs and partner schools decided to hold residents' assemblies in each sub-district in 2017 to broaden participation and increase accessibility for residents living in remote areas.

Policy stakeholders and residents have different expectations and democratic ideas regarding PB. The officer of the Department of Civil Affairs and some policy actors (e.g. councillors, heads of villages, civic organisations, community development associations) attempt to obtain resources from PB processes, whereas others want to supervise or participate in the PB stages. The government has tried to optimise the transparency and equality of the PB process and provide all information on the PB website to demonstrate that the government does not intentionally distribute resources to specific people (Interviewee H, Department of Civil Affairs).

Some community and advocate groups have mobilised their members and supporters to participate to advance their advocated policies. Some civic organisations regard PB as an opportunity to facilitate civic participation and deliberative democracy. Before the Taipei City Government promoted PB, Beitou Community College implemented the first PB session in 2013, which was initiated by a grassroots group with support from the Youth Platform Foundation, which engages in promoting youth participation and deliberative democracy. Beitou Community College devoted efforts to raising community awareness and regard by promoting deliberative democracy and PB combined with educating the public as one of its main missions. Three community universities with high-quality academic reputations were invited by the Department of Civil Affairs to join the alliance; therefore, they had the opportunity to participate in the design of PB operations and encouraged members to participate in the PB processes, collaborate with district offices, promote PB concepts, conduct training courses in neighbourhood high schools and obtain prompt responses from the district offices and the Department of Civic Affairs.

The PB processes create new deliberative spaces for the co-construction of life narratives, local knowledge and public value. The budget proposal of 'Reproduce local history and culture: A cultural and historical survey of Xinyi District through public–private partnership' is a distinctive example. Xinyi District is often considered by outsiders as a place without history. Li-Pin Huang, the PB plan proposer, developed a strong affection for the district after working in Xinyi Community College for many years. He indicated that most residents in Xinyi District did not feel that they had a deep understanding of their community. Therefore, he put forward a proposal to gather funds, through PB, to conduct a systematic cultural and historical survey of Xinyi District. The director of Taipei City Archives, Su-Chen Chan, also considered the proposal valuable because, among the current 18 guided historical routes operated by the Taipei City Archives, at least one route passes each district except for Xinyi District. After accepting this proposal, Director Chan organised several meetings with the proposer and Xinyi District officials to confirm the scope of the proposal. Mr Huang indicated that he was glad that the plan was initiated in April 2017 and implemented through public–private partnership. The results from the interviews of local seniors and the cultural and historical survey were then used to train local guides through tours, manuals and school forums (Taipei City Government, 2017b).

Some heads of villages support and participate in residents' assemblies as residents or proposers, whereas others do not support PB or simply observe proceedings from the sidelines. Instead of making proposals, some heads of villages attend residents' assemblies to further understand residents' opinions and determine whether the proposals put forward are consistent or oppose their policy positions. For heads of villages and residents who are busy or live in remote areas, PB is time-consuming and participation comes at a high cost because the proposer must attend during every stage of the PB process. A few heads of villages did not believe that promoting PB was necessary because other existing public participation channels could address residents' problems, such as having a meeting with the mayor or asking a councillor to address local problems by using the Mayor Mailbox or calling the 1999 Citizens' Hotline (Interviewee B, Head of a village in a remote area of the sub-district). The Department of Civil Affairs attempted to simplify the PB process to provide citizens with simplified participatory mechanisms to increase citizen participation.

Councillors who initially questioned and criticised PB have since attempted to understand it. An increasing number of councillors and employees from the offices of councillors have attended the residents' assemblies to understand residents' opinions, supervise the process and express their ideas or provide suggestions on PB to the Department of Civil Affairs (Interviewee H, Department of Civil Affairs). The PB process facilitates dialogue and communication between councillors and the Department of Civil Affairs, in formal and informal settings, concerning improving PB and the effect of PB on local politics. Wan (2018) indicated that in certain PB cases outside Taipei City, the existing power relations were reproduced rather than challenged. However, the experience of Taipei City reveals that PB provides another channel and equal opportunity for ordinary citizens and community organisations to participate in policy-making and reshape local politics.

At a press conference, the mayor reported that the results of PB were a 'big step towards direct democracy' (Taipei City Government, 2017a). The Deputy Commissioner of the Department of Civil Affairs reported that PB engenders substantive changes in administrative institutions, facilitates information sharing, and increases dialogue between government agencies and citizens, and enables agencies to make decisions based on the positions of residents. Furthermore, several proposals involved multiple agencies' authority, which facilitated interaction, dialogue and negotiation between governmental officers on the distribution of labour and responsibilities in the project proposal.

Each component of PB has a function in increasing the deliberative quality of the deliberative system (see Table 7.1). The original institutional design of each component's functions, whether each component has reached

Table 7.1 Functions of the PB process in deliberative systems

PB process	Crucial functions
Partnership network and meeting	Dynamically deliberating on, reflecting on and adjusting the design and implementation of PB; accumulating knowledge and experience; enhancing the interaction between governmental agencies, district offices, universities and community colleges.
Education course	Enhancing government officers', residents' and students' knowledge of PB and deliberative capacities.
Residents' assembly	Residents have equal opportunity to (1) express ideas and present proposals; and (2) express opinions, preferences and decisions that are informed by facts and based on relevant reasons. Knowledge and information can circulate among residents.
Deliberative workshops and proposal review committee	Face-to-face and two-way communication between government agencies, residents, representatives of residents and experts to refine the proposal; review and justify the public interest and feasibility of the proposal.
Public exhibition	Enable information transparency; residents have the opportunity to provide suggestions.
Proposal i-Voting	Broaden participation; facilitate further conversations.
Taipei City Citizen Participation Committee	Serves as a third-party or mediator between budget proposers and governmental agencies; increases mutual understanding between government agencies and budget proposers; learn to respect, adjust and reach compromise regarding the implementation of the proposal.
Citizen Budget Proposal and PB Information Platform	Facilitates information circulation, increases information transparency and increases citizens' understanding of PB; open budget data and budget visualisations facilitate social learning and reshape civic society discourses.

the partnership cooperation plan's goal and any changes in the role and functions warrant examination. PB has facilitated ongoing conversation on institutionalising citizen participation. In September 2018, the Taiwan Citizen Participation Association collaborated with eight councillors to hold a press conference and vision meeting, and officials from Taipei City Government were invited to attend. Before reporting the survey results of national citizen participation, the Taiwan City Participation Association led the attending councillors, government officials and civic groups in chanting the slogan, 'Citizens: big, big, big; government: small, small, small', and emphasised the six core aspects of citizen participation, comprising open government, information transparency, accountability, complete regulations, citizen empowerment and innovative tools. The Taiwan Citizen Participation Association

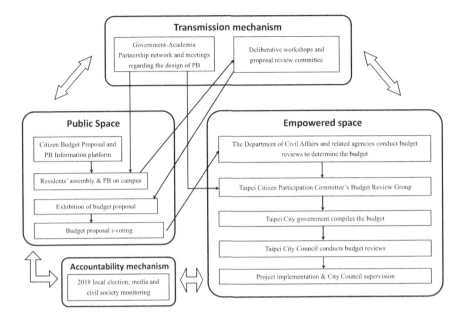

Figure 7.2 The PB deliberative system

recognised the function of the Taipei City Citizen Participation Committee, provided policy recommendations and indicated that each bureau should be encouraged to align affairs with citizen participation and invite more civic groups to discuss how to improve PB. Several councillors indicated that the government must review, adjust and institutionalise citizen participation. Taipei City Government officials responded positively to the Taiwan Citizen Participation Association and councillors at the meeting. The councillors further requested that each bureau submit a formal response to the Research, Development and Evaluation Commission of Taipei City Government (PeoPo Citizen News, 2018). The discursive practices accelerated information transmission and displayed both positive and negative feedback loops between the public space and the empowered space (see Figure 7.2).

Discussion and conclusion

The government–academia alliance approach has facilitated increased interaction between government officials and academic institutions, civic organisations, residents and neighbourhood social networks. Universities, local civic organisations and academics provide local knowledge, expertise, human resources and consultant services by collaborating with the district office and the Department of Civil Affairs to promote PB. Universities, community colleges and civic organisations play active roles in promoting the multiple epistemic–ethical–democratic functions of the different components of deliberative systems. The government–academia alliance collectively adjusts and revises the PB process through deliberation, and scholars of cooperative schools and professional counsellor teams continuously consider how to broaden participation and improve the quality of public deliberation. Several scholars have recognised that the value of the government–academia alliance model of PB is that it helps to increase public trust in the Taipei City Government's promotion of PB.[7]

University campuses and high schools have become crucial deliberative sites. The idea of university social responsibility (USR) is increasingly regarded as an intrinsic aspect of the higher education system, particularly in public universities. The government has begun to emphasise the concept of USR as an assessment criterion of funding for universities and require that universities fulfil their social responsibility. Some scholars regard the government–academia alliance approach as an opportunity to strengthen the connection between universities and local communities and fulfil USR. In addition to providing training courses in PB at neighbourhood activities centres and universities, certain cooperative schools also collaborate with the district office to hold residents' assemblies on campus, thereby increasing accessibility for students to participate in PB and create PB proposals. Residents' assemblies on campus are open to resident participation. This space enables active discussion and deliberation between the younger and older generations concerning local public affairs and improving local communities. This demonstrates that multiple approaches are available for student, university and community college engagement in PB to contribute to the deliberative system.

Instead of considering the process of PB as being manipulated by the authorities or a few politicians, members of civic groups and an increasing number of residents regard PB as an approach to participation in neighbourhood affairs. Participants of residents' assemblies collectively engage in deliberation on ideas and proposals that promote public values and public interests. These residents' assemblies become crucial deliberative spaces for the construction of life narratives, local knowledge and public values.

The evolving PB process enables fluid interaction and the production of numerous forms of knowledge, values, social relations and collaborations between policy stakeholders and trans-governmental agencies. Each administrative district is matched with local academic institutions to promote and implement PB. Furthermore, each administrative district has a different political culture; local institutions and civic organisations have different social expectations and democratic imaginations of PB, thus, each district has a unique approach to promoting and networking. Therefore, each district has demonstrated its particular characteristics of PB. Deliberative practices are developed during the PB process, which connect to other components of the deliberative systems and promote deliberative democratisation at the wider systemic level. This sparked further deliberation outside the scope of this event, and education courses have had deliberative capacity-building effects. The dynamic connections of various discussions and deliberations in various spaces and at different stages of the PB cycle enable neighbourhoods and local governances to move towards transparent and deliberative democracy.

Notes

1 The Taipei City Government established the Taipei Citizen Participation Committee to realise the political ideal of open government and public participation, obtain citizens' opinions on policy-making and effectively diminish the gap between policy and public expectations. The Committee includes members outside the Taipei City Government selected from the public, experts and NGOs seeking to enhance transparent governance, citizen participation and collaboration. Taipei Citizen Participation Committee's Budget Review Group holds monthly meetings.
2 Interviewee K, who has attended a PB education course, the residents' assembly and citizen review meetings.
3 The counsellor counters provide the following services: (1) Accept proposals for PB; (2) Provide consultation on the conception and compilation of proposals for PB; (3) Organise continuing training programs for PB, proposal forums, and registration of the residents' assembly; (4) Provide consultation on other matters related to PB.
4 For example, one proposal concerns planting vegetables on the roof of the Beitou District Office to create a garden city and share the organic vegetables with the elders in the neighbourhood. The budget would be used for relevant equipment. However, the urban planning expert suggested that planting vegetables on the land in the neighbourhood would be preferable.
5 The Department of Civil Affairs hosted education and promotion courses for recent immigrants to understand Taipei City's relevant policy implementations and to learn about deliberative democracy and the methods of proposing a PB plan. This was offered to allow the immigrants to develop policy proposals and participate in city administration. The students were recent immigrants, relevant organisations, public servants and city residents who were concerned with topics relevant for recent immigrants.
6 Da'an District collaborated with Professor K.-M. Lin of the Department of Sociology at National Taiwan University to hold five citizen assemblies in the sub-district in 2016.
7 Roundtable on PB in Taipei City during the 2018 Annual Conference of Public Administration, Taipei.

References

Anderson, B. (1991). *Imagined communities: Reflections on the origin and spread of nationalism*. London: Verso.
Bächtiger, A., Dryzek, J., Mansbridge, J., & Warren, M. (2018). Deliberative democracy: An introduction. In A. Bächtiger, J. Dryzek, J. Mansbridge, & M. Warren (Eds.), *Handbook of deliberative democracy* (pp. 1–31). Oxford: Oxford University Press.

Cabannes, Y. (2004). Participatory budgeting: A significant contribution to participatory democracy. *Environment & Urbanization, 16*(1), 27–46.

Curato, N., & Böker, M. (2016) Linking mini-publics to the deliberative system: A research agenda. *Policy Sciences, 49*(2), 173–190.

Ebdon, C., & Franklin, A. (2006). Citizen participation in budgeting theory. *Public Administration Review, 66*, 437–447.

Habermas, J. (1989). *The structural transformation of the public sphere: An inquiry into a category of bourgeois society*, translated by T. Burger and F. Lawrence. Cambridge, MA: MIT Press.

Hartz-Karp, J. (2012). Laying the groundwork for participatory budgeting: Developing a deliberative community and collaborative governance: Greater Geraldton, Western Australia. *Journal of Public Deliberation, 8*(2), 6. www.publicdeliberation. net/jpd/vol8/iss2/art6

Hasegawa, K., Shinohara, C., & Broadbent, J. P. (2007). The effects of 'social expectation' on the development of civil society in Japan. *Journal of Civil Society, 3*(2), 179–203.

Justice, J., & Dülger, C. (2009). Fiscal transparency and authentic citizen participation in public budgeting: The role of third-party intermediation. *Journal of Public Budgeting, Accounting & Financial Management, 21*(2), 254–288.

Karpowitz, C., & Raphael, C. (2014). *Deliberation, democracy, and civic forums: Improving equality and publicity*. Cambridge: Cambridge University Press.

Ko, W.-J. (2014). *i-Voting and participatory budgeting* [White paper]. Taipei City Government. https://doctorkowj.gitbooks.io/kppolicy/content/chapter_1/1_i-voting__3.html

Lin, S. (2017, February 9). Ko promotes his participatory budget process as city opens information desks. *Taipei Times*. www.taipeitimes.com/News/taiwan/archives/2017/02/09/2003664643

Lu, H.-Q., & Cai, Y.-H. (2015, October 2). Councilmen criticize 5 million dollars of participatory budgeting. *Liberty Times*. http://news.ltn.com.tw/news/local/paper/920327

Newton, K. (2012). Curing the democratic malaise with democratic innovations. In B. Geissel & K. Newton (Eds.), *Evaluating democratic innovations: Curing the democratic malaise?* (pp. 3–20). Oxon: Routledge.

PeoPo Citizen News. (2018, September 4). How could Taipei City government overcome obstacles of citizen participation in participatory budgeting? *PeoPo Citizen News*. www.peopo.org/news/377997

Smith, G. (2009). *Democratic innovations: Designing institutions for citizen participation*. New York, NY: Cambridge University Press.

Stevenson, H., & Dryzek, J. S. (2014). *Democratizing global climate governance*. Cambridge: Cambridge University Press.

Taipei City Government. (2017a). Mayor: Participatory budgeting is the most important realization of open government and citizen participation. www.gov.taipei/News_Content.aspx?n=F0DDAF49B89E9413&sms=72544237BBE4C5F6&s=22959E0BD03B4CEB

Taipei City Government. (2017b, October). Appendix I: Summary of Participatory Budgeting in Taipei. Paper presented at the International Symposium of Participatory Budgeting: Review and Prospect of Participatory Budgeting in Taipei. Taipei, Taiwan.

Taipei City Government (2018). City news: Mayor promises to continue participatory budget policy. https://english.gov.taipei/News_Content.aspx?n=A11F01CFC9F58 C83&sms=DFFA119D1FD5602C&s=17E77B8C7BF9F17E

Taipei City Government (2020). *Budget Visualised.* w2.dbas.gov.taipei/vbudget/

Wan, P. Y. (2018). Outsourcing participatory democracy: Critical reflections on the participatory budgeting experiences in Taiwan. *Journal of Public Deliberation, 14*(1), 7. www.publicdeliberation.net/jpd/vol14/iss1/art7

8 Conclusion

The co-evolution of deliberative systems

This book highlights multiple deliberative practices across various scales and periods. It explores different transmission mechanisms and associations of deliberative systems' components, the co-evolution processes of technology and the policy and deliberation practices at play. Bucchi and Neresunu (2008) believed that science and technology have become resources for new social movements to organise, act and form their identity, but they also believe that different forms of civil society participation can exist depending on the local context and the nature of the controversy. They argued that the key question is 'under what conditions do different forms of public participation emerge' rather than 'which model of participation accounts best' for expert–public interactions (Bucchi & Neresunu, 2008, pp. 454–455). In developing a co-productionist account of participation, Chilvers and Kearnes (2016) argued that 'emergent participatory experiments and practices are both shaped by – and, in turn, shape – technoscientific, political and social orders' (p. 14).

Geels (2002) also argued that technological transitions occur as the outcome of linkages and interactions of developments at multiple levels. Technological transitions as evolutionary reconfiguration processes involve changes in not only technology but also infrastructure, user practices, industrial networks, cultural construction and the regulatory landscape. The co-evolution perspective elucidates linkages, the dynamics of change and the evolution of how ICT is used and practiced in multisite deliberations and in deliberative policy-making processes. For example, the novel utilisation of ICTs and social media during the Occupy movement and 'street deliberation' practices in the Sunflower Movement created and enlarged spaces of deliberation and dialogue and accelerated the development of both information activism and the institutionalising of democratic innovations, such as vTaiwan (Chapters 2 and 5). Citizen Congress Watch's evaluation of legislative performance and the utilisation of the VOD system enable the public to scrutinise lawmakers' conduct, contributing to greater transparency in legislative debates (Chapter 3).

This book reveals a multiplicity of deliberations and how deliberative practices emerge and enable collective discussions, including institutionalised deliberative processes (i.e. vTaiwan, Join Platform), various forms of mini-publics and innovations initiated by civic society organisations and students, and deliberations within citizen activism and movements. It shows the intricate web of micro- and macro- deliberative systems, how democratic innovations and various components perform different functions, complement each other, contribute to institutions' evolution and enhance the democratic and deliberative qualities of the system overall.

In addition to the interdependence, complementarity and complexity between the components of deliberative systems, competition for legitimacy exists between different methods of deliberations. Tensions exist between the Judicial Reform Foundation's ideals of effective judicial system construction and the government's initiation of the Judicial Reform National Meeting, as discussed in Chapter 4. Based on the notions of deliberative democracy and open government, the Judicial Reform Foundation promotes increased participation, transparent laws and education. It regards deliberative forums of judicial reform initiated by civic society groups in 2016 as a major component and a key contributor to the judicial reform movement. The Judicial Reform Foundation adopts the principle of inclusion and flexibility that enables citizens to hold discussions any time. It also creates an environment that facilitates friendly and easy discussion on current questions, causes of and solutions for nonlegal professionals. However, according to the Judicial Reform Foundation, the level of inclusion, flexibility and transparency offered by the government-led Judicial Reform National Meeting is lower than that offered by the deliberative forums led by social groups. The designs of government-led national consultations have been questioned and challenged, which might pave the way to transform the tensions or competition into complementariness through cooperation.

This book also highlights the dynamic, entangled and interconnected relationship between Taiwan's democracy transition, vibrant civic society activism and revival of news forms of social and reform movements, increasing deliberative forums and mini-publics practices, and the transformation of democratic practices of indigenous peoples. The case of mining on Truku traditional territories demonstrates the co-evolution of micro- and macro-deliberative systems. Indigenous political participation and deliberations on tribal affairs and the Tsai government's pursuit of dialogue for historical and transitional justice are mutually reinforcing. Indigenous democratic practices and the relationship and interaction between indigenous peoples and the Taiwanese government have been shaped through and by social processes. The co-evolution of deliberative systems is driven by political and environmental subjectivities and ongoing plural conversations and interaction between the state and indigenous peoples. The case of the Truku tribe's fighting for traditional lands provides insights into deliberative governance involving indigenous peoples. Following Tamura's (2014) concept of 'nested deliberative systems', we can consider each tribal village and indigenous movement as parts of the macro-deliberative system and a micro-deliberative system itself, a virtual community

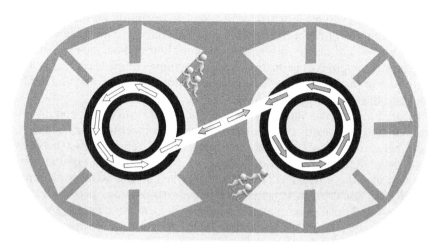

Figure 8.1 The co-evolution of deliberative systems

that transcends social boundaries as the wider deliberative system. Citizen activism accelerated the state's response to changes of entangled deliberative systems and moved to transform it (Figure 8.1). It provides a lesson to respect their traditional socio-political processes of everyday conversation and gatherings and ways of making tribal decisions that are embedded in tribal social relations and particular situations. Narratives have played a significant role in framing and collective actions.

In the face of the conflicts between dependency on mining industry and tribal environmental sustainability, and tensions between the tribal assembly based on the rule of indigenous consultation and traditional ways of negotiation and decision-making, it is crucial to grant indigenous communities the 'right to justification', which 'empowers individuals to fine-tune their preferences and be treated as autonomous beings capable of self-authorship' (Curato et al., 2019, p. 180). Rummens (2018) reminds us that 'since justice requires us to take into consideration the needs and values of concrete individuals living a historically evolving society, the democratic contestation of all actual agreements forms a crucial and constitutive part of the deliberative process' (p. 141).

In the study of the legitimacy of citizen-led G1000 in Belgium, Caluwaerts and Reuchamps (2018) found that a firmer embeddedness of the mini-public within the political system might help mini-publics' proposals to reach the empowered space. Organisers reconnect with formal politics by organising deliberations in activities in parliamentary arenas and send reports to all Belgian MPs, which has influenced the political uptake of muni-publics. A robust deliberative system needs to be sensitive to limits of deliberation per se. In the face of challenge of power, fake news and manipulation, 'the challenge is to nurture space where citizens *can constantly fight* the way the very power that underpins their democratic polities' (Curato et al., 2019, p. 176, emphasis in original). It is important that marginal or alternative innovative deliberative models are not prevented from emerging and nourishing. Deliberative democracy in Taiwan provides insights into the dynamics of division of labour, innovative practices of deliberative systems and complex connections between the mini-publics and political institutions (see Chapter 5).

Deliberative forums combine with civic society organisations' advocacy and activism, oversight by alternative media, netizens' participation, and networking, and social movements have encouraged better responses in empowered spaces and improved face-to-face communication. Adjustments to high-school civics curriculum guidelines and the Anti-Black-Box Curriculum Movement mentioned in Chapter 3 serve as fitting examples in this regard. The alliance between Civic Awakening and civic education teachers initiated the '228 Flipped Classroom – Street Class on Civic Education', comprising activities such as civic forums, evening parties, sit-ins and high school teachers' fasting meditation for 28 hours to fight for procedural justice. The transmission of citizens' actions to the Ministry of Education, legislators and politicians has transformative effects. It has even led to the government stopping the adjustment of the curriculum, creating new spaces for listening, reason-giving, and performing educational functions.

Youth active participation in public affairs and politics has systemic deliberative consequences. The occupy action and 'street deliberation' outside the Legislative Yuan during the Sunflower Movement facilitates more dialogue between citizens and authorities and highlights interconnections between non-deliberative acts and multiple forms of deliberative practices. The young generation has become more active in participating in policy-making and politics, such as advocacy and actions for legalising same-sex marriage, organising a mock referendum to raise citizenship consciousness among students, and increasing young generation and first-time voter turnout during the 2020 presidential election. The new curriculum and education provided by senior high schools have incorporated concepts of deliberative democracy, transitional justice, civic disobedience and social movements, and put more emphasis on bottom-up participation, citizen rights and empowerment. Institutional democratic innovations and online platforms initiated by civil society organisations, alternative media and social media provide spaces for youths' voices and deliberative practices, which could shape a new youth deliberative culture.

Taipei City Governments' institutionalising PB and the government–academia alliance model have successfully strengthened interactions between local governments, universities, civic organisations, local communities and neighbourhood social networks. They nourish connections between the public and empowered space and have had an impact on policy programs. PB practices have also urged councillors to listen to residents' concerns. Some council members and staff from councillors' offices attend the residents' assembly to listen to residents' ideas and proposals. The residents' assembly of PB serves as an important site for combining residents' everyday talk and deliberative practices. There are ongoing discussions and dialogues on adaptations of innovations in response to rapid and new social changes, such as the initiatives of the residents' assembly of migrant workers and PB on high schools to improve inclusiveness and incorporate plural public discourses and concerns into policy programs and community planning.

On the politics of climate change at a time when liberal representative democracy has come under pressure, Fischer (2017) argues for an alternative path of participatory environmental governance embodied in a growing re-localisation movement and global eco-localism. The vibrant civic society and local initiatives in Taiwan have good prospects for local participatory democracy and agency, which are strengthened further through everyday discussions, deliberations and daily material practices. PB innovations have considerable impact and foster ongoing communications and local transition initiatives. One example is New Taipei City Government's collaboration with Ludi Community College and Yonghe Community College to initiate PB on saving energy to empower residents to forward their budget proposal in the assembly, participate in a budget proposal deliberative workshop to clarify problems, and hold discussions with government agencies' representatives to refine the proposal. The voting stage is combined with garden party activities so that more citizens can interact with the proposal proponents and understand the core ideas behind the energy-saving budget proposal – all of which can raise residents' energy awareness. In addition, in 2019, the Tainan City Government collaborated with civic organisations to promote PB on low-carbon households and community-based adaptation in 2019. This provided local residents a platform to put forward their budget proposal and facilitated collective building of low-carbon communities. The Tainan City Government and Taiwan Environmental Education Association work together to conduct deliberative democratic training activities to empower citizens to serve as forum facilitators.

Another example is the Taromak tribe's 100% Green Energy Tribe Initiative in Taitung. It has been regarded as a part of a local struggle for tribal autonomy following centuries-long processes of colonisation and modernisation, which shows how identity politics based on their place-framing shapes and is reshaped by the community energy initiative (Lai, 2019). ENGOs collaborate with the tribal people to hold deliberative workshops to develop community energy initiatives embedded in the social, cultural and geographic conditions of tribal life. This fosters energy democracy imagination and initiatives.

Seeking meta-deliberation in times of disaster and uncertainty

The importance of inclusiveness is particularly prominent in times of crisis and uncertainty; exclusion of participation and deliberation could harm people's health rights in the face of a global pandemic and unknown challenges. China claims sovereignty over self-ruled Taiwan, and it has used its diplomatic clout to stop Taiwan from becoming a member of global organisations. Since 2017, immediately after Taiwan elected Tsai Ing-wen as president, the World Health Organisation (WHO) stopped inviting Taiwan to the World Health Assembly (WHA) under pressure from China. Taiwan was excluded from participating in WHO's emergency meeting in Geneva on pandemic prevention, which was attended by countries that had reported cases of the 2019 coronavirus disease (COVID-19) on 22 January. Taiwan confirmed its first case of COVID-19 on 21 January, but 23 million Taiwanese people were excluded from representation in the administration of global health and safety. This inability to participate on the international stage has attracted much concern from the Taiwanese public and from international news organisations. President Tsai called on the WHO to set politics aside and to grant Taiwan full access to virus updates, saying that 'Taiwan is at the forefront of global epidemic prevention. There needs to be room at the WHO for Taiwan's participation' (Reuters, 2020). Such exclusion has also united the political parties. The KMT – which rarely agree with the DPP, especially in China affairs – expressed its anger, saying that epidemic prevention knows no boundaries: 'if Taiwan is alone in being left out of epidemic prevention work, it will leave a gap; this is not beneficial to promoting epidemic prevention work around the world' (Reuters, 2020). Independent critics argued Taiwan should not be a passive recipient of thirdhand information, and it should participate in the planning and preparatory meetings of the WHO. China and the WHO are to be blamed for allowing politics to interfere with the fight against a dangerous global pandemic (Kassam, 2020).

The deliberative systems approach helps to make sense of the emergent spaces for reason-giving and claims-making in the global context, where lay-citizen participation and access to knowledge may be limited. Protest and transnational movement networks and alliances contribute to create new transnational public spheres, facilitating the transmission of ideas and knowledge claims in situations where individual states' interests dominate governance. There are multiple emergent forms of participation and citizen actions involving the public space and empowered space. For example, the Taiwanese government accused the WHO of providing 'inaccurate' information on the epidemic. In its reports, Taiwan was indicated as being a part of China, which has pushed countries, such as Italy and Vietnam, to suspend flights to and from the island. After protests by the Taiwanese government in its communiqués, Hanoi lifted the ban (AsiaNews, 2020).

The digital public sphere can be transformed into a productive space of reason (Curato et al., 2019); it can enable conversations; connect multiple spaces across time, borders and scales; and enhance the capacity of deliberative systems. The Global Taiwanese Medical Alliance (GTMA) initiated a petition, 'Support Taiwan to Join the WHO NOW', to call on the WHO to immediately invite Taiwan to the WHA 2020 and other critical COVID-19-related meetings. The petition states:

> The exclusion of Taiwan from international health dialogues is political in nature and has put 23.7 million Taiwanese lives at risk, an action that blatantly goes against the principles of the WHO and the 2020 annual theme of the WHA, namely 'Health for All: Taiwan Can Help' and the 'Right to Health' for all global citizens.
>
> (Change.org, 2020)

Such exclusion has not only 'put Taiwanese lives at incredible risk but also undermined the health and security of citizens and nationals of the Asian-Pacific region' (Change.org, 2020). The petition also emphasised how Taiwan's participation will allow it to contribute its experiences and expertise to the management of the pandemic, in addition to mentioning that both the Canadian Prime Minister, Justin Trudeau, and the Japanese Prime Minister, Shinzō Abe, expressed their countries' support towards Taiwan's meaningful participation in the WHA for the sake of global public health. A well-known Taiwanese YouTuber also posted an open letter in a YouTube video, which was addressed to the WHO on 10 February 2020. The letter asked the WHO, on behalf of the world, to include Taiwan in the fight against pandemics. In his video, he stated that excluding 23 million Taiwanese people for reasons of politics blatantly goes against WHO's vision of health as a basic human right and health for all without exception (Taiwan News, 2020). The decision of not inviting Taiwan to attend the emergency meeting drew widespread criticism from the international community. The European Union, Canada, Australia and Japan have also renewed their support for Taiwan's inclusion in the WHA as an observer. The GTMA initiated an e-petition, and 88,982 people have signed it at the time of writing this chapter (Change.org, 2020).

Furthermore, a netizen initiated a petition in January 2020 through the White House 'We the People' platform to call on the US government to support Taiwan's membership in the WHO. The petition stated that

> Taiwan has high-quality medical technology and much medical experience, and it has continuously made contributions to medical issues. To protect not only the 23 million Taiwanese people but also humanity as a whole, Taiwan should not be excluded from the WHO because of politics anymore.
>
> (We the People, 2020; Focus Taiwan, 2020)

The petition gathered 238,973 signatures as of 29 February 2020. Because all petitions to the White House that gather at least 100,000 signatures within 30 days will get a response, this particular petition is expected to as well.

In a study of democratising global climate governance, Stevenson and Dryzek (2014) argue for reflexivity and that any reflexive capacity needs something out of the ordinary:

It is in moments of disruption that a capacity to reflect and change may best be sought. Without something like total war (or even with it: war's wake has generally led to efforts to rebuild institutions only for security and economic stability, nothing more), what is possible? We suspect the convergence of a multiplicity of agents of tension and disruption may be most auspicious.

(p. 213)

Stevenson and Dryzek (2014) identify seven possible sources of necessary tension and disruption, including climate disasters, protest movements, rapid changes in the balance of discourses, norm entrepreneurs, regime clashes, the rise of China and out-of-the-ordinary global gatherings. Protest movements, rapid changes in the balance of discourses and norm entrepreneurs are mainly of public space. They argue that little significant change is likely to emerge from the efforts within empowered space without strong efforts in public space and external pressure. Deliberative analysis and institutional reconstruction are necessarily the work of many hands.

The COVID-19 global health emergency shows the vulnerabilities of epidemic socio-technical systems and has caused tensions or disruptions in multiple levels of governance. Cross-scale and trans-border dialogues and transnational networks of activism are crucial in claims-making and fighting for equal opportunity of participation and inclusiveness. Protests, social movements and alliance-building that work toward justice frequently produce imaginary and material linkages among advocates over space and across scales (Pellow, 2018). Protest movements and norm entrepreneurs have emerged, and the balance of discourse has been changing rapidly. For example, the Taiwan United Nations Alliance and other social groups met with the Chairman of the Legislative Yuan to ask the government to fight for Taiwan's participation in the WHO; policy advisers even invited legislators to lead a delegation to Geneva, Switzerland, to make a strong case when the organisation's annual WHA was held in May 2020. Furthermore, the Legislative Yuan announced, in a joint statement from all parties, its strong support for the Tsai government's continued fight for participation in the WHO. Legislators called for the WHO to abide by professional neutrality and the calls from the international community for justice and demanded the establishment of an appropriate model as soon as possible and the unequivocal acceptance of Taiwan's participation in the WHO. The statement emphasised the need for the government to actively work with friendly nations to continue striving for full participation in the WHO, including in its meetings, mechanisms and events, especially on pandemic prevention.

The emergent space to articulate marginalised discourses provides a platform for reason-giving and reflectivity in the face of China's political interests that are dominant and powerful in the time of emergency and uncertainty. Protests, campaigns, petitions and joint statements on multiple sites have the potential to facilitate dialogues, connect different sites of communications and encourage public conversations on possible ways forward. Delays in obtaining the latest information pose a danger to Taiwan and the international community, but the Taiwanese government has found alternative means of staying informed through existing networks with expert communities. WHO's spokesman, Tarik Jasarevic, responded in a press conference that the organisation is allowing Taiwan to access information about the virus and will 'have Taiwanese experts involved in all of our consultations – the clinical networks, laboratory networks and others' (Jennings, 2020).

Social media as a free and open platform for conversations, dialogues and story-sharing facilitates global connectivity. President Tsai used Twitter to share stories about how 'Taiwan can help' and indicated that 'social media helps me communicate with the people of Taiwan, but it also helps Taiwan connect with the world' (Tsai, 2020). She emphasised three major areas where Taiwan can contribute to the global fight against COVID-19. First, the Taiwanese government has donated 10 million masks and medical supplies to countries that have been most severely impacted by COVID-19 since April for use as personal protective equipment by frontline medical personnel combating the coronavirus; this was done as part of its global 'Taiwan can help' campaign to show that 'Taiwan is helping'. Second, Taiwan has been increasing production of quinine. Third, it has been sharing its use of technology to trace and investigate outbreaks. Tsai stressed that 'coming together and sharing our stories reminds us we are not alone. Together, we can be more than the sum of our parts' (Tsai, 2020). Furthermore, the US Department of State launched a 'TweetforTaiwan' campaign to rally support for Taiwan's participation in the upcoming WHA in May (Lin, 2020).

Achieving healthy deliberative systems requires radical changes in our social and political ways of life. Although there is not much time for deliberations during an epidemic prevention emergency, deliberation spaces are still emerging. Currently, people are concerned about the COVID-19 emergency and its impact on the community, which presents an opportunity for reflections on democratic and public life in times of health crises and uncertainty. In addition to the government's infection-control plans and quarantine measures, schools, public organisations and churches have discussed preventive measures and communicated to students and members the need to take precautions depending on their situation to prevent the virus from spreading locally. There have been ongoing communications and negotiations between the government, stakeholders and organisers of large-scale public activities. For example, it attracted public attention regarding whether to postpone Taiwan's largest annual religious ritual that takes place in March, the Dajia Matsu Pilgrimage, and precautions that need to be taken to prevent cluster infections. Pilgrimage activities were postponed after the religious leaders' insistence on holding the event was faced with criticism from the public. This provides opportunities to reflect on deliberation in a time of crisis and urgency – which itself may yield insights for the place of deliberation in a climate emergency.

There are opportunities in crisis and emergency situations for people to learn to adopt a talk-based approach with respect, authenticity and rationality to seek resolution. The Central Epidemic Command Centre (CECC) continues to amend epidemic prevention management measures in the process of continuously responding to questions raised through civil dissent and other ministries. Expert recommendations and voices from civil society have influenced policy-making processes, as evident in the disclosure of information during the pandemic; the re-evaluation of the quarantine locations of 247 Taiwanese evacuees from Wuhan, China (Wu et al., 2020); the demand, by 65,000 signatories, that only Taiwanese citizens can be evacuated on flights from Wuhan (Cheng, 2020); the principle of rationing surgical masks through the country's National Health Insurance system; and the debate on whether COVID-19 patients' residences should be revealed to the public, based on a balance between the values of advancing the public's interest and right to know and avoiding social panic and preserving individual liberties. Furthermore, legislators passed the Special Act on COVID-19 Prevention, Relief and Restoration on 25 February, in which a special budget was proposed to mitigate economic damage and its social fallout.

Taiwan's experience of disasters, such as the 2003 SARS outbreak, has contributed to not only greater resilience but also capacity-building, including effective public communication, with respect to efficiently and rapidly responding to new pandemic risks. The head of the Ministry of Health and Welfare's CECC, Chen Shih-chung, holds daily media briefings, and the news conference has become a crucial space for clarification, mutual communication, justification and providing information while combating misinformation. According to the CECC, the Taiwanese model of epidemic prevention includes a rapidly launched emergency public health response, a public communications campaign, and the public's cooperation in pandemic prevention measures, such as self-isolation. Discussions have emerged on what other countries can learn from Taiwan's rapid response to COVID-19. For example, *The Journal of the American Medical Association* lauded Taiwan's pandemic prevention efforts, including its speed in recognising and managing the crisis – evident in its early and strict border controls and execution of case identification, containment and resource allocation measures, in addition to frequent communications with and education of the public while combating misinformation (Lee, 2020). Furthermore, *The Telegraph* reported that 'early intervention, a clear command structure, and transparent communication with the public' have helped keep infection rates low (Smith, 2020).

Chilvers and Kearnes (2016) argue that reflexivity and humility are key elements for science and democracy in the age of emergent participation, suggesting that 'framing effects, exclusions, contingencies and uncertainties are a characteristic feature of all participatory collectives' (p. 16). Moore (2018) argues for the importance of considering 'the role of deliberation within scientific communities and institutions, particularly as it bears on the production of scientific judgements and decisions at the boundary between science and

178 Deliberative policy-making

politics' (p. 642). She emphasises the role of citizen panels, social movements and a critical civil society in both challenging and informing the production of scientific knowledge. Considering that the CECC comprises mostly experts from medical and public health backgrounds, a few researchers from the Taiwanese science, technology and society (STS) community have called for citizen participation and incorporation of different forms of expertise in the decision-making processes. In addition to medical science and public health expertise, democratic institutions incorporate social sciences, civic epistemology and lay expertise to contribute to addressing knowledge production and epistemic injustice. Participatory mechanisms could encourage lay citizens to provide observations on different social classes, life experiences and views on precautions. Citizen science and citizen epidemic prevention could reveal an epidemic's plural social dimensions and possible epidemic system breaches; facilitate comprehensive civic investigation of social concerns, controversies and capacity building; and raise awareness regarding marginalised groups' well-being (e.g. migrant workers and vagrants). Public discourses, advocacy of the common good and citizens collectively fighting an epidemic have been regarded as an emergent civic movement.

Experiencing setbacks, crises, disasters, civil resistance and party turnover might more likely induce reflexivity, meta-deliberation and social learning. Lessons from the Fukushima nuclear disaster revived the anti-nuclear movement, promoting emergent citizen actions and deliberation practices. Additionally, active dialogues and civic participation in forms of debate and knowledge production emerged, in turn facilitating meta-deliberation and evolution of governance (Chapter 5). Campaigns against air pollution and citizen science had a considerable impact on the EPA's tightening of regulations and promoting air quality improvement policy programs (Chapter 4). Extreme climate challenges and the controversy of mining on indigenous land have attracted considerable attention, leading to campaigns that promoted deliberative negotiation among stakeholders, deliberation on mining reform and reflections on dominance of developmentalism (Chapter 6). A multiplicity of forms of citizen participation and deliberation practices could complement each other and are more powerful together in performing the epistemic–ethical–democratic functions of deliberation.

Whilst the cases addressed within this book are mainly concerned with situations and claims *within* Taiwan, transnational spaces are increasingly becoming sites for competing and contesting claims to justice, rights and democracy. Dryzek (2016) argues that deliberative democracy is good at recognising and remedying its own weakness and reformulating itself in response to critics. It is necessary to maintain its orientation to reflexive thinking and epistemic humility (Curato et al., 2019). Disruptive crises and uncertainties can be considered a critical opportunity for meta-deliberation; they can encourage the seeking of reflexive participation and spaces for deliberation as well as the reimagination of democratic politics and the good life in the midst of uncertainty.

References

AsiaNews. (2020, February 8). Coronavirus: Exclusion from WHO harms Taiwan. *AsiaNews*. www.asianews.it/news-en/Coronavirus:-exclusion-from-WHO-harms-Taiwan-49245.html

Bucchi, M., & Neresunu, F. (2008). Science and public participation. In E. Hackett, O. Amsterdamska, M. Lynch, & J. Wajcman (Eds.), *The handbook of science and technology studies* (pp.449–472). Cambridge, MA: MIT Press.

Caluwaerts, D., & Reuchamps, M. (2018). *The legitimacy of citizen-led deliberative democracy*. Abingdon: Routledge.

Change.org. (2020). *Support Taiwan to join WHO now*. www.change.org/p/world-health-organization-support-taiwan-for-joining-who-now-%E8%81%B2%E6%8F%B4%E8%87%BA%E7%81%A3%E5%8D%B3%E5%88%BB%E5%8A%A0%E5%85%A5%E4%B8%96%E7%95%8C%E8%A1%9B%E7%94%9F%E7%B5%84%E7%B9%94

Cheng, C.-T. (2020, February 7). Taiwan medical workers launch petition in support of government. *Taiwan News*. www.taiwannews.com.tw/en/news/3873085

Chilvers, J., & Kearnes, M. (2016). Science, democracy and emergent publics. In J. Chilvers & M. Kearnes (Eds.), *Remaking participation: Science, environment and emergent publics* (pp. 1–27). Abingdon: Routledge.

Curato, N., Hammond, M., & Min, J. (2019). *Power in deliberative democracy: Norms, forums and systems*. Basingstoke: Palgrave Macmillan.

Dryzek, J. (2016). Symposium commentary: Reflections on the theory of deliberative systems. *Critical Policy Studies*, *10*(2), 209–215.

Fischer, F. (2017). *Climate crisis and the democratic prospect: Participatory governance in sustainable communities*. Oxford: Oxford University Press.

Focus Taiwan. (2020, February 2). Petition calling for US to back Taiwan's WHO bid meets threshold. *Focus Taiwan*. https://focustaiwan.tw/politics/202002020006

Geels, F. W. (2002). Technological transitions as evolutionary reconfiguration processes: A multi-level perspective and a case-study. *Research Policy*, *31*(8), 1257–1274.

Jennings, R. (2020, February 14). Health concerns meet politics amid Taiwan's WHO exclusion. *USAToday*. www.usnews.com/news/world/articles/2020-02-14/health-concerns-meet-politics-amid-taiwans-who-exclusion

Kassam, N. (2020, January 22). As Wuhan virus spreads, Taiwan has no say at WHO. *Foreign Policy*. https://foreignpolicy.com/2020/01/22/china-health-coronavirus-wuhan-virus-spreads-taiwan-no-say-who/

Lai, H.-L. (2019). Situating community energy in development history: Place-making and identity politics in the Taromak 100% green energy tribe initiative, Taiwan. *Geoforum*, *100*, 176–187.

Lee, I.-C. (2020, March 5). Virus outbreak: Paper lauds disease-prevention efforts. *Taipei Times*. www.taipeitimes.com/News/taiwan/archives/2020/03/05/2003732112

Lin, C. (2020, May 3). Virus outbreak: TweetforTaiwan: US's bid to get Taiwan into WHA. *Taipei Times*. www.taipeitimes.com/News/front/archives/2020/05/03/2003735718

Moore, A. (2018). Deliberative democracy and science. In A. Bächtiger, J. Dryzek, J. Mansbridge, & M. Warren (Eds.), *Handbook of deliberative democracy* (pp. 640–653). Oxford: Oxford University Press.

Pellow, D. (2018). Environmental justice movements and political opportunity structures. In R. Holifield, J. Chakraborty, & G. Walker (Eds.), *The Routledge handbook of environmental justice* (pp. 37–49). London: Routledge.

Reuters. (2020, January 24). Parties unite over Taiwan's exclusion from WHO antivirus planning. *Reuters.* www.reuters.com/article/us-china-health-taiwan/parties-unite-over-taiwans-exclusion-from-who-anti-virus-planning-idUSKBN1ZN0QG

Rummens, S. (2018). Deliberation and justice. In A. Bächtiger, J. Dryzek, J. Mansbridge, & M. Warren (Eds.), *Handbook of deliberative democracy* (pp. 132–143). Oxford: Oxford University Press.

Smith, N. (2020, March 6). Taiwan sets gold standard on epidemic response to keep infection rates low. *Telegraph.* www.telegraph.co.uk/news/2020/03/06/taiwan-sets-gold-standard-epidemic-response-keep-infection-rates/

Stevenson, H., & Dryzek, J. S. (2014). *Democratizing global climate governance.* Cambridge: Cambridge University Press.

Taiwan News. (2020, February 11). Taiwanese YouTuber posts open letter to WHO. *Taiwan News.* www.taiwannews.com.tw/en/news/3874539

Tamura, T. (2014). Rethinking grassroots participation in nested deliberative systems. *Japanese Political Science Review, 2,* 63–87.

Tsai, I.-W. (2020, April 17). *Tsai Ing-wen* [Twitter account]. *Twitter.* Retrieved 17 April 2020 from https://twitter.com/iingwen

We the People. (2020). Taking actions on supporting Taiwan joining WHO. *The White House.* https://petitions.whitehouse.gov/petition/take-actions-supporting-taiwan-joining-who

Wu, L.-Y., Chien, H.-J., & Xie, D. (2020, February 22). Virus outbreak: Two new cases related to 24th patient. *Taipei Times.* www.taipeitimes.com/News/front/archives/2020/02/22/2003731412

Index

Note: Page numbers in **bold** refer to tables and *italics* refer to figures.

Abe, Shinzō 174
academics *see* government–academia alliance model/approach
accountability 6, *8*, 67–8; elections as 87–8
Act on Sites for the Establishment of Low-Level Radioactive Waste Final Disposal Facility ('Act on Sites') 94
Administrative Institution Radioactive Waste Regulation Centre 103
advocacy organisations 30; counter-expertise 113–14
Air Pollution Control Act 79
air pollution/quality 30, 79, 178
Alliance for Amending the Indigenous Long-Term Care Service Law 24
Alliance for the Happiness of the Next Generation 58
alternative media 36–7
Anderson, B. 148
Annual Sovereign Union Forums 123
Anti-Black-Box Curriculum Movement 25, 171
Anti-Nuclear Alliance Swearing Ceremony 95
anti-nuclear protests 42
anti-nuclear waste movement 94–5; Citizen Participation Platform 103–5; civic forums 98–102; expert committees 102–3; institutional evolution 105–8; referendums 108–10
Asia Cement Corporation (ACC) 125–43
Atomic Energy Council (AEC) 39, 96, 98, 99, 107, 111, 116, 118–19; Citizen Participation Platform 100, 103–5, **110**; integrating mechanisms of public engagement 102–5

Australian Citizens' Parliament (ACP) 147–8
Awakening Foundation 85–6
Ayug tribal village 125, 128, 141–3; tribe assembly 133

Bächtiger, A. 4–5, 7–8, 63, 159
beef imports, American 62
Beitou Community College 29, 151; participatory budgeting 160
Beitou Cultural Foundation 29
Berg, M. 93–4
Boswell, J. 67
Bsngan tribal assembly 132–4; conflicts 132
Bucchi, M. 168
Burall, S. 6–7, 46, 67, 68
Bureau of Public Health, dementia-friendly communities 78

Caluwaerts, D. 170
Campaign Finance Crowdsourcing 37–8
campaigns 79–80; anti-nuclear 98–9; electoral 83–5
CCW *see* Citizen Congress Watch (CCW)
Central Election Committee 58, 59
Central Epidemic Command Centre (CECC) 177, 178
Chambers, S. 5
Change.org 174
Changhua County Environmental Protection Alliance 84–5
Chen, D. -S. 29
Chen, D. -Y. 33, 72–3
Cheng Li-chun 31
Chen Shui-bian 2, 146

Chiang Kai-shek Memorial Hall 24, 56
Chi Bo-Lin 130
Chilvers, J. 168, 177
China: free-trade agreement with 25;
    global organisations and 173
chip national identity card 77
citizen action 79–80
citizen conferences 2; after 2016 election
    55–6; anti-air pollution 30; Hsinchu
    Science- based Industrial Park at
    Ilan (HSIP, Ilan) 30; information and
    communications technology (ICT)
    and 33; online 33; radioactive waste
    12, 14; youth 31–2
Citizen Congress Watch (CCW) 13,
    49, 168; criteria for evaluation 51;
    improvement of legislative image
    52–3; local organisations 53–4;
    more seats for small parties 62;
    party negotiation mechanisms 62–3;
    performance evaluation 63;
    process of legislator evaluation
    51–2
Citizen Constitutional Meeting 34
Citizen Constitutional Promotion
    Alliance 34, 35
citizen forums 27, 30, 100, **110**, 114
Citizen is Energy 86–7
Citizen Jury on New Development
    Projects in Qiyan Community 28
Citizen of the Earth Foundation 75, 76,
    130, 131, 138, 140–2
citizen panel, nuclear waste 97–8, 111–16
Citizen Parliament 80
citizen science 42, 178
civic forums 79–80; anti- nuclear waste
    movement 27, 30, 98–102, **110**
civic society groups/organisations 9–10;
    accountability role 69; legislator
    evaluation 49–55; performance
    evaluation 85–7; WatchOut 61, 83,
    140; *see also* mini-publics
Civil Evaluation Conferences 13
Civilmedia@Taiwan 37
Clean Air Action Plan 79
climate and energy issues 28, 32–3, 80,
    84, 172
coevolution of micro-and macro-
    deliberative systems 122–43
co-governance 80–3
Congress Investigation Corps 61–2
consensus conference 2, 29; citizen
    panel 114; Danish model 28, 96; GM

food 42; National Health Insurance
    Payment 76; nuclear waste 96–8, **110**,
    111, 112, 114–16; participants 96;
    youth 31–2
consequentiality 7, 142, 148
Control Yuan: accountability mechanism
    118; mining on indigenous lands 126,
    129; powers controversial 68
@Coolloud 37
Cornell E-Rulemaking Initiative 70
Council of Indigenous Peoples 9, *50*,
    125, 126, 136, 138–9
COVID-19 pandemic 4, 173–7
cross-boundary cooperation among local
    governments 82
cross-strait relationship 25–6, 85
Curato, N. 5, 7, 8, 23, 33, 41, 62, 67, 127,
    147–8, 170, 171, 173, 178

Dajia Matsu Pilgrimage 176
Danish model of consensus
    conferences 28, 96
death penalty 30–1
decisiveness 6, *8*
deliberative class meetings 32
deliberative learning 4
deliberative systems 1; functions
    140–2; key concepts of 147–8; seven
    components 6
dementia 78
Democracy Classroom on the Street–
    Citizen Deliberation symposium 34
democratic function 11, 42–3,
    115–17, 141–2
democratic innovation 69–73, 147–8;
    see also participatory budgeting (PB)
Democratic Progressive Party (DPP) 2,
    25, 31; food referendum 40–1; future
    of nuclear energy 106, 109; New
    Frontier Foundation 26; relations with
    NPP 47–8; same-sex marriage rights
    57; 2020 election campaign 85
democratisation of science 93–119
Department of Civil Affairs of the
    Taipei City Government 147, 149, *150*,
    151–64, 165n5
digital innovations 4, 7, *8*, 69
digital technology 4, 60–1, 69; youth
    participation in the empowered
    space 60
discourse: cross-strait relationship and
    Taiwanese subjectivity 25–6; definition
    23; four types 23; market-oriented

26; in public space 41–2; reform and transitional justice 24–5; sustainable development 27–8
documentary analysis 13
DPP *see* Democratic Progressive Party (DPP)
Dryzek, J. S. 1, 5–7, 9, 23, 178
DStreet *see* 'Street deliberation' (DStreet)

ecological sustainability 115
economic development, job opportunities and livelihood 129
Education and Culture Committee 56
EIA *see* environmental impact assessment (EIA)
eID card 77, 78
elections 2; accountability mechanism 67; citizen evaluation and 53; reform of rules 46–7; 2016 legislative 46, 47; 2020 legislative 48; 2016 presidential 55; 2020 presidential 85; electoral campaigns 83–5
electoral system reform 46–7
empowered space 6, *8*, 46–64
Energy and Carbon Reduction Office 75
Energy Transition White Paper 73–6
environmental impact assessment (EIA) 125, 127, 128, 131, 136, 138, 139, 141
environmental justice: core discourse 116, 118; indigenous land rights 127–8; NNAAP and 101; *Our Island* TV programme 27
environmental lawyers 36
Environmental Protection Administration 32, *50*, 76, 79–80, 130
e-participation 71–3; anonymous nature of 71
epistemic function of deliberative system 11, 42, 73, 76, 111–14, 140–1
Ercan, S. A. 10
E-rule-making 69–71
ethical function 11, 42, 114–15, 141
Executive Yuan 24, *50*, 68, 75, 76, 79, 103, 106–8, 130, 137, 139
expert-activists 98, 111–14
expert committees, nuclear waste 102–3

Facebook 37, 39; civil partnership fan page 57; information for netizens 61; Join platform 72; mining conflict 130, 131, 136, 137;

nuclear energy supporters 109; nuclear food referendum 41; school mock referendums 59; training workshops 149–50
fact-checking 83–4
fact-finding investigation committee 135, 141, 142
fake news 68
Fischer, F. 172
Flood Control Alliance 81
food safety 38–9
Former RCA Employees' Mutual Aid Association v. Radio Corporation of America (RCA) 36
14+N Air Pollution Control Strategies Focus 79
free trade agreement 25, 34
Fuel Cycle and Materials Administration (FCMA) 96
Fukushima 38, 40, 98, 113, 117, 118, 178

Gaya 133
G1000 (Belgium) 170
Geels, F. W. 168
gender and education, role in deliberation 33
gender policy 85–6
global deliberative governance processes 28
global pandemic *see* COVID-19 pandemic
Global Taiwanese Medical Alliance (GTMA) 173–4
GM food 42
government–academia alliance model/ approach 29, 147, 149, *150*, 152, 153, 160, 163–4, 171
Government Budget Visualisation 37
grassroots organisation 24, 34–6, 74, 79–80
Green Citizens' Action Alliance 100, 101, 113, 114, 116–17
Greenhouse Gas Control Implementation Plan 80
groundwater pollution 36
G0V.tw 37–8

Habermas, J. 148
Han Kuo-yu 85, 88
Hasegawa, K. 148
Hau Lung-pin 40, 41
heads of villages, participatory budgeting and 154, 161

health insurance 2, 29
Hébert, M. 122–3
Hendriks, C. M. 7, 10, 55, 60
Homemakers United Foundation 113
Hong Kong 85
Hsinchu Science-based Industrial Park (HSIP) 30
Huang Shih-hsiu 41, 109
human rights 24
Huang, D. Y. 77

Ilan Community College 30
indigenous activism 39–40; music and traditional cultural rituals 130; and political communication 16, 123–4
indigenous communities 24–5
indigenous deliberative system 123, 142
Indigenous Historical Justice and Transitional Justice Commission 9, *50*, 125
Indigenous Historical Justice and Transitional Justice Committee 107, 114–15, 135, 136
indigenous land rights and environmental justice 122–43
indigenous peoples 9; apology to 9, 106; characteristics of indigenous deliberative systems 123; narratives and discourses 127–9; political participation 122–43; recognised tribes 124; Status Act for Indigenous Peoples 124
Indigenous Peoples Basic Act 9, 81–2, 125–7, 135; court ruling on violation of 137–8
'Indigenous Views' (TV programme) 131–2
information and communication technology (ICT): E-participation platform 71–3; online deliberation 33; Sunflower Movement 168
informed consent rights 101, 107, 131, 137–8, 140–1
'Instant Fact-Check' project 83
intergenerational equity 115
internet platforms, as public space 36–40
interpretive approach/analysis 10–11
interview research and informal conversations 14
i-Voting, participatory budgeting 157

Japan 2, 3, 38, 39, 41, 112, 113, 174
Jasanoff, S. 4, 93

Jin-Pyng Wang 25
Join Platform *see* Public Policy Participation Network Platform (Join Platform)
Judicial Reform Foundation 169
Judicial Reform National Meeting 73, 74, 169

Kanke Indigenous Sustainable Development Association 24
Karpowitz, C. 7, 159
KMT *see* Kuomintang (KMT)
knowledge: creation of 93–4, 98–9, 113; mining industry 140–1
Ko Wen-je 48, 146, 155
Kuo-Kuang Petrochemical Corp development project 43
Kuokuang Petrochemical plant 27–8
Kuomintang (KMT): democratic transition 2; future of nuclear energy 109, **110**; nuclear foods referendum 40; same-sex marriage rights 57, 59–60; and Sunflower Movement 25; Transitional Justice Commission investigation 24, 68–9; 2016 election 46; 2020 election campaign 85; *kuso* culture 37

labour law reforms 26
land rights *see* indigenous land rights and environmental justice
Lee Chun-yi 57
legislative committees, online platform and 60–4
Legislative Weekly 13, 49
Legislative Yuan 24, *50*; accountability and Control Yuan 68; digital technology and 60–1; legislator evaluation 49; negotiation mechanisms 62–3; Referendum Act passed by 41; reform of electoral system 46–9; video on demand (VOD) system 49, 51–2, 168
legislators, behavior of 47
Legislator Voting Guide 38
'Let's Supervise' function, Join platform 72
LGBT rights, same sex marriage 57–9
Lin, K. -M. 2, 28–9, 31
Lin, T. -L. 32
litigation 36, 137–8
living safety and environmental uncertainty 127–42

local governments: civic society
evaluation 86–7; overseeing 53–5

Mansbridge, J. 5, 11, 34, 42, 111, 114,
115, 140, 141
marginalised groups, women
legislators and 48
market-oriented discourse 26
Ma Ying-Jeou 28, 105
McCormick,S. 94
media: investigations as accountability
mechanism 68; READr Presidential
Candidate FactCheck Project 83–4
Me'Phaa deliberation 122–3
meta-deliberation 6, *8*, 9, 172–8
methodology 10–15
Mining Act 130, 131, 135–41
mini-publics: Australian Citizens
Parliament 147–8; development of
28–34; drawbacks and criticisms 33;
functions of 111–17; G1000 (Belgium)
170–1; open policy-making 76–8;
transitional justice through 55–6
Ministry of Economic Affairs (MOEA)
125, 129, 134–9, 141, 142
Mom Loves Taiwan 101, 117
music and traditional cultural rituals
130

Nantian Village 115–16
National Agricultural Meeting
73, 74
National Communications Commission
(NCC) 68
National Congress Watch Alliance
(NCWA) 53–5
National Council for Sustainable
Development (NCSD) 81
National Cultural Meeting 73, 74
National Development Council 71, 75
National Health Insurance Committee
(NHIC) 82
National Health Insurance Payment
consensus conference 2, 76
National Nuclear Abolition Action
Platform (NNAAP) 27, 30, 100–1,
108, 114
National River NGOs Meeting 81
natural resource exploitation 12, 122–43
negotiation mechanisms, legislative
committees 62–3
netizens 60–1, 64
New Frontier Foundation 26

New Power Party (NPP) 47–8; legislative
nominees 48–9; same-sex marriage
rights 57
Newton, K. 148
Nishiyama, K. 59
non-governmental organisations
(NGOs) 24; Citizen Congress Watch
(CCW) 49; co-governance 81;
death penalty 30–1; environmental
(ENGOs) 27, 81, 103, 114; function
140; legislator evaluation 49; National
Council for Sustainable Development
(NCSD) 81; 'outsourced' PB 146;
promoting transparency 87–8
nuclear energy, fact-checking 84–5
Nuclear Energy Rumour Terminator
109, 119n3
nuclear food referendum 40–1
nuclear power 27, 42, 97–8, 100–19
nuclear waste 12, 16, 30, 93–119; civic
forums 98–102; consensus conference
96–8; disposal disputes 94–5
Nuclear Waste Victims Alliance 105

Occupy movement 168
Occupy the Ministry of Education
protest 26
O'Flynn, I. 7
'One Fixed Day Off and One Flexible
Rest Day' 37
online civic forums 38–9
online deliberation 29, 33
online petition 130
online platforms 4, 36–40, 60–2, 64
Open Space on Ethnic Reconciliation 28
Orchid Island 93–119; AEC
mechanisms 102–5; civic forums
98–102; Committee on Nuclear
Waste Removal 105–8; flooding
and wild creek remediation 39–40;
nuclear waste disposal dispute 94–5;
referendums 108–10; Repository
Removal Promotion Committee 105
Our Island (tv programme) 27, 102

Papa Promise No Nukes Alliance 117
Parkinson, J. 5
participant observation 14–15
participatory budgeting (PB) 12–13,
16–17, 146–65, 171–2; Beitou
Community College/Youth Platform
Foundation 29; Bureau of Social
Welfare of the Taoyuan City

Government 87; campus/student initiative 154–5; citizen review committee 156–7; concerns/problems 149, 159–60; connects the sphere of micro-deliberative forums 147; counsellor counters 155, 165n3; deliberative system *163*; deliberative workshop 156; Disability Assemblies 159; energy-saving budget proposal 172; evaluation and review 157–8; functions of process **162**; government–academia alliance approach 147, 149, *150 152*, 153, 163–4; implementation in Taipei City 147; information desk service 155; neighbourhood political elites 153; new immigrant participants 159, 165n5; obstacles hinder citizen participation 148; online platform 155–6; online voting 157; outsourced model of 146; professional counsellor team 152; proposal exhibitions 157; residents' assemblies 153–155, 164, 171–2; 'rolling ways of learning' 152–3; standard operating procedure (SOP) 152; student roles 155; Taipei City 146–7, 149–51; training courses/workshops 150–1; visualisation website 151; Youth Platform Foundation 29–30
party negotiation mechanisms 62–3
Pateman, Carole 5
petrochemical industry 27–8, 43
Philosophy and Social Democracy Studio 80
Presidential Hackathon 38
private space 6
proportional representation (PR) 46
public consultations 73–6
public deliberation 7
Public Digital Innovation Space 4, 69
public opinion and elections 87–8
Public Policy Participation Network Platform (Join platform) 69, 71–3; four modes 72
public space 6, 23–43; definition 23
'Public Speaking' mode, Join platform 72

qualitative/quantitative criteria, legislator evaluation 51
questioning 51–3

recall, threat of 88
Referendum Act 40, 41, 48, 64n3, 108

referendums 40–1; future of nuclear energy 108–9; information required to make informed choices 109; nuclear waste disposal 94, 95, 101; same sex marriage 58–9; schools mock referendums 59
reform and transitional justice 24–5
Regulation Room (RegR) 70
residents' assemblies 14, 164, 171–2; participants 153–5
respect 11, 42, 71, 114–15; online forums 38–9
roadkill 42
rule-making, vTaiwan 69–71
Rummens, S. 170

same-sex marriage 56–60
Sanders, Lynn 5
SARS epidemic 4, 177
Scenario Workshop of Tamsui River Remediation 28
schools: deliberative class meetings 32; mock referendums 59; PB and 154; Sinocentric textbook 25–26 *see also* youth/young people
science, democratisation of 93–119; in deliberative systems 96–110; and policy 93–4
self-help organisation 130–43
Shenao coalfired power plant 28
Shimen Reservoir 81
Shu-Fen Lin 139
single non-transferable vote (SNTV) 46
Sinocentric textbook revision 25–6
Smith, G. 148
snowball sampling 14, 95, 127
social expectation 148
social media 36–7, 61, 63–4, 176
social movements 34–6
Social Welfare and Environment Legislative Committee 60
Speaker of the Legislative Yuan 62, 63
Stevenson, H. 6, 46, 67, 123, 174–5
Stop Nukes Now 12
'Street deliberation' (DStreet) 34, 35, 168, 171
students: activists 25–6; Citizen Parliament 80; deliberative class meetings 32; mock referendums 59; participatory budgeting 149, 151, 154–5, 157, 164

Sunflower Movement 4, 25, 34, 168, 171;
    G0V.tw and 38; New Power Party
    (NPP) 47
Sunshine Acts 68
surrogate motherhood 29
sustainable development discourse 27–8

Tainan City 54, 83, 172
Tainan Community College 30
Taipei Citizen Participation Committee
    81, 151–2, 158, *163*, 165n1
Taipei City, participatory budgeting
    146–65, 171–2
Taipower 12, 94, 99, 100, 102, 104–7,
    111, 112, 114, 116–19
Taitung Anti-Nuclear Waste
    Alliance 106
Taiwan Alliance to End the Death
    Penalty 30–1
Taiwan Association for Human Rights
    (TAHR) 24, 77–8
Taiwan Citizen Front 25
Taiwan Citizen Participation
    Association 162–3
Taiwan Civil Partnership Act 57
Taiwan Environmental Information
    Centre 84–5
Taiwan Environmental Protection
    Union 86
Taiwan Environment Protection
    Organisation 113
Taiwanese political system 49, *50*
Taiwan FactCheck Centre 83, 84
Taiwan Labour Front 26
Taiwan People's Party (TPP) 48
Taiwan Roadkill Observation
    Network 42
Taiwan Youth Citizen's Forum (TYCF) 35
Tamura, T. 123, 169
Tang, Audrey 38, 69, 70
Tao aborigines 94–5, 99–100, 105;
    activists 39–40; compensation
    107–8
Taoyuan City Government 87
Taromak tribe, Green Energy
    Initiative 172
Third Force parties 46, 47; face-to-face
    communications with students 80
three-sided negotiation meeting 134–7
transitional justice 1, 9, 24; through
    mini-publics 55–6
Transitional Justice Commission 24,
    50, 68–9

transmission 6, 67–88; and hybrid forms
    of governance **110**; three mechanisms
    67; Truku indigenous lands 129
Trudeau, Justin 174
Truku indigenous lands 16, 123–4;
    co-evolution of micro-and macro-
    deliberative systems 169, *170*; conflicts
    of mining 125–43
Tsai Ing-wen 2, 3, 9, 41, 48, 55, 73, 85,
    107, 118, 124, 132, 134, 139, 173,
    176; apology to indigenous peoples
    106, 138
'Turn around! Citizens Participation in
    Participatory Budgeting Together'
    project 30
Twitter 61, 176
228 Flipped Classroom–Street Class on
    Civic Education 171
2020 READr Presidential Candidate
    FactCheck Project 83–4

Uber 70
Uluru Declaration 123
union members 137, 138
United Nations 32, 80, 175
United Nations Framework Convention
    on Climate Change (UNFCCC) 80
university social responsibility
    (USR) 164

video on demand (VOD) system 49,
    51–2, 168
Vietnam 3, 173
virtual Taiwan (vTaiwan) platform
    69–71, 168; four successive stages 70
Voice Square 38–9

Wan, P. Y. 146, 161
Wang Guo Gan 85
Watchout 24, 61, 140; 'Instant
    Fact-Check' project 83
We Care Kaohsiung 88
Weinstock, D. 1
Wild at Heart Legal Defense Association
    35, 126, 138
wind turbine development 35
women: Awakening Foundation
    85–6; candidates in elections 46–7;
    proportion of female legislators 48
World Café model 76–7
World Health Assembly (WHA) 173–6
World Health Organisation
    (WHO) 173–6

World Trade Organisation (WTO) 41
World Wide Views on Climate and
    Energy 28
World Wide Views (WWViews) on
    Global Warming 28, 32

Xin-Min Shih, Professor 103
Xinyi District, PB proposal 160–1

Yahoo Live 37
Yi-Huah Jiang 106
Young, Iris 5
Youth Advisory Committee *50*, 82–3
Youth Consensus Conference 31–2
Youth Development Administration
    31–2, *50*

Youth Good Governance Alliance 32
Youth Platform Foundation 29–30, 160
Youth State Affairs Consensus
    Conference 31, 32
youth/young people 171; Citizen
    Parliament 80; internet generation
    63; legislative nominations 49;
    participatory bugeting 153–4, 157,
    160, 164; Philosophy and Social
    Democracy Studio, 80; school
    mock referendums 59; 2020 election
    campaign 85; Youth Advisory
    Committee 82–3
YouTube 37, 61, 174
Yuanli Coast Association 36
Yuanli Grassroots People's Forum 35

Made in the USA
Middletown, DE
31 August 2022

72809213R00113